Still
On The Run

ALSO BY BEN TROVATO

Hearts and Mines

The Ben Trovato Files

*Will The Real Ben Trovato
Please Stand up?*

Ben Trovato – Stirred Not Shaken

Ben Trovato's Guide to Everything

Ben Trovato's (mis)Guide to Golf

Hits & Missives – The Worst of Ben Trovato

Ben Trovato's Art of Survival

On the Run

Ben Trovato

Still
On The Run

First published in South Africa in 2009 by Black Hat.

This book is made up of columns that have previously appeared in print. In other words, the author is simply trying to make a fast buck without having to do any extra work. He needs to be taught a lesson. The best way to do this is to buy the book. That will teach him.

Text c Ben Trovato 2009

The moral right of the author has been asserted.
Well, it would have been if he had any morals in the first place.

The contents originally appeared in the *Cape Times*. Jihadists or lynch mobs offended by any of the words contained herein are advised to take it out on the newspaper and not the author.

This book is a companion volume to *On The Run* which has been lowering the tone of bookshelves ever since it came out two years ago. It is inadvisable to own one book without the other.

Cover photograph by Gerard van Niekerk.
Reproduction by WalkerDigital.

Cover design, page design and typesetting by Aly Vee, who was also responsible for a lot of drinking, laughing, shouting and threatening to "walk out right now".

For legal purposes this book is a work of fiction, otherwise any resemblance to actual persons, places, events or organisations is entirely intentional.

Printed and bound by CTP Book Printers
(who only agreed to it because a large sum of money was involved)

ISBN 978-0-620-44006-6

WHAT THE CRITICS SAY

'Trovato slaughters holy cows with gleeful abandon'
Pretoria News

'South Africa's comic sage'
The Herald

'A dose of Epsom salts for our new democracy.'
The Mercury

'Ben Trovato for president!'
Sunday Times

'Trovato perpetrates 'vile wittiness' – I love it'
The Star

'A remarkably astute social commentator'
The Citizen

'A rapier wit'
GQ

'Completely insane'
YOU

'I don't think my mind
will ever be the same'
The Weekender

'Offbeat and dark'
Die Burger

To my parents
who saved me from the priesthood by forcing me
to watch Monty Python's *Life of Brian*

FOREWORD

All year I had people coming up to me and asking whether I was working on a new book. When I told them I was putting together *Still On The Run* – a companion volume to 2007's *On The Run* – they nodded slowly and repeated the question.

What the hell did they want – a novel?

Here, then, is a compilation of the last of the best of my worst columns that appeared each week in the Cape Times between 2002 and 2008.

When the column first appeared seven years ago, some readers were quick to describe me as offensive, slanderous and rude. Others said they laughed so much that their morning coffee spurted from their nose.

Then there were those who loved the column – until the crosshairs swung in the direction of their own skin colour, their own religion, their own hard-earned prejudices. Suddenly, it wasn't so funny.

Once, an American fundamentalist madman by the name of Reverend Donald Spitz from an unspeakable organisation called the Army of God ordered me to say a prayer or burn forever in the eternal hellfires of damnation. Please. I live in South Africa.

Another fan advised me to take a leaf out of the book of former president PW Botha "whose generosity of spirit rose above his personal feelings for a former enemy and political opponent". I tried to be a better person, I really did, but it was harder than giving up smoking.

All the way from Walvis Bay came an e-mail saying: "You must have been beaten up terribly as a kid." Of course. That would explain a lot. I flew to Durban to confront my father but the old man denied everything and demanded a paternity test.

Speaking of misunderstandings, a Capetonian wrote: "Since so many people are asking who Ben Trovato is, may I be allowed to spill the beans on this imposter? Ben Trovato, of course, is not 'his' name and not even 'his' sex. Ben Trovato is a woman. It becomes clear after reading these columns that Brenda is a symbol of oppressed womanhood, especially those married to gin-sodden men. Only a woman writer could so cleverly get under the skin of this bully, and by doing so make this Trovato creature a thing of scorn and contempt to all women. It is all very cleverly contrived by the feminist lobby. How can we be so sure that Ben Trovato is a woman? There is a certain sensitivity about the pieces – notwithstanding the pretence of macho image – that betrays the truth: the deep-seated need to denigrate men."

Grappling with a vicious identity crisis, a doctor in London unwittingly came to my rescue. She wrote: "One has a sense of people like yourself being challenged by chaotic and violent events and trying to find a new *modus vivendi* while still retaining a sense of rationality and a wicked sense of humour."

The relief at finally discovering what it was that I had been doing for the past few years was overwhelming.

Golfing for Rats

—The Scorpions arrest former Western Cape Premier Peter Marais and former Western Cape environment and planning minister David Malatsi on charges of accepting kickbacks from Count Riccardo Agusta, developer of the Roodefontein golf estate in Plettenberg Bay. In a plea bargain, Agusta admits to having bribed the two officials.

I still remember the days when it was fairly embarrassing to be arrested. You used to pray that the cops would come for you at 4am so the neighbours wouldn't see you being dragged off and flung into the back of the van. But they never did, of course. They would always arrive just as you were putting the chops on the braai.

So you had grim-faced brutes in camouflage pulling you in one direction with the hysterical in-laws clinging to your legs while the dog, thinking it was the best game ever, ran around biting everybody.

These days, getting led away by the authorities is something to put on the curriculum vitae. Mark the calendar and alert the press. Dust off the Pierre Cardin suit and blow up the balloons. I almost disgorged my dinner when I saw Peter Marais and David Malatsi waddling up to be arrested, tossing low-rent soundbites dripping with self-righteous indignation into the gaping maw of a pack of drooling hunting dogs masquerading as the local media.

Jowly from feasting on the fleshy haunches of felonious men, these two paragons of virtue batted their hooded lids and bared their fangs in a terrible rictus of rapaciousness. It wozzen me. I didden do it. Belch.

Venal little men. Bellies distended with their own sense of importance. As the Scorpions led them away, I scanned their faces for signs of guilt. All I could see were traces of cheap lipstick. Wives. Aren't they something? Right from Hillary Clinton to Bonita Marais, they stand by their man. Had there been a Mrs Jeffrey Dahmer, she would have said: "Oh, come on, officer. It's not like he ate them raw, you know!"

It doesn't matter if you've been dipping into the till, an intern or someone else's brain, the fact remains that it is damn good PR to have a smiling woman clinging to your arm as you stride confidently into a police station to be fingerprinted and charged.

Unless she happens to be Winnie, of course.

Be sure of one thing, though. Behind the bedroom door, the smiles quickly turn to snarls. "You stupid grabby prick! How could you?" sob the distraught wives. "How could you get caught!"

Boesak tried it. Now these two lovable freebooters are trying it, hinting broadly that if they have to face trial, some nasty stuff is going to come out. They haven't even got the finesse to bury their squalid threats in the subtext of their worthless protestations of innocence. They come right out and say it, as if Marthinus van Schalkwyk and his abominable party still have enough clout to interfere with the judicial process.

In the old days it was called a Section 103ter certificate and would be issued by the State President whenever he thought that justice needed to be a tad more blind. But these days, people like PW Botha can barely order breakfast, so the system is relatively safe from this kind of abuse. And yet, these two heretics appear to be under the impression that exposing the whole rotten system would stand as some sort of mitigation for their actions.

To make matters worse, Marais seems to think he is untouchable because he is popular with the people. Let me point out that these are the same people who swear allegiance to the National Party. Holy cow. If I had my way these people would be in the dock along with Marais facing charges of first degree stupidity.

The courts will decide on their guilt. But let us be clear on one thing. The Scorpions hardly ever make mistakes. These people are capable of taking statements without once having to lick the tips of their pencils. In fact, I hear they don't even use pencils. They have pens that work straight away, without having to be shaken. Their lips do not even move when they take down statements. They know that 'corruption' is spelt with a c and during their tea breaks they read the Criminal Procedure Act and not soiled back copies of *Hustler*.

Unlike regular cops, the Scorpions have access to genuine Polaroid sunglasses and roadworthy cars.

Marais and Malatsi seem to think they can trifle with the Scorpions. Come to think of it, they both resemble actual trifles. Perhaps they were set in the same mould. Ted says that as punishment they should be coated in jam, soaked in sherry, covered with custard and cream and sent off to Baghdad to act as human trifles. Maybe then they will get their just desserts. And if they happen to escape the inferno, as I expect they will, there'll be no shortage of shady types willing to talk business with these putrescent puddings. Iraq will be perfectly positioned for countless golf estates after the Americans have created the bunkers and levelled the terrain.

Once the bodies have been moved and the blood mopped up, all it will take is a consignment of fast-growing buffalo grass, a whole bunch of little flags and a rudimentary clubhouse with diplomatic immunity to sell powerful alcohol.

One, two, three, fore! Georgie Porgie's going to war.

25 February 2003

—Malatsi was sentenced to five years in jail. Peter Marais was acquitted and the Scorpions announced their intention to appeal.

Bloodsuckers Smell the Fear

Now that the lawyers have done their worst and Brenda is out of the house, I can do things that I could never do before. Like pee on the cat, hang pictures upside down, move the couch on to the porch where it should have been from the start and then get the hell out of this appalling middle-class excuse for a house that she convinced me was home.

I have a neighbour who calls the police when taggers from the Cape Flats come sneaking through in the early hours of the morning to put their art on the giant beige concrete slabs of security that define our suburb. I can never understand why the police have to be involved. It's far quicker to get a licence for a handgun. It's also a whole lot more fun to shoot at vandals on a Friday night than it is to wait three days and then have a bunch of burly thugs in blue denting your sofa and drinking your coffee while their crackling radios attract the real criminals, i.e. the neighbours.

Anyway, the taggers would far rather we confronted them one-on-one. For a start, they are moving targets. This puts the whole thing into a sporting category. It's not like canned hunting at all. While they spray, I still have to find the breech block that Brenda hid beneath a giant pile of unwashed clothes. Then I have to locate the bullets and make sure that the thing is oiled enough not to explode in my hands.

By the time I get it together, the taggers are almost out of range. Luckily for them, you don't have to be Deadeye Dick to get a licence so I am legally entitled to fire blindly into the night. My strike rate is about the same as the Proteas, so I don't think anyone has been hurt. I've heard a few screams but nothing more than usual for a Friday night in a second-rate 'burb filled with white trash bickering over what Trevor Manuel really meant when he said we can all go out and spend the money we thought we never had. I hear it all the time since Clev stood up in parliament.

"You bought new shoes?"

"Yes, the minister said ..."

Bang!

But back to the freedom that spousal desertion has afforded me. Shedding the shackles of matrimony invariably turns men into hunters and pillagers. It's different for women, though. They turn into valium-guzzling manic depressives who waft through life like half-submerged shipwrecks drifting with the current. I'd rather be a man, thanks.

Right now, I am hunting for a new lair and last week I came close to finding what I was looking for. With Brenda out of the way I have invested in a range of gizmos, one of which tells me how fast I am walking by relaying information to a satellite which does a lightning fast calculation and bounces the data to a device I wear on my wrist. Then it is completely up to me to decide whether to slow down or speed up.

It is decisions like these that divorced men find so refreshing. The satellite never, ever nags me to pick up a box of tampons and wine for the braai with her boring brother and his stupid wife.

But that's just one of the gadgets I now wear with pride. The other is similar to a police scanner but this one is specifically tailored to journalists, lawyers, politicians and other professionals who feed off the pain and suffering of others.

Last week an entirely new genre of bloodsucker bleeped me. Now my life is infested with estate agents. I swear, all I did was think about buying a new place and they were swarming all over me. It's almost as if they can smell the fear. To be honest, I was in the belly of the beast at the time.

My financial adviser suggested that I invest in a metal detector as a hedge against the rand, so I was combing the high water mark at Camps Bay when the device began screeching like an anti-war protestor from Mitchells Plain. I followed the signal right across Victoria Road and into an estate agency that was wallowing in yet another zillion bucks worth of sales. The metal detector began lunging for the goose-like neck of one of the guests so I switched it off because this kind of behaviour is no longer encouraged in Camps Bay. These women have enough machines sucking at their flesh. They are ready for real lips. Luckily, I had them on me. But unluckily, they were quickly occupied with an exotic array of canapés and cocktails.

The trick at these functions is not to make eye contact with anyone at all. Strike up a rapport with the servants and drink and eat as fast as you can. And only then turn your attention to the jewel-encrusted throng. These people invented terms like "staggering views" so if you are a little unsteady on your feet they will assume that you are just back from a tour of the R15-million shanty on the beach.

I grew up in Palermo and went to a very good school that looked out over the bay. I remember an ugly kid called Stefan Antoni who sat in the back row. He hated girls. He would pull their hair if they came near him. For some reason, I always ended up consoling them. And when I realised that I actually enjoyed having their tongues in my mouth, I began encouraging Stefan to be as abusive as possible.

All these years later, drawn to a function by a cheap metal detector, I find that he has designed a whole bunch of fine looking houses across the city. I made a few discreet enquiries but all I discovered was that quite a few men in Camps Bay will admit to almost anything if it meant going home with me.

Stefan, if you're reading this, I am sorry for holding you down. It was Jeffrey who put the cracker up your bottom, not me. Let's talk real estate.

4 March 2003

The Dark Horseman of the Apocalypse

Somehow I have been branded a Dark Horse. I think it has something to do with an article that appeared in *Femina* magazine.

Brenda must have read it because she has been trying to win her way back into my heart for the past few days.

Isn't that so typical of women? Ditch your man because he has begun displaying disturbing signs of anti-social behaviour, and then, the moment he appears in a women's magazine, you want him back. Well, baby, there's a queue and you are at the back of it.

That's right. A disorderly line of ovulating females has formed outside my inbox. They are sending me photographs of themselves and have taken to making suggestions that I cannot repeat here. One of these total strangers even wanted me to fly her down from Pretoria for the weekend.

At this point you are probably thinking that these women are surely senile, club-footed creatures covered in hairy warts that nobody in their right mind could possibly want. Well, let me tell you something, these admirers of mine appear to be of the finest pedigree. Not all, I hasten to add. Some are clearly deranged and seem to think that because a Dark Horse once trampled all over their little hearts, they can take it out on me.

One even suggested that I seek professional help. Fine. I will allow myself to be used as the whipping boy for all you girls who have had your delicate sensibilities rent asunder by insensitive, unshaven brutes. I will be the one to suffer for the sins of others. Hang on, hasn't that been done already?

I received an e-mail today from a woman whom I cannot name because that would be a terrible breach of confidence. It would also damage my chances of getting her knickers off. She wanted to know how to approach a Dark Horse, how to tell if a Dark Horse is interested in her, and whether there is a way to tell in advance if the Dark Horse is an intellectual like myself or just another thick-necked bogtrotter who lost a testicle in a rugby accident.

I don't usually dispense free advice because there is a terrible danger that people might start taking it. But if you are interested in the silent type brooding in the darkest corner of the bar in and scribbling in a notebook, send a drink over to him. Then ignore him for the rest of the evening. Dark Horses have so much scar tissue that it takes a while for emotions of any kind to sink in.

Then they have to consider their response to that emotion. And when they finally take action, it invariably ends badly. Dark Horses act from the gut and all points below. The brain is merely ballast to allow the head to be lowered to accommodate beer, women, the toilet etc.

Another brazen hussy sent her photo assuring me that it doesn't do her justice. Her hair is longer now, apparently. And the scar left from the tattoo is hardly visible. She had something of the Dark Filly about her.

Another sent me a picture of an entire bevy of babes, challenging me to pick her out from the crowd. It was impossible. I wanted them all. She said that if I showed my face, so would she. I love games like these. They always end with bleeding head wounds and handcuffs.

I have tried to disguise the narcissistic undertones that run through this column, but I fear that I have failed dismally. And now I have to cut things short because my life has taken a sudden right turn and I find myself riding off into the sunrise with shiny silver suitcases and a badge. I am headed east, deep into the cursed heart of this fine continent. And I don't even have clean underwear.

Maybe I will take Brenda back, after all. On the other hand, if my inbox is anything to go by, there are packs of women out there who will do almost anything for a kind word. May as well let them start with the laundry.

1 April 2003

My Seed Shall be Sewn and the Barren Shall Bear Fruit

I want to have another child but I can't risk it with Brenda because of the gormless aberration she produced the first time around. Anyway, she would sooner a TB patient sneezed into her open mouth than allow me to touch her with my bargepole. So I am left with only one alternative.

"You're going to give what to who?" said Brenda, her voice rising like a jet engine picking up revs. I shuffled my feet and looked out of the window. "I'm going to become a sperm donor."

By the time I looked back she was in the bedroom packing. I was surprised. I thought at worst she would react in the same way that most people react towards blood donors – slightly suspicious but tolerant in the knowledge that they are doing a public service.

After bringing her a cup of tea heavily laced with lithium, I managed to get her to calm down enough to explain why she was behaving like Hillary Clinton on that terrible morning of August 18, 1998.

"Why don't you just go out on to the street right now and impregnate the first slut who comes along?" she shouted. Apparently this kind of behaviour is on a par with being a sperm donor. I tried to get her into a headlock to better explain my position but she was too quick for me.

I picked myself up off the floor and told her that nobody in their right mind regards a sperm donor as the father of a child born to a woman depraved, desperate or daft enough to be artificially inseminated. Brenda turned red and started breathing heavily. I mistook this for signs of arousal and had my trousers halfway down just as she launched her copy of the New Testament at my head.

"It's your stupid little sperm, isn't it? Of course it would be your child." My reasoning listed and I clutched the door handle for support.

Scratching for the high ground, I pointed out that they don't exactly have a life of their own. It's not as if millions of them abseil silently off the sheets, slip through the front door and head into the city for a night of heavy drinking and gratuitous fertilisation.

But Brenda was having none of it. She insisted that any woman who chose to defrost my bun in her oven would be carrying my child and that there were certain responsibilities attached. I was equally adamant that the moment my sperm left home, they could do as they pleased. Once they were off my hands, so to speak, I was no longer responsible for their actions.

Every sperm is not sacred, despite what Monty Python would have us believe. Anyway, I was doing this for a higher purpose. Brenda sneered. "You're out of beer money again?"

I quickly assured her that I would not be doing it for the cash. The higher purpose is that my seed would be stored and used to ensure the survival of our species when all men eventually become infertile, impotent or gay. Brenda ignored me and continued on her irrational path.

"Designer babies!" she spat. "What next? Mail-order catalogues? Mr Delivery bringing around the sample and a fresh syringe?"

Then she went off on a wild tangent about some poor girl finding out too late that my second cousin's maternal great-grandmother's son was a bipolar basket case with a string of hereditary diseases. I told Brenda that nobody would expect me to be that honest when it came to filling in the forms.

Anyway, the risk of spawning a deranged throwback is acceptable given the likelihood of an entire generation of tall, good-looking, multi-talented geniuses emerging from my 30 seconds alone with a dog-eared copy of *Hustler*. I interpreted Brenda's silence as surrender and gloated my way into the kitchen just in time to see her car reversing down the driveway.

With her out of earshot, I conceded that she might have a point. How would I feel knowing that somewhere out there were one or two or maybe even thousands of kids looking and behaving just like me?

Even more terrifying, what would happen if the lesbian at the top end of Kloof Street made a withdrawal in my name and bore a fine son, and the spinster from the bottom end near the corner café shot up with the same batch and loined a girl-fruit, and the two of them grew into horny, irresponsible teenagers who met at the Lotto machine where they fell instantly in lust and in a moment of drunken foolishness inadvertently created a two-headed monster?

Actually, I don't care. It's not my problem.

More importantly, are short, fat, stupid men allowed to donate sperm? Not that I am one, of course. But there should be some sort of mechanism in place to prevent ugly people from breeding.

With Brenda out of the house, now is the perfect time to slip off to the clinic and put someone else's life in my hands. And they had better pay me more than fifty bucks. I'm fresh out of beer money.

10 June 2003

Warm Zambians
& Violent Jacuzzis

Checking out of a Zambian hotel is like trying to get cats to put on a synchronised swimming display. It is worse than dealing with attention-deficit children who lack the hyperactivity element that makes this condition so much more interesting. The concierge looks like he has overdosed on Ritalin.

Slack-jawed receptionists are locked in thousand-yard stares. Even the porters convey the impression that they have just stumbled out of the final battle scene in *Saving Private Ryan*. And they all move with the speed and agility of a deep-sea diver. But it's not only the front desk that is in trouble.

Elsewhere in the hotel, barmen refuse to meet your eye and waiters become suspicious if you try to order a second beer. It is almost as if the locals fear that you and your foreign currency are a fragile illusion that will instantly vanish if they dare to directly acknowledge your presence, so they make contact through peripheral means which is acceptable for finely-tuned people like me, but I cannot begin to imagine what the Germans make of it. But that is not important.

The main thing is that the Zambians are very friendly people. Missing in action, but friendly, nevertheless. And that counts for a lot on a continent packed to the rafters with homicidal maniacs, sexual deviants and elderly dope fiends who will not hesitate to commit unspeakable horrors upon your person when you least expect it.

For reasons I need not go into here, I have stayed in several hotels in the past 13 days. That is an awful lot of glazed and dazed faces I have had to deal with. I am on my fourth hotel and expect to be checking out for the last time in the next day or two.

I am conserving my strength for the ordeal.

Right now, I am sitting in my room wearing a complementary bathrobe that rides high up on my hips and makes me look like a genetic throwback whose hormones have run amuck. Not very complimentary at all.

I am watching Jessica Lange being interviewed by the BBC's Tim Sebastian about her role as Unicef's goodwill ambassador to the Democratic Republic of Congo. She is appalled by the world's lack of interest in the massive blood-letting and general pestilence.

Hang on a minute. *The Simpsons* are on the other channel. There, that's better. Homer for president. I am considering wandering down to the swimming pool to sprawl about wearing dark glasses and a mysterious smile in the hope that I will be mistaken for a fading Nordic porn star and invited to an orgy. Actually, I'd settle for dinner.

Unfortunately, I am unable to plunge dolphin-like into the water since I foolishly forgot to bring my bathing trunks. I have made inquiries but it appears that the only trunks within a hundred miles of here are attached to elephants.

Or they would be if they hadn't all been gunned down and ripped up for their tusks. Last night I had my first Jacuzzi. I have always avoided this ritual on the grounds that it is terribly middle class and can only lead to a steady lowering of standards.

The device was in my bathroom and I was all alone, apparently not the best way to enjoy a Jacuzzi. Up to my neck in hot water, I inadvertently leaned against a concealed button. It was if a hundred piranhas had been dropped into the water. Clutching at myself in terror, I scrabbled for some kind of switch to moderate the feeding frenzy that was erupting all around me. If I had been on drugs the entire experience could easily have killed me. As it was, I insisted that management send me complimentary tequila sunrises until the shaking stopped.

Later, when I was prowling the hotel looking for beer to neutralise the dangerous levels of mescal in my bloodstream, I wandered into a room full of bulging narcissists moaning and gasping and thrashing about on all manner of machinery clearly designed with the more discerning sado-masochist in mind.

With my eyes closed it sounded like Saturday night at the Marquis de Sade's place. Having a gym inside a hotel is like setting up a crack house inside a police station. Normal people go to hotels so they can behave like wild animals and those of us who have no interest in working on our deltoids and tripods should not have to be confronted by such depraved scenes while foraging for booze and women.

19 August 2003

Worst Man at the Existential Wedding

B renda came into the lounge weeping on Sunday morning. This is nothing unusual because the entire family has always found Sunday to be the saddest day of the week. Easter Sunday is particularly brutal and the boy Clive can usually be found playing Nick Cave's *Murder Ballads* and quietly dismembering the stunted runt of his latest illegitimate litter of feral cats.

On Sundays I do what most men do when they feel sad, but since this is also the same thing we do when we feel happy, women become confused and begin questioning our motives.

Men do not react to anything, least of all questioning, on Sundays. This, in turn, leads to attempts to inflict bodily harm upon us to determine whether we have any feelings whatsoever.

I have felt a steady stirring in the loins ever since the advent of summer and this, combined with the sight of Brenda weeping, made me come over all strange and I fell to my hands and knees and crawled swiftly across the floor until I reached her ankles. I was about to incapacitate her by applying pressure to a little-known erogenous zone when Clive walked in and fainted at the sight of me prostrating in front of his mother.

Brenda began barking at me in tongues, accusing me of becoming markedly cruder and increasingly sexist. I sharply reprimanded her for using such clumsy English and she began weeping again.

Eventually it came out. "People are talking," she said. I nodded my head wisely. "That's where it all starts," I said. Bastards.

"No," she said, "you don't understand." Again, I nodded my head wisely, as men do when women make no sense at all. "People are saying that I don't exist," she sobbed, "that none of us exist."

I went to comfort her and managed to get a tight grip on her buttocks for a clear 30 seconds before she felled me with an elbow to the kidneys.

Clive regained consciousness and sensed something was terribly wrong. He began badgering me for love and reassurance. "Bugger off," I said. "Haven't you heard? You don't exist." Apparently this is a terrible thing to tell a child and I am still half deaf from the screaming.

Later, when Ted came over for a beer, I told him that from an existential point of view this could not possibly happen. He began nodding wisely so I explained that latter-day Orcs were going about town claiming that none of us existed. Luckily Ted has studied Descartes and it wasn't long before he convinced me that as free agents in a meaningless universe there was nothing to prevent us from unilaterally deciding that the beer, too, did not exist. And if it wasn't there to begin with, it certainly would have made a mockery of modern philosophy if it was there at the end. Only trained existentialists should use this as an excuse to finish all the alcohol in sight.

An old friend of mine is getting married today (no, really, he does exist) and I am the best man. Well, I would have been if I had not pulled out at the last minute, thereby making a laughing stock of tradition and a lifelong enemy of his lovely bride. Apparently this kind of behaviour is regarded in a very poor light in certain cultures. Well, the civilised ones, anyway. So what made me do it? It has already been established that I am a mendacious blowhard and a bounder to boot. But that is not why I let my good friend down at the last minute.

It is because I know that I cannot be trusted to behave inside a church at the best of times, least of all at a wedding, and he should have known better than to ask. The church is responsible for committing all manner of atrocities over the last 2000 years. Marrying people is just one of them. The Crusades were another, albeit on a far lesser scale.

The other deterrent was when I was presented with a breakdown of 50 things that a best man is responsible for accomplishing. This terrified me. I have spent the last month carrying around a list of three things to do. There was no way I would remember to wash the car, cut my hair, go to confession, attend the wedding rehearsal, keep the rings safe, collect the telegrams, pick up the rented tuxedos, organise a stag party, call the paramedics, stay with the groom while he has his stomach pumped and then sneak off for a quickie with the bride.

Receptions and wakes are by far the best things about weddings and funerals. There is a lot to drink and eat and single women are almost always at their most vulnerable. Had I been the best man, the maid of honour and chief bridesmaid would have been duty-bound to dance with me. Now I will have to get them drunk first and maybe even slip them one or two of the wedding gifts.

A few years ago I was the friend of a best man who asked me to do him a favour by picking up the groom. He opened the door wearing dark glasses and clutching a tumbler of whisky in one hand and a big fat joint in the other. He had done his research, you see. Apparently a marriage can be declared null and void if one of the parties signs the register while under the influence.

He was a walking disclaimer in a penguin suit and he pretty much stayed that way for the next fifteen years until the other day when she packed up the kids and drove off into the sunset with nary a backward glance.

16 December 2003

He Maketh Me Lie Down
With Lambs
– I Waketh Up With Chops

Right up front, I would like to wish everyone a happy 10 years of democracy. This is a fine moment in our country's history. But not fine enough.

When I heard that our fearless leader, dear old Thabo, was to address our disparate bunch of cocktail-sucking lawmakers on Friday, I quickly got in a fresh stash of lithium to control the mania that I was sure would sweep through my central nervous system. No such luck.

Fortunately I had a little stale Dexedrine on hand to pump up the volume, but halfway through Comrade Thabo's speech I had to ditch the dexies and reach for the Prozac. Why? Because our small but perfectly pro-portioned president began quoting extensively from a piece knocked off by Rian Malan in the *Sunday Times*.

My ghast was well and truly flabbered and if my mouth wasn't so busy quaffing beer, it would have been hanging open. I carry no torch for Mr Malan, nor do I bear him any malice.

I simply think that if the president was going to quote a South African writer, it should have been me. And I know that if the philosopher king (Mbeki, not Malan) spent more time in Cape Town he would have been familiar with my body of work.

I cheered up considerably when Brenda had a wardrobe malfunction late on Saturday afternoon. I was lying on the couch watching some or other blood sport when she walked by wearing one of these modern slinky dresses. The details are hazy but somehow the dress snagged on my hand and the entire garment came away leaving her stark naked.

It is a husband's duty to reprimand his wife when she forgets to put on underwear, and I whipped my trousers off to give her a quick rebuke. Just then, Clive walked in and quite unexpectedly set about a terrible falsetto screaming which caused the cat to hightail it right out of the house and down the road.

It turned out that this was the first time he had ever seen a naked woman. I got him in a headlock and brought him down like a wounded animal. The army taught me that the best way to calm a hysterical person is to press your knee into their throat. There was no need to demand his identification papers or political affiliation, so I relaxed my grip and allowed him to speak. Eventually it came out.

What scared him more than anything was that mom was deformed in the breast department. She didn't have Chinese fighting stars for nipples. It took me the best part of an hour and several crude drawings of the Jackson family tree to demonstrate that Janet is a genetic abnormality.

I blame the media. If there hadn't been a globally gratuitous focusing on the infamous right breast, none of this would have happened.

Even then, the kid wasn't convinced. So I brought out my collection of old *Scope* magazines which proved nothing at all because the centrefold had black stars instead of nipples.

Riding on the back foot, I carefully explained how women's bodies had evolved since 1983 and then quite inadvertently reached a point where it became necessary to explain the evolution of their minds and by the time I had finished he was rolled up like an aardvark saying things like: "No, no! It can't be true!"

I think I know why the boy is confused. It is because he is not a born free. Like the rest of us, he was born in captivity. For the first five years of his life he had free reign of the standard suburban half-acre. This included the servant's quarter, which was slightly smaller than two-eighths but was certainly big enough for Doris and her good-for-nothing alcoholic migrant worker husband and her four lovers and nine children.

Little Clive was always quite keen to have them over at the same time but he was too young to understand that this would have constituted an illegal gathering. Doris pushed her luck quite often and, even though I was a liberal, it was my civic duty to notify the nearest authorities that the *khaya* was being occupied by more than the statutory one (1) person.

But that was then. On Friday, Brenda watched the opening of parliament and was so moved that she defiantly declared that she is a Cesarean born free. This is marginally messier than Rian Malan's breech birth but more aesthetically pleasing and certainly a lot more politically correct.

And while I remain concerned about Mr Malan, it is Clive that I have to worry about. He has to learn how to hunt for himself. In the old days, it was like canned hunting. Herd the whites into one corner and then offer them all the best jobs. Now he has to go out there like an albino lamb moving with a pack of laughing hyenas.

Once things had settled down on the domestic front, I began wondering what more I could do to stimulate the economy than striking up a bilateral trade agreement with Sadiq the one-eyed barman. I need a good struggle to take my mind off Brenda's steadfast refusal to comply with her statutory obligation to have sex with me.

I am quite keen on fighting the rich, but only because I am poor. Once I am rich, and I will be one day, I won't even bother to fight the poor. The poor make a hopeless adversary because they are too busy drinking and smoking dope and having casual sex to put up a good fight. It's no good challenging them on the political playing fields either, now that Marthinus van Skulkwyk has sold his soul to the devil.

I met a person poorer than me the other day and tried to warn him about Kortbroek's Faustian shenanigans but he didn't know what I was talking about because he was expelled from school for throwing petrol bombs at Casspirs so he never learned to read properly and when it comes time to vote it doesn't matter anyway because his stolen car will have been stolen by someone else and it will be too hot or too wet to walk to the polling station and it will be a lot easier to have another hit on the white pipe and watch the omnibus edition of *Egoli* instead.

On Sunday afternoon I went out to do the grocery shopping and met a barmaid who is a half-and-half. Her first 10 years were spent in captivity, the other 10 in freedom. While weighing the bananas and pouring me a fresh pint, I asked her how she felt about a decade of democracy. Her reply surprised me. She said: "Get out of my bar, you dirty old pig."

I think she misunderstood the question.

10 February 2004

King of Spades
Nails Queen of Diamonds

With a little help from a former colleague living in early retirement in Port Nolloth, I managed to get myself on to the list of delegates attending the African Mining Conference at the International Convention Centre last week.

I wasn't a delegate, *per se*. It wasn't as if I was going to make any speeches. To be honest, I was there primarily for the free lunches. And maybe to pick up a small concession in Sierra Leone. There is something about blood diamonds that sets them apart from the common or garden stone.

Any fool can walk into a jeweller's shop and pick out something cut and polished and glued into a ring. But it takes a special kind of man to go into the heart of darkness and bring back a bag of gems that could have prolonged the civil war by at least another three days.

My plan was to mingle unobtrusively with the other delegates and eavesdrop on private conversations so that I might gain a better insight into the situation under the ground, as it were. My plan went to hell the moment I walked through the doors. I had never seen so many men in one place sporting dark suits and greedy eyes. I had taken my suit to the dry cleaners, but that was in 1987 and it had probably been sold to defray expenses. In retrospect, it might have been a mistake to wear a traditional garment that looked like it had been put together by a blind tailor on a street corner in Banjul. I thought this would help me to blend in with the natives, so you can imagine my embarrassment when I saw that everyone else was wearing Pierre Cardin.

After a little trouble at the metal detector, I managed to find my way to the conference hall where mining ministers were lining up to sell their country's mineral resources to the highest bidders.

Some of the smaller countries never really had much to put on the table. However, if nobody else was interested I was more than prepared to put in a cheeky offer to tap that shrunken vein of tanzanite. I kept putting my hand up until a delegate wearing the last of Ghana's gold around his neck told me this wasn't an auction and that if I was interested in investing I needed to be a little more discreet.

That's when I saw Dali Tambo in one of his peculiar oversized Sgt Pepper outfits standing off to one side oozing schmooze all over a couple of delegates. I waited for him to whip out one of his quaint embroidered pillows but he seems to have stumbled into something far more lucrative than presenting talk shows.

While waiting for lunch, I got talking to one of the security guards who was keen to get involved in my project. Not wanting to hurt the poor fellow's feelings, I explained that the word "mine" is an abbreviation of "mine, not yours", a phrase that helped to popularise early capitalism. This also effectively ended the conversation, allowing me to be first in line at the buffet. And a fine feast it was, too.

While wolfing my third plate of fish and pasta and curry, I sidled up to a white man with silver hair. He smelled of money. It turned out that his company was about to begin strip-mining a pristine piece of coastline on one of the Indian Ocean islands. I think he took my silence to mean disapproval, but my mouth was so full of free food that I could barely breathe, let alone conduct a decent conversation. He quickly went on to explain that local conservation groups were fully behind his project because they saw the potential benefits to the community. At that moment my mouth became empty and I used it to laugh harshly. "So you paid them off? Good job," I said, shovelling half a chicken into my gaping maw. It was probably for the best that I never got the chance to discuss matters further, because the next time I saw him he was on his knees giving the mining minister of an obscure central African dictatorship a big fat injection of foreign direct investment.

I spent the rest of the day conducting business from the lavatory. It was only the next day I read in the paper that I was among a group of people who had eaten the toxic trout. Some of the more delicate delegates were apparently treated at the scene.

At the time I thought my body was simply reacting to years of abuse. It does that sometimes. But it seemed more likely that it was reacting to the sight of Africa once again being gang-banged by a bunch of rapacious thugs in three-piece suits.

Luckily I had recovered from this brutal encounter by Valentines Day. I took Brenda to dinner and then spent the rest of the night talking and laughing and drinking Wild Turkey. The funny thing is, when the sun came up I saw that the woman I had been carousing with wasn't even Brenda at all.

Ted says I must have stumbled into some kind of parallel universe, but that didn't make sense because this woman was also not prepared to indulge me in several unorthodox requests.

I'm beginning to think the only one getting screwed out there is Africa.

17 February 2004

If Charlize Can Do It ... You Can't

Brenda has been complaining all week about her life. I honestly don't know what she has to complain about. It's not as if she gets to cook and clean and have sex and do all those other things that keep the modern housewife in shape.

She gave all that up 18 months ago, choosing instead to spend the house-keeping money on Spanish lessons and other irrational frivolities. This is why we live like hungry pigs. Well, I do. She always seems well fed and cleanly clothed. Perhaps she has a lover. Oh, well.

Of greater concern is that other people have been putting ideas into Brenda's head. People like Charlize Theron, for one. Look, it's all very well sashaying up to the podium wearing Vivien Leigh's hair and gushing all over the first three rows about your humble beginnings, but did she ever once stop to consider how much damage she was doing to the womenfolk back home?

I am sure Brenda is not the only woman in this country to start behaving above her station ever since the Benoni Bokkie took gold. It's not that I want to suppress her dreams and aspirations, but please, let's be realistic. Brenda would be among those who are turned back by immigration at JFK International because America's ugly quota is full. It is not as if she would arrive in Los Angeles and two days later she is in a Chinese laundry shouting at some poor Oriental girl about the stain on her petticoat when a theatrical agent from Sunset Boulevard walks in and signs her up right there and then to play opposite Robert de Niro in his latest Barry Ronge-approved comedy drama.

Thanks to Charlize, countless women around South Africa now believe they have a shot at escaping their pathetic little lives.

This is marginally less criminal than Mark Shuttleworth implying that every dumb brat who takes maths and science will have a fighting chance at jumping on to a rocket and floating about in outer space with two Russians and a monkey.

After watching the Oscars, Brenda went on and on about her unfulfilled potential. Then I ran out of beer and the mood became ugly. I offered to drive over to her father's house and shoot him. If that's what it takes to get you to Hollywood, I said, then I will do it. I thought this was about the most romantic thing I had ever offered to do for a woman. Then I remembered that Brenda's father had already tried to kill me on two occasions and I withdrew the offer. Nevertheless, do you think Brenda appreciated the gesture? Of course not. She proceeded to rampage up and down the living room, loudly proclaiming that it was me, and not her father, who was to blame for her predicament.

"Predicament?" I shouted. "What do you know about predicament?" I couldn't think of anything to say after that so I pretended to storm out of the room.

Another person who has been putting clever ideas into Brenda's head is Robert Mugabe. She thinks he is absolutely wonderful. On Saturday morning she put up a Zanu-PF poster above her side of the bed. I found it very disturbing. Things got even worse on Sunday when she claimed half of the garden for herself. She actually staked it out with a bunch of green and yellow crochet hooks, and when I asked what she intended doing with it, she gave me a sullen look and said: "Nothing. It shall lie fallow as testimony to my oppression."

I have never heard Brenda speak like this before. She usually communicates through a series of grunts and snarls and I was completely unprepared for such revolutionary talk. To be honest, I was afraid.

If Charlize Theron and Robert Mugabe are her role models, then where do I fit in? I thought of playing Jean-Bertrand Aristide to counter her new aristo-fascist tendencies, but the thought of having to pretend that I am being held hostage by the USA Marine Corps in the Central African Republic was too complicated to even consider.

Things can only get worse.

9 March 2004

Bosses – The Missing Link

This may come as a surprise to some of you, but I have not been spending my days reclining on the deck of my luxury yacht tapping out a weekly column and dining on deep-fried perlemoen and pink champagne.

I am embarrassed to admit it, but I have been keeping down a day job much like the rest of you white-collar criminals. Happily, this has now come to an end and I am a free man.

The worst thing about the industrial revolution is that it spawned an entirely new strain of human being whose behaviour was progressively characterised by appalling arrogance, tight-fisted rapaciousness and an unlimited capacity for treachery. Collectively, this new breed came to be known as Management.

Somehow, bosses skipped a link in Darwin's chain and instead of evolving, they regressed. Instead of becoming more complex and sophisticated, they began shedding all the qualities necessary for developing into well-rounded members of the *Homo sapiens* family.

The workers, on the other hand, became increasingly enlightened. On their way to developing a drinking problem, the proletariat developed innovative new concepts like labour unions. While the bosses spent sleepless nights wondering how to squeeze the hired hands for more work and less pay, the staff spent their nights gambling and carousing and inventing novel new ways of using up all their sick leave.

The devolution of the boss has been spectacular. There was a time when he strode the earth like a superhero, dispensing wisdom and charity in equal measure. He was the closest you could get to Plato's ideal of what constitutes a leader and about as far from the craven, venal dogs that they are today.

Not all of them, mind you. There are still bosses out there who have the capacity for rational thought and compassion, bosses who engender loyalty and respect. Like my editor, for example. And I am not saying that just because this column is the only thing standing between the Green Point shelter and me.

Actually, Brenda is the only thing standing between the shelter and me. She won't let me out of the house until I have fixed everything that I have ever broken. This is an impossible job that only a damn fool would attempt. But Brenda, being a boss and a woman, remains impervious to logic.

There is only one thing worse than having a woman for a boss and that is having a man for a boss who has too much woman in him. People who work for this kind of boss do so in a perpetual state of confusion and dismay. One minute he is pillaging donor funds from impoverished African countries and the next he is lying on his back doing gentle pilates exercises while Enya croons from the surround-sound speakers.

Some men are more comfortable working for female bosses for reasons which can often be traced back to their mothers. They enjoy being psychologically emasculated to such an extent that they can no longer even perform the most basic functions of a real man i.e. kill fish, trap leopards and enjoy strip shows without feelings of guilt and so on.

Some men think they can ride roughshod over their boss because she is a woman. This is like swimming naked at Gansbaai with a bleeding head wound during a chumming operation in shark season.

Even more foolish is to try to out-boss the woman with whom you live. There is always an outside chance that she relinquishes all control and puts you squarely in charge of everything. As unlikely as it sounds, this has been known to happen, although in almost every case it has turned out to be a trick.

If she turns to you one day and says: "Honey, I would like you to take all the decisions from now on", do not tug joyfully on your private parts and open a fresh bottle of Scotch. Instead, look at her eyebrows. This is the only way you will be able to tell if skulduggery is afoot.

While men have their Achilles Heels at the back of their feet, women have them in their eyebrows. For thousands of years, women have paid more attention to their eyebrows than to their men. As a result, women have evolved to a point where their eyebrows operate in isolation to their emotions.

When conducting a facial scan for signs of duplicity, do not even bother to look at the eyeballs. They will be steely and unflinching, no matter how heinous the fib. The truth lies in the eyebrows. They beetle, they arch, they bristle, they jostle up against one another and they wiggle and squirm like two compunctious caterpillars on the run.

But if you don't want to take my advice about the eyebrows, then go right ahead. Tell her that you would love to start taking all the decisions – that this is what you have wanted to do ever since meeting her but never had the heart to tell her because she seemed to be having so much fun controlling every aspect of your life.

But don't come crying to me when the ambush takes place. I suppose I should warn you. The ambush is a two-pronged affair, much like the old Zulu pincer movement that worked so well at Isandlwana on that hot summer's day in 1879.

It can strike without warning, but usually happens for the first time while you are driving to a party at a house you have never been to.

She: "Are you sure this is right?"

You: "Relax, honey. I'm in charge now, remember?"

She: "Of course you are, sweetheart."

(Because you're driving, you can't see that her eyebrows have gone from Whitney Houston to Jack Nicholson so she pats you on the knee and you fall for it.)

You: "You've got the map, right?"

She: "Why would I have the map? You're the boss."

(Inklings nibble at your toes.)

You: "Hey! Let's scratch this stupid party and stay home instead. What do you think?"

Ninety seconds later you're wondering how you ended up in the passenger seat with a ringing ear and a map that materialised from nowhere.

6 April 2004

Close Your Eyes
and Think of England

I was overjoyed to hear this week that trafficking in people is not a crime in South Africa. This means I can put Brenda and the boy, Clive, on the open market.

The brat has just turned 16 and needs to be exposed to the real world. He makes a pathetic drinking partner and I have no doubt that the Cambodians will be able to sort him out. From what I have heard, there is no better place for a lad to lose his virginity than in a massage parlour in downtown Phnom Penh.

As for Brenda, well, let me just say that I haven't eaten a home-cooked meal or worn a clean pair of underwear since July last year. In fact, my conjugal rights continue to be violated on all fronts.

I would happily trade Brenda for a real woman like Private Lynndie England. At least she doesn't throw up at the sight of a naked man.

Actually, I've quite enjoyed following the high jinks going on in Abu Ghraib prison. The other evening I tried to get Brenda into the spirit of the times by taking off my clothes and sneaking up on her on all fours with a paper bag over my head and a leash around my neck. She started making sounds of what I took to be arousal, then led me through the house and into what I thought was the bedroom. I had begun whimpering with anticipation when I heard the front door slam.

While reared up on my hind legs struggling to remove the hood, a pair of Jehovah's Witnesses walked through the gate and, instead of offering me redemption, began whacking me with a copy of *The Watchtower*.

When I was in the army, I rather liked the pain and ritual humiliation that was regularly inflicted upon me by corporals who were nowhere near as petite and sensitive as the eye-catching Private Lynndie. That, and being able to legally kill perfect strangers was what made being a signalman worthwhile. As a conscript learning how to drink heavily, I inadvertently violated some or other military code and ended up in detention barracks on my hands and knees crawling in an endless circle with a telephone pole resting on the back of my neck. This was not as much fun as it sounds. However, it did serve to instil in me a deep dislike of authority, blade wire, Telkom and men with the surname Ziegler.

War is an aphrodisiac and I have always believed that if enough conflict can be generated within a marriage, the divorce rate would be nowhere near where it is today. The art lies in striking a balance between hearty discord and homicide. This comes with years of practice and should not be attempted by newly-weds.

The military has always been a homoerotic institution and there is nothing quite like a good old-fashioned invasion to get the troops all hot and bothered. Iraq is no exception. There are quite a few Angolans and Namibians who, to this day, can recall their enchanting experiences at the hands of South Africa's good ol' boys.

Judging from the photographs, Private Lynndie seems to have a healthy disrespect for men. This is not necessarily a bad thing because in most cases they deserve it. I'm not talking about the Iraqis, of course. No nation on earth deserves to wake up one morning and find their streets full of yawping brutes clawing at themselves and filling the gutters with sputum. I'm talking about ordinary men, like you and me.

And I suspect this is the real reason why more and more South African men are going to Iraq. Subconsciously, we all want to meet someone like Private Lynndie who will treat us like the dogs that we are.

A recent report described Private Lynndie as a "backwoods bitch of war". And while this certainly is one of those phrases that Shakespeare might have wished he had come up with, I do not think it does her justice. Just because she comes from a small town of in-bred xenophobic white supremacists doesn't mean she is beyond redemption. Quite the opposite.

In fact, I bet if you had to visit her family's trailer and look through her photo albums, you would come across an almost identical set of pictures taken on her prom night. It's in her blood. Give the girl a break.

13 April 2004

The Toxic Waste of a Nuclear Family

Democracy has driven a stake through the heart of my family.
Like all men, there are only two things I want to know from my wife. How many men she has slept with and for whom does she vote. I believe I am not the only man who sleeps uneasily at night not knowing the answers to these questions.

The night before voting I asked Brenda who she fancied. She stared me square in the eye and said: "The chap who bakes the bread at the café." She was joking, of course. Women find me irresistible and I have no reason to believe that Brenda is any different.

Actually, I have plenty reason to believe she is different. For a start, her insistence that her vote is her secret is almost as irrational as her steadfast refusal to come anywhere near me the moment I show signs of disrobing.

Before the elections, I tried to use social occasions to draw her out by initiating political debates, but Brenda is one of those highly-strung women who is not afraid to ruin an entire Saturday afternoon braai by hanging around the Weber barking about "gender" and "equality" instead of staying in the kitchen helping the other ladies prepare the salads.

To be fair, neighbour Ted was partly responsible for ruining that particular braai when his peculiar wife, Mary, overdosed on Chardonnay and confessed that she was going to vote for the IFP for the simple reason that she thought Henry Cele was frightfully sexy when he played Shaka.

Ted was so outraged that he was unable to speak coherently, which made it difficult for the rest of us to ascertain precisely what it was that was outraging him. Brenda began prodding Ted in the chest, loudly accusing him of Zuluphobia, as if such a thing even existed outside the ANC's politburo. Ted reacted badly and started shouting things like: *Suga ma inja!* I know enough kitchen Zulu to know that this means: "Suck my dog."

Nobody in their right mind speaks like this in the renewed South Africa's former Whites Only suburbs and I was forced to eject Ted and his weeping wife from the premises.

None of this helped me get any closer to the one thing I really needed to know – how Brenda was going to vote. The touchy feely happy huggers among you will say that such information is irrelevant; that it is her democratic right to vote for the party of her choice without feeling beholden to justify or explain her decision to anyone. What utter rubbish.

How can a man be expected to trust his wife with anything, especially the car, if she is allowed to simply go off and secretly vote for a government entirely different to the one he wants in power? If it weren't for those meddling Pankhurst women, none of this would be happening.

In an effort to save the country from being plunged into anarchy, I tried to stop Brenda from voting. My plan was to daub her thumb nails with black nail varnish. Luckily, I found some tucked away at the back of Clive's underwear drawer.

The sequence of events is still hazy, but I remember a lot of screaming and a big wet hairy thing clinging to my back. When I regained consciousness, Brenda had returned from the polling booth wearing a smirk upon her face. It was a smirk unlike any other I had seen and I was afraid.

I quickly tried to form an alliance with Clive to take control of the west wing of the house but the boy threatened to turn me in to the IEC's paramilitary police. It was obvious that he had already formed a coalition with his mother, tipping the balance of power firmly in her favour.

I went out into the garden to get an olive branch so that I could extend it in the hope of giving fresh impetus to peace in the household, but all I could find was a clump of deadly nightshade which wasn't received nearly as well as I had hoped.

So now I find myself in the role of official opposition at home. I have lost my seat at the dining room table and right now I am taking precautions to ensure that Brenda and Clive do not abuse their two-thirds majority.

Unemployed and marginalised, I can only hope they behave like true politicians and forget all about me so that I can nip off to the pub at any time without undue interference for the next five years.

20 April 2004

Political Correctness – From Here to Eternity

For a long time I would skip newspaper stories if I spotted the word "homogeneous", thinking they were about gay dairy farmers. Apparently not. It is far worse than that. It is a word used to describe the increasing uniformity of our society, an alarming trend that must be stopped at all costs.

The Thought Police are already among us and it makes their job that much easier if we all dress, talk and behave the same way. Mavericks and free thinkers like Ted are being driven underground by wave after wave of political correctness that is on the verge of being legislated.

It is even beginning to affect my family. The boy, Clive, tries to slap me with his girly little hands whenever I make fun of the disabled. And Brenda is more adamant than ever that conjugal rights are a privilege I have not yet earned.

More and more, I find there are words that we are not allowed to say in polite company. The fact that it is becoming increasingly difficult to actually find polite company seems to be lost on those whose twisted Orwellian vision it is that we all become the same.

Here, then, is the A-Z of words that will soon either be outlawed or neutralised through the allocation of new meanings.

A is for Anarchy, a word used to describe an orderless political system or the filing system in the Department of Home Affairs. Also for Alcohol, a liquid which impairs your ability to operate heavy machinery. This is just one of the benefits.

B is for Barefaced Lying that accompanies applications for government funding by companies run by CEO Absolom wa-Frontman and his deputy, Wyatt Shark.

C is for Corporal Punishment, a primary pillar of the former education system which helped to create two generations of sado-masochists and assorted wife-beaters. Also for CCMA, an organisation created to punish employers for being stupid enough to have hired you in the first place.

D is for Dagga, a cash crop capable of eradicating poverty in South Africa. Used incorrectly, it arouses policemen and heightens the perception of being arrested.

E is for Eugene Terre'blanche, a mythical creature thought to be intermediate between the anthropoid apes and *Homo sapiens*.

F is for Fundamentalism, a degenerate brain disorder cured by self-detonation.

G is for Gadaffi, a term used to describe a tent-dwelling nomad. Harmless until provoked. Needs to be humoured or will blow up the world.

H is for Hate Speech, which, if done properly, could send you to jail for three years. Worth putting in some extra effort and trying for five.

I is for Identikit, a school of generic cop art designed to induce maximum paranoia among the general population.

J is for Joint, applies to statements put out by rebel groups common to central Africa. Can also be applied to the lips.

K is for Kaffirboom, a vicious, mean-spirited tree native to South Africa. Banned in 1994. Now goes under the assumed name of *uMsinsi*.

L is for Lapdog, a domesticated critter of little significance that will do anything for a handful of kudu biltong and a position in the cabinet.

M is for Manslaughter, also known as Murder Lite, a favourite among plea bargaining prosecutors who have to get home and start the braai.

N is for Nairobi, a vast cloud of unnaturally occurring carbon monoxide that provides cover for civil servants to plunder state coffers.

O is for Orania, a word used to describe an asylum run by the inmates. The opposite of Nirvana.

P is for PTA, or Parent-Teacher Association, where educationists and mothers get together to exchange racial invective in a neutral environment.

Q is for Quadriplegic, a word used to describe a person whose condition has no chance of improving, no matter how much they are ridiculed or ignored.

R is for Razor Wire, an invention designed to keep white people together in small, manageable herds.

S is for Sex, an activity rendered redundant by marriage. Also for Straight, an aberrant sexual deviancy in which men are attracted to women (rarely occurs in Cape Town).

T is for Tik, a form of medication that some students use to stay awake during history class and the entire summer.

U is for Usury, an offshoot of capitalism designed to ensure that the poor remain in debt for generations to come.

V is for Vuvuzela, a heinous instrument destined to remain untouched by Caucasian lips.

W is for Womb, everybody's starter home. Comes with a standard nine-month lease. Often a breeding ground for trouble.

X is for Xanthippe, the nagging cow who made Socrates's life a living hell. Emulated by women everywhere.

Y is for Yarmulke, the doily worn by Jews to avoid being mistaken for Muslims.

Z is for Zymurgy, a fancy name for the science of standing around with a thirsty look on your face watching your home brew ferment.

15 June 2004

Haircut Saves Man From Sex-Crazed Abalone Addict

Last week Ted and I went into the Cape Point nature reserve on a perlemoen poaching expedition when something went horribly wrong and I woke up 48 hours past my deadline covered in rotting kelp with a crotch full of sand fleas and some kind of rodent gnawing on my foot.

My obsession with perlemoen began one morning a couple of weeks ago when I fried one up as a special anniversary treat and delivered it to Brenda as she woke. The effect was remarkable. She locked the bedroom door and set about the most alarming shrieking and whooping I have ever heard coming from a white woman. I doubt she could even hear me banging on the door begging to be let back in.

When I finally smashed my way through the window, I found a naked Brenda hunkered down on her haunches in the far corner sweating heavily and sucking on the perlemoen shell with a crazy look in her eyes. My courage failed me and I stood there, shoulders hunched and sullen of eye, like a Spanish bull who knows when it is beaten.

I have since changed all the locks and hidden the keys. The next time I get some of this satanic shellfish into Brenda, I want to be right there to take full advantage of her remarkable metamorphosis. Ted keeps warning me to be careful, but I have long recognised sex as a blood sport and always prepare accordingly.

When it comes to making advances of a carnal nature, whether on your wife or somebody else's, the most important thing to remember (apart from the protective goggles) is to have a haircut before you go in.

Not many people know this, but men have lost more fights through having long hair than blunt swords. Look what happened to that elvish ponce in *Lord of the Rings*. It took a troll to save his gay little butt.

William Wallace painted his face blue and gave King Edward a damn good thrashing at Stirling, but then he grew his hair and thought he could get away with sleeping with hundreds of Celtic sluts. By the time he got to Falkirk, his hair had been yanked by so many jilted women that the first blow in that fateful battle of 1298 dislodged his entire temporal lobe from both cerebral hemispheres and shortly afterwards he was caught and executed by the bastard British. Braveheart, my arse. Anyway, look at Scotland today. He needn't have bothered.

Hippies are another hirsute bunch who lost a revolution because they refused to cut their hair.

And that's why people like George W Bush and the Pope make regular trips to the barber. They know that if they hope to keep Americans off crack and Catholics off contraceptives, they cannot afford to have the Internet full of pictures of them being dragged around by the hair by jealous White House interns or frustrated Vatican altar boys, even if it is on a subscriber site.

But back to me. It was after my trip to the reserve with Ted, when the debauchery reached unprecedented levels, that I decided to clean up. So, with loins fully girded in anticipation of a little early spring action with a post-perlemoen Brenda, I went off to get de-fleaed, have a tetanus shot and visit the hairdresser.

Not being the leader of the free world or the head of a heavily over-subscribed cult, I choose not to go to barbers. Again, not many people know this, but the word "barber" is a corruption of "Berber", a North African tribe which deals with long hair by removing the offender's head.

I have a hairdresser who knows better than to talk to me. For too long I allowed myself to be at the mercy of strange women who said things like: "So where are you from?" and "So what do you think of Cape Town?" even after I had repeatedly told them that I am from Cape Town. I mentioned this to Ted and he said I was thinking of hookers, not hairdressers. Some friend he is.

Why, I don't know, but I always decide to have a haircut just as I am careening off one of those crippling benders that men go on when they have nobody around who cares enough to stop them. This happens more often than you might think.

Fighting off the dry heaves while the synapses splutter and fuse is not always the best time to be bent over backwards with your head in a sink while an unidentified androgynous biped wearing leopard-skin pants and tight frilly top massages your scalp in time to an ambisexual band made up of bottle blonde teenage vixens with swollen breasts and shrunken morals.

Being a liberal, I try not to be rude to people of indeterminate gender. Instead, I chew the inside of my mouth to a bloody pulp and keep my eyes closed so that the popping of the ophthalmic veins does not disturb the other poor swine getting their heads rubbed by the rest of the hip-swaying transsexual mutants on the payroll.

It gets worse. The wash is over. Now it is time to wear a Day-Glo pink sheet and sit in front of a giant mirror without moving your head more than one millimetre in any direction.

Your body a lurid amorphous blob, you find that your face doubles in size. By the end, you cannot even bring yourself to look into the mirror. You resemble some sort of queen from the gay insect kingdom without any of the perks, like allowing the warriors to suckle your breast so that they may go back out there and conquer new kingdoms.

This is what happens when you get into the habit of channel hopping between *National Geographic* and *Emmanuelle II*.

3 August 2004

Drug Scandal at the Fish Hoek Olympics

I n my part of the country, the coldest day of the year fell on Women's Day. However, I will refrain from drawing any inferences.

Being sensitive to gender issues, I thought it might be a good idea to help Brenda thaw out by staging our own suburban Olympic Games. I rang up Ted for some ideas and straight away he said we should give Gina a call. He described her as a fiery redhead who apparently does Greek, which fitted in perfectly with the whole Athens thing.

When I asked Ted if she could speak English, he said he wasn't sure but the advert said she was "a totally inhabited lady". Brenda also has that lived-in manner about her, so I told Ted to invite her to join us.

The boy, Clive, volunteered to make a replica of the Parthenon using bricks from the back wall of the police station down the road. Okay, that's not strictly true. He never volunteered. I told him I would burn his favourite skirt and make him listen to Leonard Cohen if he didn't cooperate.

While the brat was busy, I nipped out to buy the ingredients for a typical Greek lunch. When I got back, Brenda shouted at me and said there was no room in the fridge for 15 litres of ouzo and a small tin of olives.

Because it was Women's Day, I let her go off at me for longer than usual before coming at her with the sharp end of the broom. Using some sort of Tai Chi manoeuver which I had never seen before, she brushed the weapon aside and was about to sink her teeth into my face when Ted arrived with Gina. She looked more lower Sea Point than upper Plaka.

Clive said his Parthenon would never be ready in time for the opening ceremony, which I thought was an authentically Greek touch so I gave him a bottle of ouzo and sent him to his room.

Before the games began, I called for a minute of silence to mark the death of the New National Party, but Ted ruined the moment by imitating the sound of a howler monkey caught in a gin trap. Brenda wanted to know if it was coincidence that on the day Smarty von Skunkbroek switched off his party's life support system, a couple of provinces announced that thousands of ostriches had to be slaughtered. I snatched the ouzo out of her hand and reminded her that we had guests.

Gina checked her watch and said her rate was R500 per hour or part thereof. There had obviously been some sort of misunderstanding, so Ted took her to the spare bedroom to fully explain the significance of Women's Day. Ten minutes later I heard the front door slam and Ted returned alone. He was having some trouble walking and refused the offer of a chair. This was just as well, because there is no time to sit when the Fish Hoek Olympics are underway.

The first event was an ouzo drinking competition. It was declared a draw because nobody gave any indication that they would stop drinking. Ever.

The second event was golf. Brenda snorted like a sick animal and said that golf was not an Olympic sport. I tried to correct her but she parried effortlessly and replied with a thrust to the solar plexus that left me winded.

Since it was Women's Day, I resisted the temptation to launch a counter-attack and instead took Ted out on to my verandah overlooking False Bay. By a stroke of good fortune, three medium-sized Southern Right whales were lolling about within range of my tungsten steel driver. Ted got seven points for hitting two of them, but I took gold by getting a hole in one.

Ted tried to argue, claiming that a whale's blowhole was smaller than a golf ball and that a hole in one was technically impossible. I called him a filthy lying dog and the mood turned ugly.

Demanding that I take a drug test, Ted ordered me to urinate into a cup. I was still sorting out my aim when the newly-wed Jehovah's Witness couple from across the road came over to complain about the noise. I thought we were under terrorist attack and grabbed Brenda from behind. Using her as a human shield, I worked my way towards the kitchen where the machete is kept.

With an overpowering stench of aniseed pouring from his mouth, Ted announced that the archery event was about to begin. He lunged for my loaded speargun and, in the true pagan spirit of the Olympics, advanced on the Jehovah's Witnesses. Then he went and disqualified himself by shooting before they had a chance to run.

The rules of this event were clear – the target must be moving at all times. As it happened, Ted missed by a few centimetres. By the time I had released Brenda and reloaded, the happy couple was safely home scanning back copies of *The Watchtower* to check if what they had just encountered marked the beginning of the end of the present system of world government.

I doubt that it did, but it certainly marked the beginning of the end of my friendship with Ted. The booze-addled heretic decided that the only thing missing was an Olympic flame, so he set fire to my collector's edition of *Soldier of Fortune* magazine and ran through the house shouting garbled words of encouragement for South Africa's athletes, even though we had agreed hours earlier that they were doomed to fail miserably in everything they attempted.

Once the smoke had cleared and the cat had been extinguished, Brenda cracked a fresh bottle of ouzo and said she had an idea for a new event. Despite being severely incapacitated, Ted and I rounded as one. We reminded her, in words of many syllables, that, for thousands of years, women had not been allowed to participate in the Olympics. Athletic training takes up a tremendous amount of time and the Greeks understood better than most that if women were allowed to take part, somewhere there would be men going without food or sex.

However, Ted and I agreed that as it was Women's Day, we would make a special exception and allow Brenda to compete in the Striving for a Non-Sexist Society event. For Brenda to win, she had to convince us in 30 seconds why she should not go to the kitchen and make a round of toasted bacon and peanut butter sandwiches. It was close, but she had to make do with bronze. Ted took silver and passed out. I'm still waiting for my medal. And my sandwich.

10 August 2004

Africa's Big Five
– The Ultimate Happy Meal

I returned from Namibia with the brat, Clive, to find that Brenda had turned into a svelte wench with a tiny waist and bronzed face. She had also somehow managed to shift about 50kg of useless blubber from her hips to her breasts. She looked like a cross between Marie Stopes and Dolly Parton.

The transformation was so dramatic that the boy collapsed and grabbed hold of my legs when she opened the door for us. I tried to kick him off but he clung there like some kind of blubbering mollusc, completely ruining my hopes of opening the floodgates to the untapped reservoir of pheromones that I have always suspected lies dormant within my wife's unyielding bosom.

However, the cold-hearted bitch recoiled visibly when she saw my new rugged Desert Survivor look. Lying in bed that night, I tried to covertly inspect her body for surgical scars. Moments later, in the bathroom washing the last of the pepper spray from my eyes, I caught sight of myself for the first time in weeks. Many hours spent under the savage Namibian sun soaking up the meaning of life had left my head swollen to three times its usual size. I looked like a medicine ball with eyes.

When I threatened to report Brenda to the Gender Commission on the grounds of gross insensitivity, she snorted and tossed her freshly burnished mane and suggested that my bulbous head was more likely the result of 1500 cans of lager.

This is utter rubbish. Namibian beer is brewed according to German purity laws. This means the more you drink, the longer you will live. It goes without saying that your looks improve substantially at the same time.

If drinking too much beer turned you into a lardaceous blimp, you would have to be mad to drink excessively. Especially if you live in Camps Bay, where a fresh generation of beautiful young things is starting to appear in the cocktail bars like some kind of blue-eyed spawn from Dr Josef Mengele's slow-release programme.

Purity laws notwithstanding, the amber elixir of the Namib seems to have reacted badly to something I ate. While travelling through that godforsaken country in the hope of turning the fruit of my loins into something vaguely resembling a man, I was unable to shake an insatiable hunger for biltong. It started innocently enough with a few strips of cow, but this turned out to be a gateway to the harder stuff.

By the time I had a few chunks of springbok inside me, it was a simple matter of moving on to gemsbok, kudu, oryx and even dik-dik, which are so small that you can fit almost the entire buck into your mouth.

My craving for ever more exotic strains grew by the day, and by the time the Namibian Game Hunters' Association reported me to the authorities, I was moving at high speed with a portable drying rack in the back seat strung with the flesh of a baby elephant, a dwarf rhino and two smallish leopards. Eating the Big Five was so much more satisfying than spotting them.

However, absorbing the desiccated DNA of so many different species comes at a price. Although I was fortunate to escape developing animal-like tendencies (growling, headbutting, joining the police and so on), my skin erupted in a giant blotchy rash and my lips blew up like bicycle tubes.

After one particularly heavy binge on honey badger and warm beer, I stopped outside Outjo to decompress and found myself fighting off a small white bird trying to get at the decaying meat wedged between my teeth. It wasn't a pretty sight.

This is why I was so disconcerted by Brenda's reaction to the new physique I had developed on my road trip. Most South Africans, whether they live in Cape Town or Pietermaritzburg, emerge from winter looking like joyless, dissipated slugs. Not the very poor, of course. They remain their sleek selves all year round.

Women across this great country are right now prodding their dimpled thighs and thinking: "I must get rid of this before summer." Among these women is an alarming percentage who are prodding their sleeping husbands and thinking the same thing.

Some might say the thing uppermost in the minds of all right-thinking

South Africans should be the looming civil service strike. Well, it's not. And not just because "government worker" has taken pride of place in the local pantheon of oxymoronic phrases either.

Strikes, like push-up bras, are no longer sexy. They no longer inspire in us the desire to rise up and militate against the Man. Karl Marx and Leon Trotsky are out. Karl Lagerveld and Leon Schuster are in.

Downing beers makes so much more sense than downing tools. Besides, ever since I opted out of the system, I have grown to fear the unemployed and despise those with jobs. This has left me in an invidious position, whatever that means.

The important thing is that we all start to get our bodies back into shape. Brenda has had some things sucked out of her and other things shifted around.

If more people took the trouble to have collagen implants, Botox injections and a little liposuction around their haunches, we might get more visitors from civilised countries like Sweden.

Very few Europeans want to feel like they are witnessing a beaching of orcas every time they venture near our coast. Nor do we want visitors from other parts of this continent thinking we are the sole cause of famine in Africa.

So my message is simple. Lose the gut. Lose the butt. Make Charles Darwin proud. Summer is almost here and if you can't make the effort to resemble something vaguely human, don't come and lie on our beaches.

Especially not in Fish Hoek, where I am mounting a harpoon on my deck as we speak.

14 September 2004

Save Sudan
or the Dolphin Gets It

People come from all over the world to visit the Western Cape and soak up the stunning scenery. Among them are those who go all the way to Fish Hoek, not so much to enjoy the surroundings, but more to kill themselves.

Oh, yes. Us valley folk are very proud of our status as the suicide capital of the province.

But things took a strange turn during the early hours of Friday morning when a posse of dolphins deliberately beached themselves not far from the Bayside Café. I never saw it myself, but word on the street is that they had to fight their way through mobs of manic depressives heading in the opposite direction.

By all accounts, it was an ugly sight, what with the dolphins whistling and squeaking and the basket cases moaning and wailing. Luckily, the jostling never lasted long. The dolphins made it to the beach and the capitulators made it into deep water with minimal disturbance to the circadian rhythms of the seafront dwellers.

I woke just in time to see the navy round the point in their shiny new kick-back Corvettes and begin live firing exercises that made the whales miscarry while simultaneously taking care of the flounderers who had realised too late that they wanted to live, after all.

Nan Rice, who speaks fluent dolphin, was on hand shortly after her regular shrimp-free breakfast to issue a statement condemning everything that can blink or doesn't own a set of gills.

Had I been quicker off the mark, I would have darted down from my eyrie and taken one of those suicidal dolphins hostage. Like most God-fearing people, I have demands that I would like met.

Snatching an elderly engineer from the streets of Baghdad has a certain primitive cachet, but I have no doubt that if I had to post live pictures on a website of me holding a dolphin in a headlock with a rusty bait knife to its throat, I would be able to get myself a Cuban passport and a powerful boat.

I would then be in a position to demand unhindered passage to Sudan, a country that Washington does not consider to be a safe haven for militant Islamic rebels. This is wonderful news. The general raping, killing and looting I can deal with, just as long as militant Islamic rebels are not involved.

If I am to get involved in an abduction and potential beheading, even if it is just a dusky dolphin, I don't want any militant Islamic rebels stealing my thunder. I want to commit an act of tourism that the world will never forget. God knows those Khartoum characters need it.

Hopefully, my mission will be accomplished before those interfering peacekeeping bastards arrive. Two weeks ago, the UN Security Council authorised the African Union to mobilise three thousand troops to raise the national morale and bring down the cost of local prostitutes.

Richard Snyder, the US State Department's senior representative on Sudan, caught unawares while caucusing with senior White House officials in his private Jacuzzi, said Washington was ready to provide material support once the African Union had submitted its plan. Thanks to years of training, he only started laughing once the cameras had been switched off.

On hearing the good news, Nigerian president and African Union chairman, Olusegun Obasanjo, switched into a fresh set of robes and straight away went on record as saying that the AU would hold an emergency meeting to decide by early 2008 if it could mobilise the troops, many of whom were sick in bed or still drunk from the night before.

After sending a runner to get a fresh batch of air time from the dodgy Arab on the corner, Cde Obasanjo noted that Sam Nujoma, after eliminating the homosexuals from his army, could contribute 17 men.

Robert Mugabe was in for 13 000 war veterans, all of whom were too small to be issued with anything but handguns.

Botswana offered a Harvard-trained scientist who had developed a drinking problem and could no longer be relied upon to keep quiet about the real reason behind their currency's strength.

Mozambique's offer of its entire army was politely turned down because nobody trusts anyone who speaks Portuguese, black or white.

And Rwanda's only fighting fit battalion was keen as mustard to try out their new prosthetic limbs.

While marshalling the African troops with one hand and asking white countries for at least $200-million for logistics with the other, which presumably includes ammunition and condoms, President Obasanjo said, helpfully, that "one man's autonomy is another man's decentralisation."

I have no doubt that this will speed up the process immensely. Teenage rebels high on blood lust and unspecified hallucinogens have an innate understanding of such concepts.

All of this makes me think that beheading dolphins might not be that effective in my fight for world peace. Besides, dolphins have incredibly thick necks and I would be at it forever, forcing me to look at my broadband streaming options and that's not something anyone in their right mind wants to do.

I have a new plan. I intend spending time in the Company's Garden training squirrels to carry explosives on their backs. Rodents make the most effective suicide bombers because they are instinctively drawn towards food.

And until America realises that what we want are more helicopter gunships and less genetically modified maize, the squirrels will keep on coming.

28 September 2004

Colin & Jesus
– Separated at Birth

Waking on Sunday morning incapacitated by hunger and half-mad with ethyl alcohol poisoning, I went outside to purge from the north face of the balcony. And that's when I saw them.

Thousands upon thousands of people in the streets, all heading out of Fish Hoek. It was obvious that I had slept through the sirens and warnings, and was now the only one trapped inside the valley while some sort of deadly Andromeda strain crept silently through the suburb.

Panicking in mid-purge is never a good thing, as Jimi Hendrix discovered. However, I am married to a woman who wouldn't come to my assistance even if I were on fire, blinded by cobra venom and stumbling directly towards an open window in an apartment on the 30th floor. This means I have had to learn how to save my own life when it is in jeopardy, like when I am choking on a particularly robust purge.

I have fortunately perfected the art of administering a self-inflicted Heimlich Manoeuvre by running into the sharp edge of the kitchen counter. Yes, I have shattered my sternum and ruptured my spleen more times than I care to mention, but I am still alive – although on Sunday I wasn't sure for how much longer, given that even the old, sick and ugly were getting the hell out of the area.

In times of urban crisis, it is usually this demographic that is content to put their feet up and watch a bit of Jerry Springer while happily waiting for death to take them.

Then I noticed they were all wearing baggy shorts and silly hats, a strange attire for people fleeing from some unspeakable abomination. I said three Shaloms and a Hail Mary and headed down into the belly of the beast to get some answers.

Instead of fearful looks and cries for help, I got a whole bunch of cheerful greetings and words of encouragement. I nearly purged all over again. Turns out that the great unwashed were not abandoning the Deep South ahead of an epizooty of epidemic proportions. Oh, no. What they were doing was participating in the *Cape Times* Big Walk. The hold this newspaper has over people terrifies me. It's almost biblical.

Something else happened over the weekend that reminded me of the Old Testament. It was the funeral of Colin 'The Saint' Stanfield, portrayed by the corrupt enforcers of the so-called law as a drug-dealing gangster who served time for tax fraud.

The event of the year was held under two enormous marquees in an open field in Valhalla Park, a part of the Cape Flats where no white man has ever gone before.

After blacking out my two front teeth, I shaved my head, slapped a giant self-adhesive spider-web tattoo across my neck and walked boldly up to the Police Firearms and Alcohol Unit vehicle parked near the gates. Even though it was pretty obvious what I was waiting for, the officer behind the wheel refused to hand over my complementary 9mm pistol and bottle of Klipdrift. Perhaps we were meant to bring our own.

Disguised as someone who could be linked to either organised crime or organised religion, I made it past the two acolytes wearing matching Fabiani suits, dark glasses and earpieces and in to one of the circus tents that had been hired to help give Saint Colin the send-off he deserved.

Inside, people on plastic chairs were transfixed by a priest who seemed to be possessed by some kind of ecclesiastical demon. I have seen junkies withdrawing from heroin in a more controlled manner, but apparently this is how sermons are delivered in the Badlands.

I noticed a large woman wearing a blue T-shirt emblazoned with the message: "We salute you Colin Stanfield." She was watching me with suspicious eyes. Not wanting to blow my cover, I gave her an elaborate gang sign using both hands and most of my fingers. It must have worked, because she rushed over and showed me to an empty chair. Perhaps she thought I had Parkinson's.

Then the priest began shouting: "Colin and Jesus! Colin and Jesus!" over and over until I could no longer distinguish between the two. I felt a hallelujah bubbling up in my throat but quickly suppressed it when we were asked to stand and sing, "What a friend we have in Colin."

Two thousand people rose as one. They couldn't possibly all have been on the payroll. It was astounding.

Later, speaker after speaker reminded us of how Saint Colin of Stanfield had supported the community, paid their rent, put their kids through school, bought candles for the church, kept impoverished lawyers in business through modest payments of R20 000 a day and so on.

There's nothing like a little evangelical idolatry to work up an appetite, so I made the sign of the crossbow and headed for the food tent. There I found a herd of industrious women preparing food for the multitude. There seemed to be a lot more than a couple of loaves and a few fishes on offer, although I did have some tuna on a roll, but scoring a free lunch in this area was a miracle on its own.

While taking food from the mouths of the poor and kicking grubby urchins off my shins, I recalled an Institute of Security Studies report from four years ago that said Colin was worth more than R30-million. So I swallowed my guilt, along with a third tuna roll, before hightailing it out of there the moment I heard the stretch limousines fire up their engines.

The cavalcade was endless and it became impossible to tell where the family ended and the unmarked vice cars began, with the result that I followed the wrong vehicle and became hopelessly lost in about nine seconds.

Luckily, a disoriented preacher jumped into the car and showed me the way to the graveyard. On our way there, we came across traffic officers diverting the cars. In the distance, I could see a convoy escorted by flashing blue lights heading our way.

"Must be Mbeki," I said. "Too slow," said the priest. He was right. It turned out to be our man, Colin. The priest urged me to go through stop streets, red lights and right over an elderly Muslim fellow on a zebra crossing so we could get to the cemetery in time.

The Maitland cemetery extends through at least four postal districts and we wasted valuable minutes standing around a grave full of surly men who turned out to be nothing more than uptight Catholics.

I was sombre of mood when I arrived at the right spot, largely because a traffic cop who had never made it on to the payroll refused to allow me to take a shortcut through the cemetery where a high-speed run would have won me pole position at the hole. Instead, I had to stand at the back.

This put me 300m away from the action and right next to a Caucasian gentleman wearing a white tennis shirt, blue polyester slacks held up with a snakeskin belt, a regulation-issue moustache and dangerously short black hair. I thought he was a decent Colin-fearing mourner right up until the moment he whipped out his VHS camera with modified telephoto lens and turned to his friend and said: "Boet. How do we know it's really Stanfield in the coffin?"

You know you are going to heaven when even the police make the effort to film your funeral.

12 October 2004

Chicken Noodle Fellatio for the Soul

I was hacked recently. I thought this kind of thing only happened to the Pentagon and other institutions that allocate seats on the axis of good and evil, but apparently not. Some spotty-faced spawn of Satan deleted four years of messages on my Hotmail account and then killed three of my Yahoo addresses.

On the very same day, my cellphone went missing. In the space of a few hours I was rendered utterly and hopelessly incommunicado.

I made straight for Sea Point and accosted the first Nigerian I came across. He must have been Kenyan because he refused to give me drugs but he did offer me a damn fine cellphone instead. My joy was soon crushed by the realisation that nobody had my new number and the only number I could remember was my army number, and that's only because a staff sergeant once carved it into the back of my hand with a blunt bayonet.

When I told Brenda that we would need to find a whole new set of friends, she gave me one of her special withering looks and said, in what I assumed was mock surprise, that I had surely made a back-up of all my numbers and e-mail addresses.

I laughed in the way that a United States Marine might laugh just before gunning down a wounded Iraqi, and told her that the last time I needed back-up was late on a Friday night outside Smuggler's Inn on Durban's dark and dangerous Point Road.

She seemed genuinely interested in my story so I began recounting the events of that terrible night but stopped when I realised that she had fallen asleep with her eyes open.

Women do that when their loved ones confess how close they have come to death. It's some sort of coping mechanism.

Feeling isolated and disconnected, I turned to Telkom. After all, they are in the business of putting people in touch with other people. The first person they put me in touch with was a technician who spoke no recognisable language and bore the face of someone who had fallen head-first into the shallow end of the gene pool.

After he left, I swept the place for bugs. I also checked for listening devices. Getting hacked has sent my paranoia levels soaring to unprecedented levels and I no longer trust anyone, especially not someone who works for a monolithic monopoly that plans on siphoning enormous amounts of cash from my bank account every month just so that I can reassure my mother twice a day that I am not on Equatorial Guinea's extradition list.

On top of it all, the cat has developed some sort of mad bum disease which it insists on rubbing against me at every opportunity. It's like having a Chacma baboon with a frottage fetish in the house.

At the same time, I have been struck down by the dreaded lurgi. There is no fun at all in spending an entire week sweating and retching and shaking, and even less fun when you beg your so-called spouse for a diagnosis and all she comes up with is delirium tremens and a rictus grin.

Brenda's singularly unsupportive response to my condition puts paid to the lie that women have a more developed instinct for nurturing the sick. Look, there may well be women out there who turn into a cross between Florence Nightingale and Pamela Anderson the moment their husbands fall ill, but Brenda is not one of them.

Chicken noodle soup and low-intensity fellatio are all we really need when we are feeling poorly. What we don't need is biting sarcasm and a poisonous viper in the bed.

To make matters worse, I live in a suburb where the sick are treated like lepers, or even worse, like Congolese sellers of beaded wire art.

Camps Bay has no place for a yellow-eyed, mucus-stained wreck of a man, especially not at the onset of summer, when all the happy shiny people are trying to get high and laid at the same time.

The pretty folk are quick to back away when they see me lurching down the strip in search of a pharmacist who is prepared to go to the trouble of getting off his skinny white ass just so that he can make a profit of nine cents. And that's before tax. Yet, I find it hard to sympathise with anyone who has unfettered legal access on a daily basis to some of the finest narcotics known to mankind. Any male animal that loses his ability to hunt is quickly ostracised by the pack, unless he is a hyena, in which case the pack simply stands around and laughs cruelly. Brenda has a bit of hyena in her.

And that's why I went out and acquired myself a second-hand motorcycle. Once I had hosed the blood and brains off it, I took it to the dealer for a service. Like all dealers, whether they be in the drug or automotive trade, you can expect to be ripped off. What I never expected was to be charged R500 an hour for labour. That's R4 000 a day. R20 000 a week. R80 000 a month.

I was outraged and dashed off a letter to my local member of parliament who I expect will have announced his resignation and set himself up as a mechanic by the end of the week.

No wonder I'm sick.

23 November 2004

The Couch Who Spoiled Christmas
– A Horror Story

There are only 18 shopping days to Christmas. And there are roughly 4 800 shopping days until I contract one of the many dread diseases that afflict the elderly. I am beginning to wish the two could be reversed. Brenda has decided that we need to share more. I suggested bodily fluids; she suggested shopping. The result is that I now spend my free time mall-hopping.

Mall-hopping is not for the faint-hearted. It is at the very apex of the consumer pyramid and should not be attempted by amateurs. Unless, of course, they are accompanied by a true professional. Like Brenda.

It all began when the mad woman said we needed a new couch. Good idea, I said, I'll make one. I went off to fetch the tools and when I found the toolbox three days later, I was shocked to discover that the years had not been kind to my equipment. All that remained of a once-pristine portable workshop was a pair of rusted pliers, around two million nails of different sizes and a hammer without a head.

Inexplicably, Brenda hadn't taken my offer at all seriously and was instead poring over maps of the city charting the fastest route between malls. I began to feel like a participant in some sort of gruelling reality show for capitalists and immediately went into training.

With Clive's old pram as a substitute trolley, I raced through the house using furniture and household pets as stand-in shoppers. My strike rate was impressive, but I have never really enjoyed contact sports unless they involve other naked consenting adults.

Armed with a hip flask and a mantra, I thought I was prepared for what lay ahead. A couch. How difficult could that be? The shops are full of them.

So when we entered the first mall on the first leg of the expedition, the first thing I saw in the first shop we came across was a couch. A whole room full of couches. There were couches everywhere. It was like a couch convention. I was overjoyed. Not only did Brenda refuse to stop, but she made a point of looking in the opposite direction.

Apparently women are unable to buy the first thing they see, even if that is the very thing they are looking for. Along with the extinction of the dinosaurs, this ranks as one of the most baffling mysteries of our planet.

Passing shop after shop teeming with couches of all shapes and shades, I implored Brenda to at least slow down and take a look through the window. No such luck. I was beginning to think the only reason women take men shopping is because they need someone who can remember where the car is parked.

Brenda is one of those women who do not communicate lightly while on a Code Red mall-hopping mission. Her face sets like quick-drying cement and she imparts information strictly on a need-to-know basis. If other shoppers got wind of the fact that she was looking for a couch, everyone would want one and we would be crushed to death in the stampede.

Breaking radio silence, Brenda slipped me a piece of paper with murmured instructions to swallow it. I was about to obey her command when she rabbit-punched me in the kidneys and hissed: "Read it first, you fool."

On the paper was a single word. A word, I was to discover, that makes the shoulders of seasoned shoppers droop with despair. That word was "Coricraft".

If the Holy Grail so sought after by King Arthur and his knights had been a couch, it would have been a Coricraft. Actually, you stand a far better chance of coming across Jesus Christ's finger bowl in the Sea Point branch of Cash Converters than you do of getting your hands on a Coricraft couch before 2005.

It's not that they don't exist. Every Coricraft branch in every mall has dozens of couches. It is just that you are not allowed to buy them. Most furniture shops have signs saying "Sale" on their couches. Not Coricraft. Their furniture has signs saying "Not For Sale".

This turns shopping into even more of a Zen thing than it already is. If you walk into a showroom and there is a couch that is not for sale, does it exist? There are no easy answers. And even if there were, you wouldn't get them from the sales staff.

Walk into any branch of Coricraft at this time of year and ask for a couch. You can even ask for it by name, because Coricraft treat their couches as if they were people. This means that you are guaranteed of an Alice in Wonderland experience when you walk through the doors and ask to see Rachel or Wesley and the sales staff treat you like a piece of furniture.

I watched as couples stalked the aisles, snapping at each other like competitors in *The Amazing Race*. They would stop bickering just long enough to sit on Teddy, stroke Francis or lie down on Elizabeth. Then they would summons a shop assistant with a view to making a purchase. The assistant would look at them as if they were trying to order *pate de foie gras* at a pavement café in the Darfur region. Come back in July next year, they would say in voices heavy with scorn.

Every time the assistants passed one another in their quest to escape customers, they would roll their eyes. I stared at one girl for so long that she was forced to look at me, and then I rolled my eyes at her. Instead of rolling hers back at me, she called security and had me escorted from the store where a deaf, drunk woman blindsided me and stuck her hand up my shirt and tried to rub my belly like I was some sort of good luck Buddha-figure.

"It will take more than that to get a Coricraft couch," I shouted, and fled for the car.

30 November 2004

Let Them Watch Us Play Golf

Global warming ruined my Sunday. I took Brenda and the brat down to Camps Bay beach for a breakfast picnic and I was in the middle of buttering a Portuguese roll when we were engulfed by a mini-tsunami. It struck with no warning whatsoever.

And while there was no loss of life, I did lose 400 grams of imported ham, a block of Italian cheese, the Sunday papers and what little remained of my dignity. Loudly condemning the Americans, I snatched up my water-logged towel and stormed off the beach.

When I got home, I reached for my club. In the old days, I might have used it against Brenda the moment she walked through the door. These days, however, I blow off steam by using it for what it was designed. Hitting stupid little white balls. At least they don't call the cops on you.

I decided to take up golf after I heard that the environmentalists were opposing new golf estates for no other reason than they deface the natural environment, guzzle enormous quantities of water and benefit only the elite. These are spurious reasons by any standards. Environmentalists themselves consume a fair amount of water and, from an aesthetic point of view, their scruffy beards, unshaven armpits, lentil-breath and woolly jumpers leave a lot to be desired.

The problem is that when Ted and I went off to join a golf club, we found that none of them would have us. Ted said things would have been different if we were women and launched into a misogynistic tirade lasting well over an hour.

Now, whenever we go for a round of golf, we have to park out of sight of the clubhouse, cut through the fence and jump straight in on the 4th or 5th hole. We usually arrive without any balls because Ted thinks it is great sport to throw them at passing cyclists. Most times we are fortunate to find a couple of balls lying right there on the fairway, so we can start our game immediately. This is almost always followed by a lot of angry shouting and waving of clubs. The good thing is that golfers are generally a puny lot and Ted and I simply push them over and carry on playing.

However, times are changing and many golf clubs are now allowing darkies to become members. For some reason, black golfers are in far better physical shape than white golfers. Ted says it is because they have spent so much of their adult lives working out in the prison gym.

What I like about golf courses is that they are smooth. You can run as fast as you want in any direction and you won't trip over any unsightly fynbos. And there are no pointless trees standing around using up valuable oxygen. Deforestation is heavily underrated as a means of conserving the planet's natural resources, and golf estate developers understand this better than most.

The spoilsports in the Western Cape who are calling for a moratorium on golf estates have clearly never felt the pleasure of walking out onto the fairway on a crisp spring morning and feeling the bite of the first chilled Chivas Regal as it slides down your throat. They have never experienced the thrill of dragging an elderly couple from their golf cart and wheelspinning on the green. They have never known how much fun can be had simply by watching your caddy struggle to carry the golf bags, a cooler box, a portable braai and two hunting rifles.

Semi-automatic weapons are becoming the latest must-have accessories for the serious golfer. These days, few people are prepared to wait for that decrepit captain of industry to wrap it up with 28 shots and move on to the next hole. A flesh wound inflicted from 500m away enables you to play through a lot faster.

Then there are the Egyptian snow geese that copulate loudly in the rough, emerging only to ruin your putt by defecating uncontrollably all over the green. In this case, a shotgun works better than a standard rifle.

When I am on a golf course, I enjoy knowing that I am helping to raise the national morale. Whenever a group of ragged urchins and their unemployed parents press up against the blade wire to watch me play a shot, I can see in their eyes that I am a role model to them. I am a manifestation of their aspirations. As long as there is one man out there playing golf, even if it is by himself, they will have hope.

It is my dream to develop a golf course stretching from Hermanus to Amanzimtoti. It would have 9 450 holes and would take some time to complete, but just think how far it would go towards instilling a little ambition among the great unwashed.

I may even start charging. Five rand per person for a shot of renewed hope doesn't sound unreasonable. And, like any developer with a social conscience, I would plough the profits back into the community.

A chain of golf shops selling wine by the gallon should do the trick.

25 January 2005

Taking a WEE Gamble on the Gee-Gees

I lost my shirt at the J&B Met. Literally. A syndicate of punters chased me down and tore it from my back after I drank too much and began taunting them mercilessly after their horse ran stone last. I barely escaped with my life. In retrospect, I should have let them rip me apart.

I was so certain Badger's Delight would win that I emptied out my bank account, and Brenda's savings account, and Clive's college fund, and cashed in my policies and put it all on the filly. As it turned out, the race was rigged by the bookies and a carthorse from the Cape Flats walked it.

When I got home and told Brenda that we were officially destitute, she thought I was joking and playfully tried to wrestle my wallet away from me. Even though it was empty, real men don't give up their wallets without a fight and we ended up crashing though the front windows and onto the lawn where the neighbours hosed us down as if we were dogs. By the time the paramedics left, Brenda had more or less come to terms with the fact that we were broke. She wept a little and then went off and stared for a long time at nothing in particular, as the indigent are inclined to do.

I couldn't understand why she was taking it so badly. After all, there haven't been this many impoverished white people in South Africa since the British set fire to the farms and put all the women and children in concentration camps. After the Boer War, countless families drifted off into the hinterland, still proclaiming to be God's chosen people when in fact they were little more than wagon trash.

The level of white poverty bothered the government so much that it commissioned the Carnegie Corporation to investigate why all these genetically superior people had no money. The Carnegie Poor White Study found no evidence that they were all betting on the horses, but it did agree that something had to be done to uplift these penurious people, if only for the sake of strengthening white political power. This was just what the nationalists needed to hear, and it was only much later that someone at the Carnegie Corporation said: "Oops. Look what we've done."

Even then, it took another 50 years for God to finally come clean and admit that his chosen people are actually Patrice Motsepe, Tokyo Sexwale and Cyril Ramaphosa. What I need right now is to become a beneficiary of White Economic Empowerment (WEE), a new government policy that has not yet come up for discussion.

Unlike Black Economic Empowerment, WEE should not be broad-based. In other words, WEE should not apply to people who think they are white simply because they are not black.

Being white is a state of mind, not a skin colour, and fierce interrogation would be necessary to determine whether or not a person meets the criteria to qualify for WEE.

I would qualify straight away because I am an Inadvertently Disadvantaged Individual (IDI). In other words, I became poor through no fault of my own. That three-legged bastard horse is to blame. Others who would automatically benefit from WEE are men who have been financially ruined by divorce lawyers acting in the best interests of their shamelessly venomous clients.

It goes without saying that women are automatically excluded when it comes to benefiting from WEE because when a man falls on hard times he is not in a position to slip on a short skirt and wander off down to the corner to generate a little easy tax-free cash.

White career criminals who have been forced out of work through an over-saturated market would also qualify.

As soon as parliament promulgates the White Economic Empowerment Act, I intend making damn sure that I am first in line. I am clearly a victim of the economic injustices of the past, Saturday in particular, and there is no reason why I should not be given vast tracts of prime plutonium-rich land so that I may fulfil my dream of building weapons of mass destruction in order to level the playing field, so to speak.

1 February 2005

A Vicious Cycle

Alcohol is not a depressant. If it were, I would spend most of my time thinking up new and original ways to kill myself. Instead, every time I drink, all I want to do is kill other people. I would like to hear the experts explain that one.

Perhaps I should be more specific, lest people stop inviting me to dinner parties on the selfish grounds of wanting to avoid a post-prandial blood-bath.

When I drink, it is mostly cyclists whom I wish to kill. Any normal person who has spent the past couple of weeks in Cape Town will know what I am talking about.

What part of single file don't these bullet-headed androids understand? Do they really think that by riding nine abreast, they are indestructible? Don't they know that there is no safety in numbers in this case? Such brutishly dumb behaviour simply enables us to increase our strike rate with minimal effort.

Cyclists are not as harmless as they like to make themselves out to be. I have seen what a high performance Kevlar racing bike can do to a car. Some people think that scratches are mere surface wounds not worth a second thought, but when you take your modified turbo-charged Cortina out on the road for a bit of Sunday afternoon hit-and-run sport and end up with rake marks from bonnet to boot, things don't seem so funny any more.

Last year Ted and I won the Cape Argus Cycle Tour. But even though we crossed the line tied for first place, we spent the next six months fighting off trumped up drug charges and allegations that we jumped into the race 200m from the finish. What kind of imbeciles did they take us for? Thanks to the double jeopardy rule, I can openly say that it was more like 50m.

We had every intention of entering again this year, if only to prove to the anally retentive organisers that we are so much more than a pair of cheating dope fiends. Ted had even drawn up a training programme that we embarked on as far back as Friday evening.

Any idiot knows that carbo-loading is vital for athletic success, but we badly misjudged our fitness levels and by late Saturday night we had run out of beer and were forced to resort to a bag of non-herbal remedies we discovered while digging up the bottom of my garden in order to strengthen our forearms for the long ride ahead.

On Sunday, we narrowly missed the start by a couple of hours. Ted's wife Mary told me later that she had tried to wake him for the race, but that he appeared devoid of vital signs. She had someone come around to pronounce him clinically dead at 8:06am. An incorrect diagnosis, as it turned out.

It took a bit of work, but Mary managed to revive him through a secret technique that wives use to prevent husbands from avoiding their full quota of abuse and neglect.

When I eventually got Ted on the phone, he seemed to have forgotten about our plan. He thought I said come around and watch the dyke race, so he arrived with some kind of portable device that he swore can turn the most hardened lesbian into a real man.

I called him a despicable gender-insensitive whore, a statement I was forced to retract when he whipped out a jar full of amyl nitrate, an essential component of the picnic hamper for those of us who found ourselves at the side of the road watching thousands of grown men and women sweating heavily in skin-tight Lycra pants and homosexual shoes.

Every organised sporting event in South Africa attracts bad elements, and I told Ted that I was concerned about openly ingesting narcotics in front of roving bands of paramedics, paralegals and other perverts who, like flies to a dead dog, are attracted to cycle races by the promise of high-impact injuries involving buttocks and genitals.

Ted said there was nothing to worry about. He said these vultures invariably brought their own drugs and assured me that we wouldn't have to share any of ours.

Besides, he had heard that the World Anti-Doping Agency had recently legalised the use of illegal substances by spectators at events like cycling, chess and bowls. It made sense. Who, in their right state of mind, could possibly bear watching Gary Kasparov take 90 minutes over his opening move, or watch 38 000 cyborg clones doing nothing more dramatic than looking tired and clicking into another gear?

Self-medication livens up the process for spectators and riders alike. I believe that everyone who entered the race sooner or later found themselves itching to disembowel the next moron who cried, "Come on guys!" or even worse, "You can do it!"

I could see in their faces that they welcomed our, "Faster, you lazy faggots!" and "You're going the wrong way!"

Through judicious use of the jam jar, we progressed from sniggering at the leaders to laughing so uncontrollably at the losers that we pulled every muscle in our faces and ended up in a tent with pink plastic oxygen masks lashed to our dribbling mouths.

Ted later said they weren't oxygen masks at all, but that a pair of hormonally-rampant, silicone-lipped divorcees from the Free State had sexually molested us before making off with the jam jar. I suspect he imagined the whole thing because I distinctly remember being inside a tent.

But that still doesn't explain the bite marks.

15 March 2005

Dial 46664
– No Code Required

With Brenda gone and Clive on some sort of healing workshop for troubled teens, I had every intention of acting my age and going to bed early with a good book on Saturday night.

Then Ted ruined everything by arriving at my house with an overnight bag. Well, he called it an overnight bag but it looked more like a small refrigerator that plugged into the cigarette lighter.

By nefarious means, he had managed to get his hands on a couple of tickets to the 46664 Concert at Fancourt and thought it was a splendid idea to drop by unannounced and drag me halfway to Durban for no good reason at all.

I told him emphatically that I wanted no part of this foolishness but the next thing I knew, I was up to my elbows in the overnight bag whipping past Caledon at 185km/h.

As the designated navigator and person responsible for shouting things like "sharp left coming up" and "we're going to roll", it took us longer than expected to reach Fancourt.

At one point we found ourselves outside the reinforced steel gates of De Anker, home of the eccentric recluse, PW Botha. We badgered the Caucasian guard to let us in but he claimed the Grand Wizard wasn't home. I took it that "home" was a metaphor for mentally all there.

By the time we reached the venue, most of the local acts were over. Ted said this was a blessing so I dragged him from the car and denounced him as an enemy of the people. Nobody around us began stoning him so I helped him to his feet and we made our way past the thugs manning the entrance.

There were a few thousand people between us and the stage. This is no good for those with failing eyesight and a depleted overnight bag, so we used our usual tactic to get to the front. This involves Ted wrapping a dishcloth around his head and shouting in what he hopes people will mistake for Arabic. Then he runs directly into the crowd with me behind him making ambulance noises. I have never been able to tell if people mistake us for Islamic fundamentalists or escaped lunatics, but it works every time.

We got to the stage just in time to see Johnny Clegg leap out of his ethnically correct wheelchair seconds after a roadie injected 250cc of adrenalin straight into his indigenous heart.

"This is great stuff," I yelled. Ted tried to take it away from me, but I insisted that I was talking about the music. Johnny was a man possessed. He was like a whirling dervish, raising his leg above his head and slamming it down with a force that rattled my liver. Then he turned his back and I saw it for the first time. A bald patch? Surely not! I grabbed Ted and demanded verification. Ted said it looked like a crop circle.

"That's what it is," I shouted, and scrambled for my phone to call the *Daily Voice*. I got through to the newsroom and quickly gave them the headline: "Aliens Land On Johnny Clegg's Head." There was a pause, and someone asked if I wanted oyster sauce with my stir-fried chicken. No wonder my cellphone bill looks the way it does.

Then an impi of Zulu youths ran on stage carrying what looked like an enormous joint. It eventually broke up into more manageable sections which turned into cultural weapons so I lost interest and began watching Ted doing some sort of dysfunctional dance while mouthing the words to a song he had never heard before.

It was then that I realised we were surrounded by white people. Everywhere I looked, there were white people. I felt threatened. Maybe it was because I was so close to Johnny Clegg that I felt black. Don't be silly, I said to myself. If I were black, I would have interests in the mining industry and representation on half a dozen boards. I would certainly have more than R20 and an expired condom in my wallet.

I got Ted into a headlock and asked him about this racial anomaly. He said it made perfect sense. Five thousand whiteys at a concert meant five thousand well-stocked residences with nobody at home.

I was in the process of calling him a judgemental jingoist when Johnny collapsed in a heap behind the drum kit and a dark-skinned diva by the name of India Arie took to the stage. She began crooning about dying home-less children and it wasn't long before most of the crowd drifted off looking for a quiet place to open their wrists. In between songs, she said: "Are y'all still with me?" Ted asked if she was blind.

Then India announced she was so moved at being invited to perform in Africa that she had written a special song right there and then on the flight over here. Well, hell, India, we've all scrawled meaningless rubbish on barf bags at one time or another.

Interviewed afterwards about what she thought of South Africa, she said Knysna was "way cool" but that she had to get back to the States tomorrow. I don't blame her.

In the meantime, Ted had snuck off to the car for replenishments and the guttural cries that heralded his return marked the start of Annie Lennox's set. She was wearing a leopard-skin top, made from real leopard, beautifully offset by a cluster of Sierra Leonean blood diamonds.

Ted was dribbling like a sex-starved madman, which, being a married man, he is, but Annie scared me. At one point she began baring her teeth instead of her midriff, and then started singing about heartache and loss. This was wasted on an audience which had clearly spent most of the day smoking the Knysna heads instead of admiring them from a distance like normal people do.

The high point, and the reason I agreed to accompany Ted in the first place, came when Annie was enticed off-stage by a bag of depressants.

There is nothing like watching the tattered remnants of Queen to boost one's *schadenfreude* levels. The drummer resembled someone who had had just been dragged out of a retirement home for trailer park trash. Brian May had a perm that looked like it was hired from a company specialising in cryogenics. And Freddie Mercury's replacement clearly starred in badly-dubbed German porn movies in his spare time. They were great.

The only people who really disappointed me were the in-bred freaks to my right who looked like they were there in the hope of claiming maintenance from Steve Hofmeyer, who never pitched up even though he hadn't been invited.

22 March 2005

'A towel is the most massively useful thing an interstellar hitchhiker can have.' – Douglas Adams

My car was broken into the other night and it looked like the thieving bastards had invited guests around for the occasion. The interior was strewn with empty pie packets, used condoms, a broken whisky bottle and a couple of dozen empty beer tins.

I immediately called up Ted with instructions to bring over the bloodhound and the big weapons. There's nothing quite like arming oneself to the teeth and heading out in full pursuit of one's property to make one feel proudly South African. It's the Anglo-Saxon equivalent of affirmative action.

When Ted arrived he took one look at the inside of my car and threatened to shoot me right there and then. He demanded to know what kind of a white man I am and proceeded to hold me solely responsible, in a very loud voice, for the fact that there is majority rule in South Africa today.

It turned out that the devastation inside my car was the result of a night out celebrating my birthday with Ted – the same Ted who was now threatening to gun me down in front of the neighbours.

How was I to know? I had only just woken up. Besides, my powers of recollection are no longer what they used to be. And this is precisely how nature intended it. Some memories are best forgotten, especially when you are married.

On closer inspection, somebody actually had been inside my car. The cubby-hole was hanging open and so was the ashtray, neither of which I ever use unless I am transporting contraband. For some reason, police at roadblocks these days never think to check these two places. They're quick enough to wrestle you to the ground and shine a torch up your bum, but don't expect them to investigate the obvious.

Feeling the need to extricate an apology from Ted, I attempted to snatch the weapon from the holster on his ankle. A shot went off in the ensuing struggle, wounding a Congolese car guard in the leg. He limped over and thanked us for letting him off lightly. It must be a Hutu thing.

The only items of value missing from the car, apart from a bunch of loose change that I keep on hand to toss into the path of oncoming traffic whenever I find myself surrounded by street children, was a plastic container of petrol and a beach towel emblazoned with the American flag. These are essential to the survival of any motorist.

If you run out of fuel in a Christian neighbourhood, you can use the petrol to make it to the next garage. If you run out in a Muslim neighbourhood, you can use it to set fire to the towel and the residents will carry you shoulder-high to the next garage. If you run out in Muizenberg, you can drink the petrol and be embraced by the community as one of their own. If you have your own towel they will treat you like a god.

The robbery never bothered me as much as it should have. Being a graduate of the Jacob Zuma School of Financial Management, albeit possessed of strong Buddhist leanings, I am in the process of selling off my assets so that I may lead a simpler, more pure life.

This is why I am not unduly troubled by the theft of my towel. I wish the thief well. He has served to lighten my load. I only hope that he tries to sell it to a fun-loving fundamentalist at the next al-Qaeda fundraiser.

Now that Brenda is somewhere out there scanning the obituaries for signs of my untimely demise, thanks to her Marburg-infested birthday cake, I am at liberty to get rid of her possessions. Spousal desertion automatically invokes this right.

I have gutted the kitchen and taken a chainsaw to the marital bed. For some people, half a bed is better than no bed at all, even if it means strapping yourself in every night so that you don't roll off into the far corner where the dog will find you and have its way with your leg as dogs are inclined to do.

In the absence of Brenda's contribution to household expenses, I have gone out and got a day job that frequently stretches late into the night. It's going splendidly, even if the smoking room sounds like a trawler's engine room and looks like a ward for the criminally insane. I am prevented from divulging more details though a craven combination of corporate allegiance and a deep-seated fear of a boss who looks like he heads the Sea Point chapter of Fight Club in his spare time.

Now that my status as a family man has been so brutally ripped from beneath my feet, I see no need to continue paying a rent so high that it could have got Faust out of trouble. Here in Cape Town, two bedrooms with a sea view and a long lease are worth far more than anybody's soul. And estate agents, Satan's little helpers, know this better than most.

I own a piece of land in Hout Bay. It is heavily overgrown with alien species and I expect that any day now it will catch fire and the entire suburb will go up in flames. If the wind is blowing in the right direction, property prices will soar.

Even though perlemoen poachers are too wet to burn, the devil's spawn know that a divine act that levels a few hundred shacks with sweeping sea views will drive up their commission of an offence against a whole bunch of non-people who can't even get to the bank, let alone apply for a bond.

Right now, I need to get a good price for my land. And every time someone is murdered in Hout Bay, my own personal Lord of Vermin tells me that I need to drop my price. This is not an option. So I would like to appeal to the folk of the valley to get bigger dogs, higher fences and drugs that keep them awake all night.

Should they fail to keep themselves alive until I sell my land, I will encourage the overflow from Imizamo Yethu to move in. I reckon the plot could take 30 shacks at a squeeze.

Who knows, I may even find my towel.

3 May 2005

Hot Fuzz & Cold Pressed

The plan was to get to Riebeek Kasteel and participate in the Olive Festival. Ted wanted to go dressed as a giant olive, but that wasn't the kind of participation I had in mind.

"Nevertheless," he said, "should I go Picholine or Calamata, green or black?"

"Most definitely green," I said. A place with a name like Riebeek Kasteel is probably not ready for something resembling a dangerously over-inflated Idi Amin walking the streets and scaring the children.

Fortunately, the importance of finding an olive costume was overtaken by more pressing concerns. When he arrived to fetch me on Friday afternoon, the entire left side of Ted's body had shut down. He thought it might be gout but I said it was more likely that he had suffered some kind of stroke.

Not sure how much longer Ted had to live, it was even more imperative that we got moving without further delay. I hoisted a crate of beer onto his good shoulder and pushed him in the direction of the car.

The weekend started coming unglued before we had even left town. Being semi-incapacitated with a potentially fatal aneurysm, Ted had reluctantly asked me to drive. This involved a fair amount of stalling and wheelspinning while I battled to get the measure of his flaccid clutch. Eventually he snapped and began sawing at the wheel in an attempt to get me to pull over, but I fought him off easily.

As we swung onto the N7, I reached into the back seat for something cold and wet and saw that Ted had a sleeping bag rolled up on the floor. Being oestrogen deficient and thus not possessed with the capacity to think far enough ahead to book some sort of accommodation, we had decided at the last minute to take our own beds.

Sleeping bags are very gay and for that reason I refuse to have anything to do with them. I have seen grown heterosexuals progress from sleeping bags to sashaying around the kitchen swinging their hips to Barbra Streisand while whipping up a delicious soufflé for one.

When I mentioned this to Ted, he asked what I had in mind by way of bedding. "Blankets are for Basotho warriors and other real men," I said, gesturing with a masculine nod towards the rear of the car. "So where are these blankets?" asked Ted. A long moment went by before I answered in a small voice: "At the front gate."

Ted giggled in the way that men with sleeping bags do. Little did he know that I had no intention whatsoever of sleeping out in the open. I would get him drunk and then slide into his sleeping bag while he was unconscious. See how easily this sort of thing can happen? Insidious things, sleeping bags.

Riebeek Kasteel is only 70kms from Cape Town, yet it took us far longer than it should have to get there. Ted's bladder seemed to be largely responsible for our slow progress. Even though we were getting four kilometres to the six-pack, I still had to pull over after every three litres or so. Perhaps it was the altitude.

At one point we drove through Riebeek Kasteel, through Riebeek West and were well on our way to whatever godforsaken town lay even deeper into that jetblack night when I realised something was wrong. I hit the brakes and counted the empties. By my reckoning, we should have been there half a case ago.

While Ted was stumbling through the undergrowth relieving himself yet again, I began rooting in the boot for fresh supplies. Ted started shouting something but I couldn't hear a word over Seal and Jeff Beck's version of Jimi Hendrix's *Manic Depression*.

I was in full throat in the middle of the chorus, sounding more like a walrus than Seal, with my hands full of cold, wet things when the police van pulled up next to me.

Ted panicked and somehow managed to get his landing gear caught in his zip. What with Ted screaming and Beck's guitar wailing, it was hard to hear what the young white constable was trying to say to me.

This meant that I had to lean right into his window breathing beer breath all over him and ask him to repeat what he had just said. Luckily I had been drinking, otherwise I might have ordered him to step away from the vehicle and spread his legs. If you're sober enough, you can get away with that sort of thing on a dark country road.

The rookie cop wanted to know if we had seen any accidents along the way. A strange question, considering that our entire car was a moving violation and it was clear to everyone but the blind and the deaf that my navigator was the victim of some sort of freak accident, even if it was by his own hand.

Like a good citizen, I told the officer that I had seen nothing and waved them on. "Y'all have a good evening now, you hear?" I said, before telling Ted to put his bleeding genitals away and stop being such a girl.

Eventually we found the house we were looking for. It was full of people full of red wine and other sparkly things. I'm not sure if they ever completely knew who we were, but they welcomed us as only dislocated hillbillies can.

Right away, we set about celebrating the humble olive. However, there was a downside to paying repeated homage to this oleaginous expatriate. At one point, the other half of Ted's body froze up, seriously curtailing his ability to keep up with the rest of us. One of the locals directed him to a nearby vet for a shot of ketamine. We made Ted promise to get some for all of us.

By the time we managed to escape, nearly two days later, we were the colour of unripe olives, mentally impaired and minus our cellphones.

I can hardly wait for next year.

10 May 2005

Tokyo – So Much More Than a City in Japan

A new television show began last week and ended with a former convict turned multi-millionaire publicly destroying the future of a fresh-faced young white man.

The poor swine was just one yuppie among 16 who had been selected from thousands to have their hopes dashed on national television.

His name was Tristan, condemning him from the start. What mother in her right mind names her son after some medieval moron who was despatched to Ireland to fetch an Irish tart called Isolde so that his uncle, King Mark of Cornwall, could marry her only to fall in love with her himself after getting her drunk on some or other aphrodisiac and then dying of grief after marrying someone else who lied to him?

Our Tristan, from the local version of *The Apprentice*, was doomed to crash and burn from the moment that Tokyo Sexwale, showing no apparent long-term effects of his time on Robben Island, walked into the boardroom and separated the men from the women.

This was presumably done to minimise the risk of unwanted pregnancies and accidental homicides that might inconveniently pop up on prime time television later in the series.

Then the boys got together in their dark suits, had a few drinks, gave each other high fives, tried not to wet their Gucci shoes in the rising tide of testosterone and elected a team manager. They elected Tristan, who was clearly unfamiliar with the story of Piet Retief. Our hero was ecstatic, slapping a few more duplicitous black hands before going on to thank his mom. For what? For naming him after the most tragic figure ever to emerge from the court of King Arthur, with the exception of Lancelot who was a closet homosexual with a self-image problem? Yeah, thanks mom. If you ever give me a couple of brothers, be sure to name them Icarus and Oedipus.

"We are going to change history," shouted Tristan. One of his team, who bore more than a passing resemblance to Dingane, said something in Zulu. Tristan high-fived him and his eyes glazed over as he imagined himself as Tokyo Sexwale in the very near future. That didn't work, so he imagined himself as Donald Trump. Much better.

On the other side of the gender divide, the girls were also drinking and trying to high-five each other, but missing most of the time. Girls are genetically co-ordinated to kiss, not slap hands, but sadly there was very little mouth action going on. Well, not on camera, anyway. There's a very good chance that those bits were cut. I have seen what happens when a group of over-excited girls get together and leak pheromones all over the carpet. It's not exactly suitable for family viewing.

The black girls broke into their ethnic tongue, leaving the white girls to squeal and gush as white girls do when they haven't a clue what's going on. It's an inherited mechanism designed to bamboozle men into marrying them.

At dawn, the narrator informed us that Tristan likes to start early. "With the smell of dew on the streets of Johannesburg …" droned the disembodied voice. I beg your pardon? Dew hasn't been smelled on the streets of Joburg since gold was first discovered there. Blood and vomit, yes, but not dew.

I think it was more a case of Tokyo likes to start early. You don't get to have teeth like that by lying in bed until midday while a R50 hooker nurses your crippling hangover. People like Tokyo wake up and buy companies, not crack. People like Tokyo don't worship false profits. They don't wake up in police cells and call their pimps for bail. They pick up the red phone and call God directly to thank him for taking such a personal interest in their lives. Then they call their mothers. If he had been named Tristan Sexwale, he would still be in prison.

So, by dawn's early light, the two teams met in a suitably Tuscan environment to be given their first task. The boys told Tokyo that they had named their team *Amabhubezi*. I can't say for certain what it means, but I think it has something to do with a lion. I'm not sure what this bunch of metrosexuals has in common with the king of the jungle, but perhaps there is a gay pride parading about in the remote reaches of the Kruger Park.

You might have thought that the girls would have called themselves something neutral like Teazers. Instead, they opted for *Umbokodo*, which has more to do with striking a rock than striking a compromise. Personally, I think the world needs more strip clubs than it does violent resistance movements based on the myth of gender inequality.

An upbeat Tokyo told the teams there were 10 000 informal traders on the streets of Johannesburg. That would have done it for me. Had I been a contestant, I would have whipped out my cellphone and called a taxi to take me to the airport right away.

At the very least, I expected that the task would be to see who could expose the most illegal traders, with the winner being the team that secured the highest percentage of convictions and deportations.

Bizarrely, though, the winning team would be the one that increased a street trader's profits for the day. That's right. Encourage them.

"It's all about ethics," said Tokyo with a smile that must have driven the warders wild.

The boys hit the streets with gusto. One of the black contestants suggested they take some time to get the feel of the environment, the sub-text being: "Let's check out who's armed and who's not."

One of the whiteys, devoid of any survival instincts whatsoever, went up to a woman selling mielies and began explaining the Golden Calf economic theory to her. I had no idea what he was talking about, but I expect him to do the right thing and take the rap when the health department busts her next week for selling freshly slaughtered baby cows right there on the pavement.

The girls ended up hawking loose cigarettes and fruit and veg, a fine metaphor for the life and death nature of the game. The boys tried to sell airtime and a couple of eggs. Nobody thought of going up to Lagos Larry and helping him to shift product.

And, as the teams scuttled through downtown Joburg raising and dashing the hopes of informal traders, Tokyo was reclining in his Italian leather swivel 'n' tilt and polishing his first silver bullet.

At the end of the day, the teams came together in the executioner's chamber, a room constructed from the finest Burmese teak and decorated with an organic sensibility that extended to wallpaper designed to look like shelves full of books. This is what I like about reality television. No pretence whatsoever.

The girls won hands down, of course. Being the losing team's leader, Tristan had to give up two people for the chop. Both were black men. Angry, eloquent black men. If these guys had been around when Judas made his move, Jesus might have lived long enough to experience a midlife crisis.

The tables turned and the last we saw of Tristan, he was slinging his bag into the back of a long black car and driving off into eternal obscurity. What better day to shatter a young man's dreams than Youth Day?

I love this country.

21 June 2005

Pass the Buck
– Then Shoot it in the Head

In the old days, when the country was run by a cabal of ill-tempered white men in pork-pie hats and warthog moustaches, government departments awarded contracts to companies controlled by men who knew their way around the Bible and the gun. Both had proved equally successful in keeping the heathens at bay while the business of civilised men was conducted.

Then came 1994 and the embarrassing realisation that they might not, after all, be God's chosen people. Funny handshakes and veiled references to Blood River were almost overnight no longer the preferred currencies of trade between the public and private sectors.

Suddenly the hawkers were banging on the front door and a new wave of civil servants was pouring in through the back. *Revelations* might have been full of giant locusts but there was nothing that could have prepared them for this.

The criteria for securing government contracts no longer included an ability to recite the *Book of Job* while dismantling and reassembling an R-3 rifle in under 30 seconds.

The one good thing that democracy has brought to South Africa is a revival of the tender system. This never occurred out of any deep sense of fair play, but was instead born of necessity.

Previously, civil servants were permitted two standard-issue children – girl (1) blonde; boy (1) blond. Dark-haired offspring were kept in their rooms until they were old enough to become train drivers or alcoholics.

Now the dynamic is different. Civil servants are expected to have as many children as it takes to fill a minibus.

The only four female civil servants still at their desks have had their husbands neutered. All the rest are on maternity leave.

Prior to the rainbow era, many South Africans could be found hard at work in villages and townships practising to be good civil servants. The results of their noble efforts can be seen today squeezed into taxis around the country.

This means that at any given moment, every company – apart from the Koeksuster Kollective in Orania – has a certain number of employees with an uncle, cousin, brother or father in one or other branch of government.

Back then, when state departments resembled Ku Klux Klan meetings, civil servants never had extended families. The men tended to assault and molest their immediate blood relatives only. There just wasn't the time or space to invite others in for their share of domestic abuse.

But now that everyone in the public and private sectors is related to one another in some way, it has become increasingly vital that the tender system is rigorously implemented.

Not to prevent corruption, but to prevent internecine conflict from spilling across the provincial borders when one relative is favoured over another. Previously, it was quite safe to give your uncle the contract to supply schools with lengths of bamboo (whipping: for the purposes of).

But no longer. Nepotism has become an altogether more complex affair. And although the principle of extended families is based on love, there is no mention of peace. That's where the hippies were different. All that free love and raising everyone else's children as your own was largely inspired by enormous quantities of lysergic acid diethylamide, but they always stopped short of hacking one another's heads off with blunt machetes when it came to resolving family squabbles.

So the tender process is used these days as a mechanism to minimise the chances of losing a limb to your first wife's brother while on leave in the Tugela Valley.

But somebody has to be given the contract, so a complicated system has been devised. For example, in the mining industry a king of diamonds is usually enough to beat a pair of cousins. Nobody is leaving anything to chance and everything is put out on tender.

In one of the Sunday papers, there was a business snippet headlined: "Springboks to be bought and culled." I have often dreamed of going to a rugby match with a high-powered sniper rifle and bringing down that muscle-bound meathead with the floppy blonde fringe. I probably couldn't afford to buy more than one, but that's all I needed, so I called up Ted and told him to get the gun ready. Then I read the rest of the story and had to call him back and cancel the hunt.

The first paragraph read: "The Department of Defence's tender B/G/011/05 calls for people to buy, cull and remove 200 springbok at its ammunition depot in De Aar, Northern Cape." Interested psychopaths were invited to call Colonel KP Majola. The last line stated: "Night shooting is preferred."

The prospect of gunning down the national animal was almost as inviting as wiping out the national rugby team, so I called Ted back and told him to get the gun ready again.

At first I wanted to do my killing during the day. That way we could pick out the weakest in the herd and put bets on getting a clean head shot. Ted pointed out that it would be more fun to mount powerful spotlights on his bakkie and drink heavily while chasing the fast-moving vermin through the streets of De Aar. We could take turns driving while the other fired blindly into the night in the hope of hitting something, maybe even the ammunition depot itself.

It's possible that Colonel Majola could be swayed into giving us a couple of mortars or even rifle-propelled grenades. That way we could blow up whole clumps of the dumb brutes. But if not, then I am going to tender for a few hundred rounds of incendiary bullets. I want that Northern Cape sky to be lit up like Fallujah on a busy night.

One way or another, I'm gonna bag me a Bambi.

Yeehaaa!

5 July 2005

Lying, Flying and Almost Dying

Last weekend I told Brenda I was going away on a fishing trip with Ted, but that was merely a cunning cover story. My real plan was to rendezvous with the husky-voiced vixen I recently met in Hermanus while on a covert whale-counting mission.

She had sent me a coded message containing the GPS coordinates for a secret landing strip in the Overberg. Grabbing my trout rod, I gave Brenda a kiss on the cheek, dodged her retaliatory straight-arm jab and ran for the car.

Passing through Hawston at 210km/h, I realised that GPS coordinates make no sense at all without a GPS. The reason I have never invested in one of these devices is because they are very gay. Real men need only the sun and the stars as their navigational tools. Unfortunately, it was heavily overcast so I phoned the vixen and told her to meet me in the Caledon museum. It seemed like the safest place to be. There was nobody in it. Just a few pieces of old furniture, a double bass without strings, a bunch of unidentifiable artefacts in a display cabinet and a few black and white photographs on the walls, including one of Miss Susie Coert, a teacher at De Vos Malan School, standing next to a chair with what looked like a dead raccoon on her head.

There was also a photograph of Caledon in 1910. I walked back to the front door and looked out. Nothing had changed.

My phone rang. It was the vixen. She was at the museum and wanted to know where I was. Holy mackerel. If she's at the museum, then where am I? Probably inside somebody's home. I left quickly.

"Follow me," she said, giving me a kiss that brought me to my knees. I am unaccustomed to affection, and physical contact of a non-violent nature can easily incapacitate me. But Caledon is not ready for the sight of a white man genuflecting before a blonde-haired, green-eyed, mini-skirted she-devil, so I got into my car and we set off at high speed.

An hour later we pulled into the Birkenhead, which I had always been led to believe was a ship that ran aground near Gansbaai. Instead, it turned out to be a brewery. Or perhaps it was a shipwreck that had been converted into a brewery. Or a brewery that had run aground. It was hard to tell.

Taste these, said the Illicit Consort, as the bartender began filling dozens of glasses with different kinds of beer. By the time we wrapped things up and headed for the airstrip, I felt more wrecked than the Birkenhead. Waiting for us was a man in dark glasses and even darker mood.

"You're late," he shouted. Great, I thought. We're flying with an angry pilot. This is almost as bad as being on the operating table and just before the anaesthetic kicks in, the surgeon leans over and says: "I know about you and my wife."

After bouncing down a donkey path, the pilot took us up to our cruising altitude of 10 metres. A polite request that we climb a little higher was met with a stream of invective. The only word I understood was "radar". At one point he seemed to lose interest in flying and let go of the controls altogether. The Illicit Consort took the wheel and led us through a series of alarming dips and lurches before the pilot snapped out of whatever dreadful flashback he was having and took over again.

The Consort scrambled into the back and began explaining, in vivid detail, the rules of the Mile High Club. The pilot seemed oblivious to my foot smacking him in the back of the head, so I sat back and allowed myself to be inducted into this elite organisation. Below us, the sea was teeming with whales, sharks, half-eaten perlemoen poachers and other exotic forms of marine life. I couldn't have cared less.

Back on the ground, the Consort and I raced off before the pilot could discover the damage we had done to his plane. Four hours later, we were threatening the desk clerk at the Arniston Hotel with dire consequences should he fail to give us his best room without delay.

The events of the weekend are a little sketchy. I recall meeting a couple of philandering doctors who seemed more interested in my kidneys than my life story, and at one point there was a wedding reception, but I'm pretty sure it wasn't mine. For a start, it resembled a wake attended by retired security branch cops. The official photographer was taking pictures with a cellphone, the groom looked like a Mennonite virgin and his bride was giving me the lazy eye. The situation had trouble written all over it. The Consort saw this and dragged me back to the room and locked me inside until the unhappy event was over.

A day or two later we returned to civilisation via Elim, a Moravian enclave with hobbit houses and no people. No alcohol, either. The only signs of life we encountered were three small children wearing hoodies and carrying plastic guns. It can't be easy aspiring to be gangsters in a mission town. There just aren't the right role models. When we left, they smiled at us and waved their guns in the air. Poor little bastards. Even when they are finally big enough to shoot and rob someone, they won't be able to resist the impulse to take him to hospital afterwards.

Somewhere along the way we stopped at a bottle store and took advantage of a courtesy bucket full of grapes soaked in Witblits.

I awoke to the sight and sound of a barking kraken with hate-filled eyes and a head of writhing snakes. I was home.

27 September 2005

Trust Me – I'm a Doctor

When my column first appeared, Outraged of Oranjezicht led an orchestrated charge of poison-pen letter writers accusing me of being a racist, sexist, homophobic misogynist. This hurt me deeply. For about five seconds.

I never again heard from these self-appointed guardians of public morality. I expect they came around to my way of thinking. Now, a new adversary has set out to tarnish my reputation.

J Maxwell of Rosebank has publicly accused me of lying and cheating in the wake of last week's column in which I admitted to lowering my fidelity guard and committing a brash in-transit heist on a violently beautiful Hermanus wench, robbing her of her hitherto unquestionable virtue and leaving the town awash in rumour and speculation.

I wrote about it secure in the knowledge that Brenda wouldn't read it. She is one of those people who believe that quality newspapers such as this one are responsible for creating an artificial sub-stratum of pseudo intellectual mountebanks who write letters to the editor in the deluded belief that someone actually gives a damn. People like J Maxwell, in other words.

What Maxwell seems to forget is that if a man has an affair and his wife doesn't hear about it, then it never happened. It's the classical Zen paradox that relates to falling trees and absent ears, only in this case it involves nudity and a fair amount of shrieking and whooping.

Maxwell dares to suggest that I am sending the wrong moral message to our young people. For a start, I don't know any young people. Clive doesn't count. He is a teenage aberration with a heteroclitical interest in women's clothing and possessed of a grotesque addiction to the music of one of Satan's disciples operating under the name of Marilyn Manson.

Maxwell should realise that our young people spend their free time ingesting enormous quantities of methylenedioxymethamphetamine and riding each other bareback whenever mom steps out of the house for a quickie with the golf pro.

And those are the good kids. The rotten apples go to university to study politics and actuarial science.

Men who practise the dying art of deception should be regarded as role models and not condemned as depraved animals, as Maxwell would have it. However, it must be said that when it comes to drinking and dancing and chasing the nymphs in the train of Dionysus, not all men are infected with satyriasis to the same degree.

I know a member of the medical fraternity who, even though he is up to his well-worn elbows in an extra-marital affair, still cannot help himself from hitting on other women. When it comes to him, the last line of the 1964 version of the Hippocratic oath should read: "May I always act so as to preserve the finest traditions of my calling and may I long experience the joy of shagging those who seek my help."

It should be remembered, however, that the predatory philanderer is different to the serial philanderer in that he is attracted to women who have just ended a relationship or are starting a fresh one. This is when women are at their most confused and vulnerable.

This is also when you will start hearing prescriptive lines like: "As your doctor, I advise you to sleep with me." You would be surprised at the number of women who fall for it.

The serial philanderer is less discriminating when it comes to selecting his next conquest. Although driven by the same primordial need to spread his seed or upgrade his lifestyle, he is not as narcissistic as the predatory philanderer. He quickly loses interest once he has succeeded in bringing his quarry to its knees, so to speak.

The predator, on the other hand, is a carnal recidivist. Blind to changed circumstances and deaf to repeated warnings, he returns to the scene of his crime of passion to try his luck once again. Often, the only way to dislodge a predatory philanderer is to put a 9mm bullet into his buttocks. His doctor will then advise him to stay away. Unless, of course, he is a doctor. In which case he has to be shot in the head.

Predatory and serial philanderers are specialists in their respective fields. Most men, on the other hand, fall into the general category of weekend philanderer. These are amateurs who drink too much and cannot remember where they were or what they said to whom. This kind of muddled modus operandi almost always spells disaster and goes a long way towards giving men a bad reputation.

Despite what Maxwell says, I am not a bona fide philanderer. This is because Brenda is not a bona fide wife. Since she refuses to take her connubial responsibilities seriously, the sexual statute of limitations on my marriage has expired. This means that I am morally and ethically entitled to offer my services pro deo to whoever takes my fancy. And if she does not take my fancy, I shall not impose it upon her. That would be just plain wrong.

Maxwell is misguided. I am a devoted husband and virtuous to a fault and I would not be dallying with an emerald-eyed vixen if my so-called wife had not turned into a human glacier.

Sex therapists suggest that one of the ways to spice up your marriage is to invest in a pornographic video, which, as two consenting adults, you are at liberty to watch in the privacy of your own home. I might not know much about sex, thanks to Brenda, but I do know that watching a square-jawed German take off his trousers to reveal an 18-inch willy is not going to turn my marriage into the lubricious fiesta that it ought to be.

I've got more chance of interesting Brenda in a little Saturday night saturnalia if I go to the nice Nigerian man standing outside Adult World and invest in a selection of his wares.

It's her mind that needs expanding, not my member.

4 October 2005

Polygamy for Beginners

I am in the process of introducing prospective second wives to Brenda. As wife number one, she is entitled to have a say in this matter. It is vital that the two of them get along. There is little point in having two wives if all they are going to do is bicker and squabble endlessly.

It's bad enough having one wife who does that all day long. Imagine the horror of having two of them at it. So this weekend I decided to bring the Illicit Consort home.

At first she was reluctant, saying that she feared for her life. I told her to relax. I had timed the meeting to coincide with Brenda's ovulation. I once asked Brenda to make me an egg for breakfast and I ended up with a burst eardrum and a dislocated elbow, but when she makes an egg in a biological kind of way, she softens considerably.

I wouldn't go so far as to say that she is fun to be around, but certainly her propensity for domestic violence is reduced to a more manageable verbal level. I think that instinctively her body is telling her that it is ready to mate, but her mind is so powerful that it overrides any natural urges that still linger.

I expect that once wife number two is ensconced in the family home, Brenda will begin vying for my attention in a big way. Women are like that. They are similar to that dog in the Bible who wouldn't give up his manger for baby Jesus even though he didn't particularly enjoy sleeping in mangers. I suppose he liked babies even less. Can't blame him, really.

Last week, Brenda celebrated the news of my impending conversion to polygamy with such vigour that I had to take her to have her stomach pumped. I was astounded to discover that a smallish woman could hold that much vodka. She's still a bit groggy from the sleeping pills, which allowed me to move in for a quick grope and get out before her sluggish brain could transmit the attack signal.

I decided to bring the Consort to the house on Sunday. If the ovulation failed to mellow Brenda, then at least she might think twice about launching a pre-emptive strike on what everyone except Palestinian militants and clergymen regard as a day of rest. The Consort had to fortify her nerves with three bottles of wine. I suggested she might be overmedicating, but quick as a flash she pointed out millions of Catholics were doing the same thing in churches around the world at that very moment.

Symbolically drinking the blood of Christ is one thing, but there's no need to pig out to such an extent that He has to go for a transfusion.

"Best you don't start on the wafers lest ye be accused of cannibalism," I added, prising her fingers from a fourth bottle of Cabernet Sauvignon.

By the time I helped her from the car and through the front gate, she was slurring her words and staggering like a shell-shocked war veteran. The first person we came across was my feral son, Clive. He was in the garden putting the final touches to his latest project, a miniature weapon of mass destruction designed for domestic use only.

I doubt he is stupid enough to actually ever use it. Mind you, that's what the Japanese said about President Truman and today there are still three-headed babies being born in Hiroshima. I gave the brat the sharp end of my shoe and he scuttled out of the way, hissing and spitting.

I turned to the Consort to apologise for having spawned such an aberration and saw that she appeared to have fallen asleep on her feet with her eyes wide open. I recoiled at the sight and my scream brought Brenda to the front door where she found me slapping the Consort in an effort to break through the wine-soaked bout of narcolepsy that had rendered her mute and immobile. Brenda misunderstood the situation, thinking I was attacking a defenceless catatonic who had inadvertently found her way onto our property, and came at me with an uncoordinated series of quasi-oriental kicks and punches which I easily parried, cuffing her playfully across the side of the head every time she came within reach.

The Consort woke in a state of deep confusion and began lunging at my exposed flank. It is never a pretty sight when women lose control, but often it can be quite funny at the same time.

I was ducking and diving and trying not to laugh when the disturbed offspring blindsided me and sunk his teeth into my calf. The battle raged back and forth between the begonia bed and the dysfunctional water feature, and I was beginning to get the upper hand when the armed response unit swarmed over the garden wall and separated us.

By the time I had prised the razor-toothed runt off my leg and wiped the blood from my eyes, the Consort and Brenda needed no introductions. They were breathing heavily and fixing each other's makeup.

Make no mistake, I'm all for a little female bonding, especially when it comes with a foot-tapping soundtrack and German dialogue, but there was something about their manner that left me feeling decidedly uneasy. What if King Goodwill Zwelithini's harem is not made up of happily heterosexual honey bunnies? What if the royal boudoir is, in fact, a Sapphic hotbed of tribadistic anomalies slick with baby oil?

Maybe this wasn't such a good idea after all.

1 November 2005

Damp Dog Day in Durban

Brenda seemed to think it important that I get parental approval before taking the Illicit Consort as my second wife. This sort of thing isn't normally expected of the paramount chief of the white tribe of South Africa.

Usually, a simple chat with the ancestors would suffice. However, I come from a long line of Dutch potato sellers and even if I could speak their language I doubt very much that their opinions would be worth anything. I decided to take a Kulula flight to Durban because the airline is easy to find in the phone book, unlike Aeroflot which doesn't even have a listing. Flying with Kulula is a bit like taking a trip into Lewis Carroll's imagination.

Not now, of course. I'm talking about when he was alive. The female cabin crew look like they moonlight for Teazers and the black cabin controllers look like hijackers. Well, I suppose they would, what with being black and all.

They are also very helpful when it comes to the safety instructions, informing passengers that should the plane appear to be crashing, they should put their heads between their legs and kiss their ass goodbye. Kulula is cheaper than SAA because they don't give you free snacks and drinks, instead making you pay for everything but the oxygen that you get to suck into your lungs in the few seconds you have left before being incinerated in a giant fireball.

Our rented car was white and that's the best thing I can say about it. The boot was welded shut and the interior smelled like wet dog. I discovered soon enough that the whole of Durban smells like wet dog.

I was trying to reach Umhlanga but took a wrong turn and ended up in downtown Lagos. The Consort panicked at the sight of so many black people and began winding up her window but the handle fell off.

"Relax," I said, swerving around a burning Fidelity van and side-swiping a sangoma chasing a goat down the middle of Grey Street. "They mean us no harm."

The Consort screamed as a man wearing animal skins knocked on her window and gave us a traditional Zulu greeting. I responded in kind, drawing a finger across my throat and giving him a thumbs up with the other hand.

Eventually we broke free and made our way to Broadway, a street in Durban North that I remembered from my childhood. I told the Consort that Broadway was once lined with Mdoni trees full of shrieking Indian mynahs and that they had probably been cut down because the mynahs kept defacating on the cars parked on either side of the road.

The Consort was appalled. She feels very strongly about child abuse and demanded to know why the Indians sent their children up into the trees in the first place.

I clutched my temples. "Mynahs," I said, "not minors."

We didn't speak again until we reached our hotel. For some reason, we had been given a self-catering room. This made no sense at all. The whole point of staying in a hotel is that someone else does the cooking at night and mops up the bodily fluids in the morning.

That night we abused the mini-bar until there was nothing left but a packet of peanuts and two iceblocks. Just after 3am I suggested to the Consort that we go to the beach. It was an idea whose time had come and nothing was going to stop us, not even the steel fence topped with spikes and electrified wire.

After a little encouragement, the Consort agreed to check if there really was a high voltage current coursing through the wire. She reached up and grabbed it with one hand.

I quickly stepped back in case she fell on top of me. There was no point in both of us getting electrocuted. She showed no visible signs of shock. Then again, she was beyond feeling anything at that point.

I think she might have shorted the entire security system, which was a good thing because security is the last thing you need when you are swimming naked in the middle of the night off a deserted beach on the isolated fringes of one of the most violent provinces in the country.

The Consort scaled the fence like a cat burglar. I followed, snagging my Levis on one of the spikes as I jumped. With my pants ripped to shreds, we fought our way through dense bush until we hit the beach.

Tearing off what remained of my clothes, I ran into the ocean and immediately got trapped in a powerful undertow. The Consort came to my rescue, dragging me back to the beach by my hair.

There's nothing like a near drowning experience in shark infested waters to ruin a romantic mood. Having lost our clothes, we stumbled naked back to the hotel where the night porter pretended this kind of thing happened all the time.

We made it to the room and slept like dead animals. Waking early, around noon, we self-medicated to quell the eye-bubbling hangover and set off for the parents.

The rest of the day passed in a blur of aggressive questioning, saliva tests and a general calling in of loans stretching back 20 years. At the end of it, the Consort was given the nod and we got the hell out of there. The flight home swiftly turned into a nightmare when two young white women in the row behind us began taking turns to go to the lavatory, where they were clearly ingesting some sort of substance that made them babble incessantly in voices hoarse with amphetamine damage.

These two potty-mouthed lesbian crack whores upset the Consort so much that she sought refuge in the galley where an air hostess with the face of a retired lap dancer tried to feel her leg.

I doubt that I shall be going away again any time soon.

8 November 2005

How Stupid Can You Be?

I stopped trusting people a long time ago. I remember the moment as if it were yesterday. I had just turned 18. Somebody dragged me away from the punch bowl and told me that there was no Easter Bunny, no Tooth Fairy, no Father Christmas. That my mother and father had been lying to me all along. I was so traumatised that I developed a drug habit right there and then.

A few days ago, I decided to give people another chance. Not my parents, of course. It takes a lifetime to forgive that kind of treachery.

What happened is that I decided to sell my motorcycle at a vastly inflated price. If someone was prepared to pay R9 500 for my 1974 Yamaha XT500, then I would happily take his money. Using Cape Ads' free service in order to maximise profits, I sat back and waited for the gullible hordes to start calling.

The first person who phoned sounded dead keen. He asked about the condition of the bike and I lied like anyone else selling second-hand goods. He asked when it would be convenient to come around and have a look at it. Inexplicably, I had forgotten that I was in Hermanus and the bike was parked outside my flat in Sea Point. I could hardly tell him that any time would be hopelessly inconvenient and that it would be best if he simply forgot about the whole thing and went on with his life.

"I'm out of town," I said, "but feel free to go along and take a look at it." I gave him my street address and told him where the bike was parked. He pointed out that he would have difficulty making a decision without actually taking it for a test ride. And that's when it happened.

I don't know if there was something in the beer I was drinking, but I was spontaneously imbued with overwhelming faith in my fellow man. I told him he could take it for a ride, that the XT500 doesn't actually need a key. That he could start it with a 50c coin, or his house key if he preferred.

"When you're done, put it back where you found it and give me a call." This was followed by a silence that can only be described as deafeningly incredulous. I asked him to please not steal the bike and requested his name, which I forgot within two seconds of him telling me. I told him that if there was any monkey business, I would be able to trace him through his cell number. He laughed and said he could always get a new number. I laughed. Then he laughed some more.

"Call me," I said, and laughingly went back to my beer. I stopped laughing around about the time that I arrived back in Sea Point four days later. All that remained of my bike was an oil stain on the tar.

I was rent asunder with sadness, not because of my own brutal stupidity, but because me and that bike went back a long way. We had been up mountains together. We had fallen over together. We had evaded traffic cops and angry motorists. We had done everything a normal couple does except bicker or throw plates and glasses at each other. And we never slept together. But apart from that, we were happy.

But, as in most relationships, there comes a time when you need to trade your partner in for a new model. One who doesn't leak all over the floor. One who doesn't have to be kicked into life over and over again until you are sweating heavily and purple in the face. One who doesn't throw you off if you open up too quickly.

Marriages are destroyed through the betrayal of trust. Countries have been invaded. Governments toppled. Companies get taken over in the dead of night. Watered down tequila is sold openly in bars. "I trust you" has overtaken "I love you" as the most deadly and duplicitous phrase in use today. Trust has become a four-letter word in the slippery hands of those who prey on the weak and vulnerable. Look, I'm not saying that I am weak and vulnerable. Far from it. I always wear long pants and I have never eaten quiche. I eat lambs and other small animals. And I have never once had second thoughts about snapping the spine of a kabeljou as it twists on the end of the line fighting to get at my jugular.

Several other people phoned about the bike in the days that followed, and the words: "Sorry, it's been taken" have never rung more true.

So this is a call to arms. As your commander, I expect every man, woman and child to be on the lookout for a black unlicensed XT500 with dysfunctional lights and a broken speedometer. It also comes trailing a string of outstanding warrants, but you wouldn't know that just by looking at it. Unless the thief is as dumb as I am, it's likely that the Durban number plate is already a souvenir on someone's bedroom wall.

If you spot my bike, I expect you to make a citizen's arrest. Even if you are travelling at high speed on the freeway, I urge you to run him off the road. Try to minimise damage to the bike. There is a reward, of course. Vigilante justice doesn't come cheap these days. Bring me my bike, or even one that looks like it could be mine, and you will receive an autographed copy of my latest book, three cases of beer and a weekend away with Brenda.

22 November 2005

Shooting Birdies
& Black Knights

Writing a book about golf has brought with it many benefits, one of which is that I have been declared persona non grata at Fancourt. Another is that I was given VIP status at the Nelson Mandela Invitational at Arabella last weekend.

Assuming I was being invited to play, I rushed off to Cash Converters and invested in a putter, two sand wedges and a driver that looked like it could send a ball to the moon. I also bought one black glove from a Sea Point hustler who tried to sell me two for double the price. That's affirmative action for you. Bastards.

Before I even had a chance to get my car out of the disabled parking bay, I was given the opportunity of practising my swing on a previously disadvantaged gentleman who seemed to think that a yellow bib gave him the right to look at me in an accusing fashion. Back home, I wiped the blood off my putter and rifled through the press kit that had been sent to me. I was appalled to discover that the tournament was presented by Coca Cola and hosted by Gary Player. As a seasoned journalist, I knew that al-Qaeda couldn't be far behind. I have no doubt that Osama bin Laden drinks Coke when nobody is watching, but it's an altogether more serious matter when a fatwah is declared on our small but perfectly formed golfing icon.

In the event that the organisers had failed to invite the mandatory quota of disabled Muslim lesbians, I stopped off at the gun shop and bought myself a Proudly South African bullet-proof vest. All I needed was a caddy.

While I was considering the most ethical way of forcing a young black man to carry my bag for as little money as possible, Ted arrived at the house with a sack full of beer.

I guzzled a six-pack and explained that I could take him, Brenda or the Illicit Consort with me to Arabella. The brat, Clive, was due for his bi-weekly electroconvulsive therapy session, so that was one less thing to worry about. Ted smacked me on the side of the head and began explaining the finer points of golf tournaments. I smacked him back and told him that as a man who has just written a book on golf, I did not need advice from the likes of him. He got up and began questioning my credentials, so I smacked him even harder and this time he just lay there and drank his beer from a supine position.

His point, once he could articulate it through his smashed mouth, was that the Nelson Mandela Invitational is based on the fourball system. I grabbed him by the throat and demanded to know how each golfer could play four balls and still be done by Christmas.

Kneeing me in the crotch, Ted pointed out that a fourball meant we could all play. Me, him, Brenda and the Consort.

The trouble started from the moment I hit the orange traffic cones outside Arabella. Brenda shouted at me to go back and pick them up. Ted said there's no going back, ever. The Consort urged me to go faster. Suddenly I was surrounded by men in moustaches and day-glo orange vests performing hand signals that made no sense. After a mutual exchange of racial epithets and at least one reference to Gary Player's mother, we were directed to the VIP parking area.

While Ted was trying to commandeer a golf cart, the Consort began demanding to know how an icon like Nelson Mandela could give his name to a golf tournament.

She was shouting something about the Mother Teresa Classic and the Pope Benedict World Series when a man with a serious face came up and asked her to be quiet. I jabbed him in the ribs with my sand wedge and told him to back off. "We are golfers," I said. "Now get out of our way."

The competition had started without us so we jumped straight in at the 7th hole, throwing our balls as close to the green as we could get them. We were still putting when a ball came out of nowhere and hit Brenda in the head.

I was dragging her out of the way so that I could play my shot when a fast-moving knot of men arrived. They demanded to know what we thought we were doing. "It's hard to say," said Ted, addressing himself to the leader of the pack.

"Why are you dressed all in black?" The little man with the face of a turtle looked at us in disbelief. "You fools. Don't you know that I am the Black Knight?"

The Consort began laughing so robustly that she tripped over her putter and crashed to the green. A dissolute version of Peter Pan appeared out of nowhere and helped her up. "Who are you?" she asked, clutching on to his hand a little too tightly.

"I am Ronan Keating," he said, smiling just enough for the sunlight to bounce off his teeth. Sensing that he was being upstaged, the Black Knight elbowed the Irish upstart aside, drew himself up to his full height, looked me squarely in the kneecaps, and said: "I am a living legend and I am the saviour of needy children."

Seeing that we were inexplicably unmoved by this information, he added: "I also have Nelson Mandela's cellphone number." Just then, a large black man walked onto the green. "Bring my bag," barked the little golfer.

"Sorry boss," said Vincent Tshabalala. "Those days are over."

29 November 2005

Delivering the Last Rites of Passage

My deviant offspring, Clive, is on the brink of turning 17. This must have triggered something in his so-called brain because he has begun misbehaving to an alarming degree.

The brat has always given me trouble. When he was born we all thought he was a girl but it turned out that he had tucked his willy between his legs like one of those drag queen abominations.

Once the nurse had wiped the blood and gore from his puny little body and handed him to me, I gave him a good smack and warned him never to impersonate a woman again. The nurse snatched him back and smacked him harder. We passed him back and forth, smacking and laughing, until Brenda sprang from her bed and intercepted him. I thought she wanted to join in the game but all she did was snarl and bark and rub his stupid red bottom as if that would help him grow up into a real man capable of playing a blood sport and fiddling his taxes.

I should have married the nurse instead of Brenda. I knew there was something different about Clive from the moment he failed his Apgar test. The nurse told me afterwards that he had the lowest score of any baby she had ever seen, including those born from vodka fiends and estate agents.

The Apgar test works much like basketball in that the infant is awarded two points for every score. Clive cracked the heart rate, thanks to the healthy beating. He lost one point for breathing because he screamed solidly for three minutes without once drawing breath. When it came to muscle tone, I was appalled to discover that the runt couldn't even arm wrestle me even though I was using my little finger on my left hand. No points there. None for colour, either. He was suspiciously dark. I demanded that they bring me another baby – a whiter baby. I can't even remember ever having had sex with Brenda, let alone impregnating her. The very idea is inconceivable.

Just as I was about to storm the nursery to acquire a more Caucasian replacement, they performed the final test on him. Stimulation. Clive reacted so well to stimulation that the sister had to put a screen around him and ask people to go back to their beds. That's when I knew he was mine. I overheard a doctor use the word "priapism".

Brenda panicked but I restrained her with a headlock and reassured her that this was a good thing. That was the first and last time I was convinced that I had a son and not a daughter. Years of mollycoddling, eating sandwiches with their crusts cut off and piano lessons with a priest who played Santa Claus at the mall every December sapped the poor bastard of the one drop of testosterone that he was born with.

He showed no interest in killing animals, taunting lesbians, abusing the hired help or any of the other things that make South African men what they are today. Instead, he developed a penchant for camouflage skirts and began hanging around his mother in the kitchen learning how to bake gay little tarts while swinging his girly hips to Brenda's favourite Abba album.

At the age of 16 his voice had still not broken. Unfortunately, Brenda got wind of my plan to sneak into his bedroom one night and give his testicles a healthy Catholic tug. She threatened to have me jailed, a prospect that made my sphincter tighten and my resolve weaken.

All of this has changed in the last week. With the approach of his 17th birthday, Clive appears to have become possessed by some sort of incubus. On Friday evening he sidled up to me in a crab-like fashion and asked if he could accompany me to the shop. I go to the shop every Friday evening for milk and bread. If we haven't run out, I wait until Brenda is out of the kitchen and then pour the milk down the sink and give the bread to the dog. Brenda caught me out when she found 30 or 40 loaves of bread moulding behind the garage. Apparently the dog died a few years ago.

I wasn't all that keen on Clive embarrassing me at my local shop, so I said he could come if he stole R100 from his mother's purse. He was back in a flash, thrusting two fifties into my hand. This is the same boy who would press the panic button whenever I forced him to watch wrestling instead of that mindless violence on the Discovery Channel.

The shop was thick with smoke and full of shouting men and squealing women. Clive grabbed my arm and said: "We must call the fire brigade!" I grabbed him by the throat and guided him to a stool. "First we have to steady our nerves," I said. "Then we'll call the fire brigade."

A shopkeeper with a 36D chest gave him the lazy eye and asked what he wanted. "Milk, please," he said. I laughed and cuffed him playfully across the head. "He means a milk stout," I said, helping him off the floor.

By the end of the evening, Clive's voice had broken and he was sucking shooters out of the barmaid's belly button. "I think I like girls," he growled.

It turns out that he also likes cigarettes, tequila and stealing the car when my back is turned. I won't even get into the skilful lies, artful deception and condoms in the sock drawer. I am mystified how a callow teenage virgin can overnight turn into a capricious hedonistic boy-slut.

Brenda is devastated and blames me for being a pathetic role model. I was having none of it. "What about Jacob Zuma?" I asked indignantly.

That shut her up.

6 December 2005

Rumble in the Jungle

I knew it was time to get out of Cape Town when it took me an hour to drive from Sea Point to Camps Bay. All I wanted was a brace of beers at Café Caprice and maybe a chance to taunt the odd passing anorexic.

"Yo, babe!" I usually say. Then, when they turn and smile coyly at me, I shout out: "Why you so fat?" It gets a laugh every time. Unless I hit a bulimic, in which case they throw up right there on the spot, which isn't so funny, especially when your calamari has just arrived.

Most of the prime parking on the strip was already taken. Not, as you might expect, by swarthy slum lords from Gauteng and human traffickers from the city council, but by a line of F1 racing cars emblazoned with the GQ logo. What kind of staff cars does this magazine provide? I suppose there has to be some sort of serious perk to compensate for having to work for a heartless brute like Craig Tyson.

Deprived of beer and an opportunity to mock the self-destructive, I went home and told Brenda that we had to leave town. Clive was still refusing to talk to me after I sent his nymphomaniac cousin, Roxanne, back to her mother in Windhoek. I had walked in on them after coming home after a bit of last minute Christmas shoplifting. They were rolling about on my bed – my bed, mind you – clutching and clawing at one another and making the kind of sounds that one would expect to hear at the Okaukuejo waterhole just before sunset.

I am the first to admit that Clive needs to lose his virginity. It may be the only way to get his facial hair to grow. But even I have boundaries and, to me, first cousins are off limits. This principle was instilled in me by my father and I have the scars to prove it.

Brenda jumped at the idea of a vacation. "Let's go and visit my parents in Durban," she said. There was a time that, on hearing these words, I would clutch my chest and crash to the floor. This was more fun in the early stages of our marriage when Brenda would get down on her hands and knees and urgently say my name over and over again, pumping my chest and blowing into my mouth. Then she would run to the phone and call the paramedics and when I heard the ambulance arrive I would jump up and go and hide in the basement and stifle my laughter as I listened to her trying to justify wasting their valuable time.

Those happy days are long gone. One time I had a fake heart attack, she rolled me over so she could vacuum beneath me. That's why I dispensed with the theatrics and agreed to go to Durban .

I always try to prepare myself for the stinking fug that shrouds Durban like an enormous steamed towel at this time of year, but I invariably end up gasping like an emphysema patient and sweating like seven pot-bellied pigs moments after stepping off the plane.

Brenda's father picked us up at the airport. A large taciturn man with wild white hair and a beard to match, he drives an ancient Land Rover with no aircon and a bell hanging from the rearview mirror that rattles and rings like a Hare Krishna at full throttle.

We arrived at the house in Durban North delirious from the heat and jangled by the bell. While Brenda and Clive struggled with the luggage, I hacked a path through the impenetrable jungle my mother-in-law calls a garden. The foliage is so dense that I half expected to come across the decomposing bodies of visitors who had lost their way over the years.

Chopping my way through a herd of elephant ears, I brushed aside a boomslang and burst through the front door. Brenda's mother was in front of the television watching an oddly compliant Saddam Hussein being readied for the noose.

Suddenly she leapt to her feet. "A pack of filthy lies!" she screamed. "The whole thing is rigged!" She launched into a tirade about the edifice of propaganda that shores up America and then, as George Bush's picture flashed up, she clutched her face and bent double, as if she had been kicked in the stomach. She began cursing and stamping her feet. Alarmed, I ducked back outside and grabbed Brenda by the arm.

"Your mother is behaving like an escaped lunatic with Tourette's Syndrome. I think we should leave." Brenda said this was perfectly normal behaviour around news time.

Her mother is one of those people who believe that JFK's assassination was staged by the Illuminati so that Fidel Castro could continue working for the CIA.

I walked back inside and stood on a cockroach the size of a mongoose. It made the same sound a crayfish makes when you break its head off. Brenda's father stalked past me, muttering something about taking the life of a sentient being, and disappeared into his room to meditate.

We got to sleep in the *khaya*. Now that domestic workers have their own lawyers, nobody wants the hired help to live in. Let them do the washing and the ironing and the cleaning and then bugger off back to the township. Minimises the chance of a lawsuit.

They've been broken into three times in the past month and once the alarms are set and the minefield activated, there's no way we can get back into the main house after curfew.

Right now it is way past midnight and Brenda is asleep. I am outside on a camp stool, laptop balanced on my knees, a beer between my legs, my body slippery with sweat.

The fractured lights of KwaMashu in the valley. Strange noises from the jungle. Gunshots in the distance. Somewhere, a woman screams.

2 January 2006

Riding Waves of Nausea at Face Brick City

Last Friday seemed like a good day to resurrect my surfing career, since my current one doesn't seem to be panning out at all. I was going to head for Llandudno until I heard that the beach was awash in human excrement. This is no ordinary excrement, mind you. It is the excrement of Very Rich People.

Oddly enough, having a mansion with sweeping sea views and two Porches in the garage is no guarantee that your body will process Beluga caviar and West Coast oysters in a form any more acceptable than it would a half-eaten ham sandwich retrieved from a bin on the Sea Point promenade.

In that way, the homeless are no different to the obscenely wealthy. The homeless, on the other hand, don't leave Llandudno beach awash in faeces every time Eskom trips.

I have to get out of the Western Cape. The elections have been over for almost a week and still nobody can tell me who is in charge of Cape Town.

I told Brenda that I was going away on a surf trip and she laughed so hard that I thought she was going to have a hernia. I playfully elbowed her in the stomach to help the hernia along and went off to find my surfboard.

When it comes to surfing, there is really only one place to go in South Africa. Jeffreys Bay. I camped there once with a girlfriend about 100 years ago and it was an unmitigated disaster. That's why I never thought twice about not inviting Brenda or the Consort to accompany me.

Taking a woman on a surf trip is like shooting up heroin inside a police station – it's bound to end badly.

For a start, she never understands why it is so important that she sits on the beach in a howling offshore wind getting drenched by intermittent squalls and set upon by rogue seagulls and stray dogs.

It is so that she can watch, in open-mouthed awe and adoration, as you ride waves that strike terror into the heart of ordinary mortals. Instead, she goes and sits in the car and calls up her ex-boyfriends to pass the time. Then, unable to get back to the beach because a 15-foot storm swell has just arrived from Madagascar, you have to watch as a knot of foam-flecked surfers forms around your car.

Surfers have no code of conduct or ethics of any sort whatsoever when they are on land. They are more unprincipled than even rugby players or musicians when it comes to women.

Women, in turn, quickly lose all sense of moral rectitude when surfers are in the area. Apparently there is something about the sight of a man with long blonde hair and a tan, wearing a skin-tight neoprene wetsuit, that sends their inner compasses spinning.

By all means, take your girlfriend or wife on a surf trip. But then be prepared for a knife-fight. It might be easier to simply lock her in the boot of the car while you go surfing. However, there is a good chance that this sort of thing is illegal in the new South Africa. Chaining her to the bed, however, is still permissable.

The drive to J-Bay took longer than expected because it was further away than I thought. On my way there, I passed a turnoff to a place called Suurbraak. What kind of vicious, hollow-eyed panhandlers would name their town Sour Vomit? There was another one a bit further along. Ystervarkfontein. I can see the marketing brochures. "The opportunity of a lifetime! Invest now in stunning Iron Pig Fountain!"

The laughter died in my throat the moment I drove into J-Bay. What was once a quaint seaside town smelling of resin and tetrahydracannibanol now stank of cheap perfume and boerewors.

Super Tubes has become Face Brick City. The aloes are dying, the shells are gone. The surf shops are no longer full of hippies standing about wondering what they came in for. Instead, they are stuffed with enormous jellied women with moustaches and thick-thighed brutes wearing denim shorts held up by big buckled belts stretched by ballooning beer bellies, all shouting in a harsh, guttural tongue.

"How did this happen?" I cried softly to myself. Softly, because nobody would openly speak English in J-Bay unless they had a death wish.

With tears welling up in my sensitive *soutpiel* eyes, I got back into my car and drove to the far end of town, the bad end, where I found a ramshackle bar that had a sand floor and a palm frond roof. "The spirit of J-Bay lives on," I said less softly as I walked in and ordered a brace of cold beers.

My joy was short-lived. The bartender looked like Shane Warne, but that wasn't the disturbing part. I wasn't even particularly bothered by the fact that he would immediately be disqualified had he to ever enter a race for heterosexuals only. After all, some of my best friends are gay.

What really upset me was that he refused to change the music, no matter how much I begged or threatened him. Everything he played sounded like a bastard hybrid of Worsie Visser and Steve Hofmeyr. I found it deeply troubling.

Let me just say that I have nothing against Afrikaners. The inclination to ridicule and discriminate against others is nothing new. I do it all the time. But why, oh why, have they been allowed to overrun every coastal resort from St Lucia to Langebaan and beyond?

The trail of rusted fish hooks, broken brandy bottles, sad battered wives, sucked chop bones and 4x4 wheel tracks stretches all the way back to a single heavily-bearded pipe-smoking Groot Trekker who decided to park off at the coast instead of doing the right thing and heading for the Transvaal.

There was only one thing for it. Go surfing. I drove to the Point, where the waves are gentler than Supers. My wetsuit must have shrunk because when I bent over to put on my leash, it split down the seams causing my flesh to ooze out like an overripe sausage.

Then I almost killed myself jumping off the rocks to paddle out and when I got to backline I discovered that the locals don't allow outsiders to catch waves so I tried to come back in and got washed along the reef for two kilometres.

Drenched in blood and pin-cushioned with toxic sea urchin spikes, I tossed my surfboard into the last patch of dune vegetation that hadn't been turned into a guest house, got into my car and drove home.

At some point I hit a roadblock. Orange traffic cones. Flashing lights. Thugs in camouflage. Police caravan for law enforcement officers to smoke the evidence. Braai for the confiscated perlemoen. Nothing out of the ordinary. Then I saw her. Every white male motorist's worst nightmare.

A black woman in a uniform. Don't misunderstand me – some of my best friends are black women who wear uniforms. But she was different. This one was enormous and yet still managed to walk with a thin man's swagger.

She was at my window before I had time to hide my unlicensed firearm, get rid of the beer between my legs and dump the herbal remedy that was burning out of control between my fingers.

I looked at her and smiled the smile of the bust. She never smiled back. What she did, though, was ask me the one question I have never before been asked at a roadblock.

"Do you have any pork products?" she said.

This is why I don't emigrate.

7 March 2006

Narco-Loading With the Spiders from Mars

It has only now come to my attention that Eskom has been plunging much of the Western Cape into darkness on a regular basis. I thought it was just me, because ever since I moved to the wine-growing region I have been experiencing my own rolling blackouts.

When I informed Brenda in a grave voice that I was suffering from seizures brought on by postprandial hypotension, she barked like a lunatic and instead of rushing me off for an electrocardiogram, she started calling me Julius Seizure and mocked me relentlessly by staging her own dead faints whenever I looked at her.

I eventually had to stop looking at her to preserve my own sanity. I don't even know if she is still in the house. Perhaps she has moved out. Oh well. It's about time I did some load shedding of my own.

I had every intention of riding in last Sunday's Cape Argus Cycle Tour, going so far as to begin an intensive training regimen on Saturday evening. As always, Ted and I planned to emerge from the bushes at the bottom of Queen's Road in Sea Point and sprint for the finish where we would cross the line together and be hailed as the world's latest cycling sensation.

At some point, Ted suggested we carbo-load the last of the methylene-dioxymethamphetamine. This we duly washed down with a couple of Tafels and went to the garage to fetch the bicycles that we had borrowed off the back of a Gauteng-registered trailer in Camps Bay late on Friday night.

My next recollection was Ted standing over me. I recoiled at the sight. His eyes were huge and his face looked like a melted Frisbee. The race was long over.

Eventually the truth came out. It wasn't Ecstasy that we had carbo-loaded. Apparently the gentleman from the Congo was fresh out of hallucinogenic stimulants so Ted had bought Thorazine instead but didn't want to tell me because he thought I might be angry.

"Angry?" I shouted, grabbing him by the throat. "The Chinese use Thorazine on their dissidents, you irresponsible fool!"

Luckily for Ted, one of the side effects of ingesting a dangerous neuroleptic is a disruption in the functioning of the frontal lobes. It is not easy sustaining a meaningful level of discourse after receiving a chemical lobotomy.

We looked at each other and drooled indifferently for a while. Then Ted suggested that we could still put our training to good use. I tried to ask him how, but found myself unable to formulate the word.

He seemed to read what little remained of my mind. "We are needed at the Zuma trial," he said, collapsing sideways into a pile of oil rags. A black spider with the face of a small monkey ran across his head, paused to look him in the eye, and disappeared behind a garden spade.

"Spider," I said, two hours later. With tremendous effort, Ted raised his hand and brushed it across his face.

"Yes," I thought, willing Ted to understand. "Zuma certainly could use two more mentally-impaired morons in his camp."

By then Ted had lost interest. That's the one good thing about Thorazine. It imbues you with such deep apathy that you no longer care about anything at all. It wouldn't surprise me to discover there is Thorazine in this country's drinking water.

We sat quietly in the garage experiencing multiple blackouts. There was nobody around to ask if it was Eskom or our neurological transmitters that were shutting down. Thanks to the Thorazine, we didn't care.

A day or two later, Ted asked if the spider was still on his face. I laughed. This is a good sign, I thought. An hour later, I was still laughing. This is not so good, I thought.

While I was trying to stop laughing, or crying, it was hard to say which of the two I was busy with, Ted discovered that he was lying on the Sunday papers.

There is something deeply comforting about the Sunday papers. Especially if you don't read them. Ted turned to the books page to see if my critically acclaimed (mis)Guide to Golf had made it into the Non-Fiction Top Ten. Ted lives in eternal hope that one of my books will make me rich.

For some reason, he thinks that once this happens he will never have to work again. He has the logic of a woman.

This time, Ted's howls of outrage were even more vociferous than usual. The Thorazine must have started wearing off.

"Look at this!" he shouted, screwing the page into a ball and throwing it at me. "Patrick Holford has taken five of the top six slots!"

"Patrick who?" I said. "Exactly!" Ted yelled, rising to his knees.

Fear churned in my belly. The last thing I needed was another Dan Brown to come along and hog the bestseller lists for months on end.

Unwrapping the ball, horror quickly replaced the fear. Holford is not the creator of a literary masterpiece destined to change the way in which we see the world. He is something far worse. He is a food writer.

Patrick Holford writes about dieting, about food allergies, about optimum nutrition for your child's mind. On his website, he says: "The Holford low-GL diet is set to revolutionise weight loss. With this simple yet highly-effective programme, you can beat food cravings and hunger, shed unwanted pounds *and* enjoy delicious meals."

I was destroyed. In South Africa, the only people who can afford to buy books are rich people. Rich, fat people. And they will keep this Holford bastard on the Top Ten for years.

I looked at Ted and he nodded. There was only one thing to do. Take the rest of the Thorazine and move in with the spider.

14 March 2006

This Magazine is Empty – Bring Me a Fresh Round

I am in a quandary. I have never once bought a men's magazine and I don't know whether to feel enormous pride or intense guilt. Perhaps I should differentiate.

There are two types of men's magazines. The first falls squarely into the category of porn. This includes *Hustler*, *Loslyf* and *Farmers Weekly*. The second deals with subject matter of a far more aberrant nature, such as cars, health and computers.

Cosmopolitan is also a men's magazine, although not many men realise this. One of the reasons I have such a deep insight into the feminine psyche is because I read magazines like *Cosmo*. Not openly, of course.

Ted came around on Saturday night with a clutch of cold beers and I told him that I was thinking about buying my first real men's magazine. The argument started almost immediately. Ted pointed out that women buy women's magazines because they are full of women and womanly things.

"It follows, then," shouted Ted, wedging a bottle into his eye socket and ripping the cap off, "that men buy men's magazines because they are full of men."

We sat there for a while glaring at each other in silence, me reluctant to defend myself against his homophobic tirade and he incapable of speaking because his mouth was full of beer.

When he had finally finished guzzling he looked at me with his good eye and said: "Oh. My. God. You've bought one, haven't you?" I looked away, trying to hide that quick hot flush that mea culpa brings to one's face. Not being familiar with Latin, Ted misinterpreted my shame as coyness. And there is nothing more gay than coy.

I leapt to my feet with every ounce of righteous masculine indignation that I could muster. "Fine!" I shouted. "I bought one!"

Unfortunately, I had to go and fetch it from the toilet, an action with deeply disturbing connotations of its own.

My sexuality was redeemed when Ted saw the magazine was still wrapped in plastic. It was a health magazine. On the cover was a photograph of a man-child stripped to the waist. His body told of many, many hours spent in the gym. His eyes told another story. They said: "Library? What's that?"

Protruding from the cover was a hard, cylindrical object. Ted said: "This isn't one of those scratch and sniff covers, is it?"

The unsightly bulge turned out to be a stick of free deodorant. Ted barked harshly and began slapping himself across the side of his head. I moved away and adopted the Prancing Tiger stance, then resumed the drinking position once I realised he was simply having one of his non-violent epiphanies.

"What a brilliant marketing ploy," he said. "Tell your readers that the reason they can't get laid is because they smell bad."

I couldn't argue. Studies have shown that the stinkers have sex far less frequently than the non-stinkers. The really smelly ones often remain virgins for their entire lives. I don't care. That's their problem. As long as they don't rub themselves up against me, I don't mind how rotten they smell.

Ted said that he, too, had never bought a men's magazine. I had my doubts. When I took the beers away, he admitted he had once bought a *Penthouse* but after realising it wasn't a property magazine for the elite he took it back to the shop but they wouldn't return his money because the pages were stuck together.

His eyes were so big and mad that I agreed this must have been the printer's fault and we decided there and then that we would go back to the shop and burn it to the ground.

However, we became so distracted by my new magazine's cover that we inadvertently drank the Molotov cocktails we had been mixing. "This is a health magazine, right?" asked Ted.

"Of course," I said, "can't you tell by the teasers?" Ted is a bit like a dog. Dogs will hear a word like "beach" and start slobbering and running for the door. For Ted, the word is "Teazers".

I hosed him down with my portable AA-approved fire extinguisher and once he had scraped the foam from his face he wanted to know why a men's health magazine was writing about "More Sex Than You Can Handle!" and "Seven Ways To Cheat Death!"

I grabbed him by the throat and wrestled him to the ground. "They are two sides of the same coin! Why can't you see that?"

He broke free and crawled under the pool table to suckle on a beer. After a while he slunk out and we began paging through the magazine. The first article we came across reassured men that they have nothing to worry about if they are big boned. Ted pointed out that *Cosmo* reassures us that we have nothing to worry about if we are small boned.

"You read *Cosmo*?" I shouted. Ted blushed furiously and passed out. I was going to call the paramedics but then I came across a feature that told me precisely what to do in this situation.

I quickly applied a Breitling watch to his wrist, rubbed a little Loreal Men Expert Vita Lift with Shea Butter and Silicone on his hands, poured a spot of Vanish on his soiled shirt and slapped some, well, I didn't have any of that stuff, so I just slapped him.

11 April 2006

What Rough Beast Slouches Towards Langstrand to be Born?

An unborn baby has single-handedly destroyed press freedom in Namibia. Okay, so it might be a little premature to blame the foetus. But once the brat gets out and realises the tremendous power that it wields, the world should brace itself for another Josef Stalin or, if it is a girl, Margaret Thatcher.

For those who are unaware of the latest horror being perpetrated in our former colony, this impending crisis has been sparked by the presence of one William Bradley Pitt and one Angelina Jolie Voight (the Voight fell by the wayside after she and her father lovingly described one another as sexually depraved and mentally disturbed).

The world's most perfect cyborgs have shacked up in Langstrand, a godforsaken stretch of mist-shrouded coast between Swakopmund and Walvis Bay. Their neighbours speak in a harsh guttural tongue and live in ugly triple-storey houses that blight this bleak landscape. Rotting seals litter the beach and scorpions are everywhere. This is where she has come to have her baby.

In a 2003 interview, Angelina said: "Everybody jokes that whenever I go to a country, be prepared in case I come home with a new child. I want to have a home that represents the world as I see it, which is children with all different religions from different parts of the world."

Brad pictured himself turning 45 while trying to stop the Arab orphan from setting fire to the Israeli orphan as a pack of feral orphans from central Africa bludgeoned one another with their bottles while the two Korean orphans (North and South) set aside their differences and began feasting on the cat. It became blindingly obvious to Brad that he had to impregnate his girlfriend if he hoped to prevent his home from turning into a hellish version of the United Nations, and also if he hoped to ever have a white baby. As a secondary precaution, he had to ensure that she gave birth in an orphan-free area. An isolated spot on the fringes of a jackal-infested desert seemed about right.

What Brad hadn't realised was that the world had grown monumentally bored with pictures of burnt-out cars and dismembered corpses, and was now demanding photographs of him in a Speedo and Angie showing her big fat tummy.

The paparazzi duly flew into Namibia and made their way to the coast. Once there, Angelina's bodyguard welcomed the media by inviting them to have their legs broken should they try to snap the happy couple.

Namibians fought long and hard for their freedom from oppression and the government wasn't about to tolerate any more threats of abuse from foreigners. It was clear that the photographers had to be thrown out of the country immediately.

Years of inhaling mica dust, prolonged bouts of heatstroke and overexposure to Windhoek lager have finally rotted the minds of those in power. Desert madness has taken its toll on all who waddle through the corridors of power. Dante's *Divine Comedy* has nothing on what is going on inside the Tintenpalast right now.

"Abandon Hope All Ye Who Enter Here" – The Germans were among the first to succumb to the curse. Then came the South Africans and their doomed attempt at forging a legitimate puppet government. Now it is Swapo's turn.

The increasingly unstable Sam Nujoma, who still controls the country from his mansion in the hills, has loathed foreigners ever since he was forced to live among them in exile.

In this case, however, he must have told president-by-proxy, Hifikepunye Pohamba, to lay off Angie and Brad. Perhaps Sam has seen their movies, although this is unlikely since he is widely known to despise all films with a non-agricultural theme.

There is a chance that Sam has a crush on Angelina. Or even Brad, heaven forbid. Anything is possible. Sam is behaving strangely out of character. His abhorrence of anything homosexual goes way back, possibly to an incident in his childhood. Does he not know of Angie's penchant for getting nekkid with other girls? Perhaps this is simply an image too powerful for any homophobe to resist. I struggle with it, even though none of my best friends are gay.

The hunting down and deportation of the foreign press came after Angie and Brad threatened to leave the country if they continued to be disturbed. This is a threat issued by two people who make their living by pretending to be other people. They are paid enormous amounts of money to not be themselves. Who the hell do they think they are? Hard to say, really.

And why would they want to inflict Namibian citizenship on their newborn? The poor kid is going to need visas for virtually every country it is dragged to. While an American passport might get you killed, an African passport is going to land you in endless queues and marshy pools of bureaucratic quicksand.

Personally, I would rather risk death.

25 April 2006

White Men Can't Strike

There have been so many exciting things happening in this great country of ours that I felt compelled to invite Ted over for a meeting so we could come up with new and innovative ways of improving the lives of our fellow South Africans without regard to race, gender or political affiliation.

"So you've run out of beer, then?" said Ted, snorting loudly. I objected to his cynicism and asked what he was snorting about. "About half a gram," he said.

He was joking, of course. Ted turned against chemicals the day South African Breweries turned against Justin Nurse.

"We need to caucus," I said.

"A raucous caucus or a dorkus caucus?" Ted asked. A lot of the time I have no idea what he is talking about. It is often best not to ask.

Three hours later he arrived with a boot full of beer and a car full of wife. I opened the front door to find Mary reared up on her hind legs like an angry polar bear.

"What do you want?" I said.

"I want to speak to Brenda," she said. "Sorry," I said. "Brenda's not speaking at the moment." I made the mistake of stepping aside to allow unfettered access to five cases of Tafel lager on legs. "Not to you, she's not," said the bear, waddling into the house.

Ted was already in the safe zone, sucking heavily on a beer and laughing at the same time. It wasn't a pretty sight. I am trained to recognise the symptoms of marital hysteria and was about to smack him across the side of the head when he made a startling admission.

"I am the Third Force," he said, beer dribbling down his chin. Pressed for details, Ted admitted that he had joined the security guard strike in Cape Town.

"What were you thinking?" I shouted. "White men can't strike." Ted looked at me long and hard, then lay down in a spontaneous fashion.

"I was a security guard once …" he began, his so-called eyes misting over with a nasty combination of nostalgia and pterygiums.

I took him gently by the throat and explained that sitting in a thorn tree with a sniper's rifle on the outskirts of Lubango did not make him a security guard. He begged to differ. I cannot stand to see a grown man beg so I released my grip and grabbed a beer by the throat instead. That's what I like about alcohol. You can abuse it as much as you want and yet you will never hear it complain.

Ted told me he had arrived early for the SA Transport and Allied Workers Union march. Parking, apparently, is at a premium at these events. These days nobody really wants to march further than they have to. Especially in winter. This is why the comrades set the trains alight the moment they disembark at Capitalist Central. It's the only way to warm up before heading onto the mean streets to fight for their rights.

Ted said he got there early enough to see the last wave leave Bob's Bar on their hands and knees barking like dogs. He said he tried to unionise them but lost sympathy for their cause when a transvestite bit him on the ankle. Then a pack of feral street kids began harassing him so he went back to the car and defused the situation by handing out cans of glue he keeps under the passenger seat for emergencies.

Ted said dawn began doing its overrated pink thing just as the first of his fellow protestors arrived. He said they were wary of him until he brought out a bottle of Klipdrift and showed them his yellow flare that would have saved the lives of his platoon had it not slipped down his trousers on May 3, 1978.

Then, he said, a middle-aged white gentleman wearing a red jacket and spectacles appeared out of nowhere and introduced himself as Tony Ehrenreich. Ted said Cape Town welcomed all visitors, even if they were from Germany, and gave him directions to the cable car.

Ted said Tony the tourist was still struggling to formulate a reply when hundreds of excited black men began surging around them. Excusing himself, he said he had to go back to his car to fetch his placard.

When he got to his car, he saw that he had locked his keys inside. "This was a terrible situation," he said. "A protestor without a placard is like a

Catholic with a condom."

So he smashed his window. And the idea took like wildfire.

"Now you know," said Ted mournfully. "I am the Third Force."

"Never mind that," I said. "Unless you work for PG Glass, nobody will ever suspect you. Right now, we have to form our own union."

Just then Brenda and Mary breached internal security and walked brazenly into the safe zone. Ted and I rose as one. "How dare you?" I said. Brenda bent down and removed the canister of pepper spray from the holster on her ankle. Ted and I sat as one.

"Men," said Mary, "are ruining it for the rest of us."

"Men," said Brenda.

Defending his groin and swivelling his face so that he might avoid being turned to stone, Ted got to his feet, fell over and got to his feet again. "What if women were called upon to protect people and property with nothing more than a balaclava, a baton and a beast of a boss?"

"Women," said Brenda, "wouldn't be that stupid."

"Women," said Mary, "would marry the boss in community of property, market the balaclavas in a range of pastel colours and use the baton in the best possible way."

Ted and I looked at each other. We kept looking at each other until the women sighed and went back to the kitchen.

23 May 2006

The Soccer Fans Were in the Group D for Drunk Category

I took the abominable fruit of my loins to the Waterfront on Sunday to make a little extra cash by nicking ladies' handbags from fancy restaurants.

On our way to Balducci's, we saw a sign in the CNA window: "Your Dad chose to have you." It was aimed at guilting the adolescent market into buying Father's Day gifts. Clive got all excited and grabbed my hand. He wanted to know what he could get me. I wanted to know why he was holding my hand in a public place.

"I don't want people thinking you're my catamite," I said, smacking him sharply across the back of his so-called head.

"I just wanted to get you something to thank you for choosing to have me," he whimpered.

I laughed and laughed until I felt my spleen beginning to rupture so I stopped. "Choose to have you?" I wheezed. "Are you insane?"

When I explained that he was the result of a night of drunken carousing, the brat turned ashen and had to sit down. I reassured him that when he was conceived, I had been under the impression that I was cutting loose on his mother's best friend. It was only when I woke up a day or two later that I realised it was, in fact, Brenda.

Clive seemed to perk up a little upon hearing this humorous anecdote but it turned out to be nothing more than a precursor to full-blown hysteria. Funnily enough, Brenda had an almost identical reaction when I shared this little nugget with her.

People were beginning to stare as if I were some kind of monster.

"Listen here," I said, taking him gently by the trachea to prevent him from drawing another lungful of scream. "Since I made you by accident, I am legally entitled to kill you by accident."

He started turning a very gay shade of blue so I let go and offered to take him to the soccer World Cup instead of killing him.

"We're going to Germany!" he shouted, jumping up and down and clapping his girly little hands.

By the time my fourth beer arrived, I think he must have realised that we weren't going much further than the Sports Café. I ordered him a Jägermeister as compensation and turned my attention to the dying minutes of the Serbia & Montenegro v Holland game. There must have been absolute carnage on the pitch because the entire Serbian team had already been sent off, reducing Montenegro to 11 players and giving Holland a clear advantage. The Dutch scored once, which in itself is unusual because when I visited Amsterdam I saw locals scoring all the time. And that was just in a coffee shop.

The game over, the eastern Europeans took their Slobodan Milosevic haircuts and shifty genocidal demeanours out onto the street to look for a Bosnian Muslim immigrant to kick to death.

I ordered a brace of beers and settled in to watch Mexico take on Iran. It was a Group D match, the D presumably referring to those countries that fall into the Doomed category.

The bar began filling up with people who looked as if they lived in Group D countries and I switched tables so that my back wasn't exposed. Citizens of the Doomed are notoriously unpredictable when they are thrust together in open competition.

When Mexicans get excited, they want to drink tequila, dance on tables and ravish nubile young senoritas. When Iranians get excited, they want to nuke Israel. Sometimes I don't know which is worse.

It was a brutal 90 minutes. By the time Mexico scored their third goal, the Iranian supporters were holding the entire bar staff hostage. That explained the slow service. My throat was parched from swearing in broken Spanish and I needed a beer quickly. Clive seemed to be cheering up and said he would have another Jägermeister after I assured him that it was an energy drink made from fruit and spices.

I accosted the nearest bearded extremist and insisted that the waiters be beheaded so that we could at least get behind the bar and help ourselves.

When he realised that I was a non-Jewish South African, he apologised and announced that the Jihad was over. Everyone feels sorry for us because we are not in the World Cup. We, on the other hand, are overwhelmed with relief.

Having your national soccer team whipped by seven pregnant women from the Gambian Society of the Blind is one thing. But to lose 15-0 to Togo while the entire world crawls about the floor helpless with laughter is a humiliation on an altogether more serious scale.

A victorious Mexican wave ended with the Iranians storming out into the street. One swarthy type with a cigarette in each hand, two in his mouth and one behind his ear shook his fist and shouted that he was going back to his hotel to enrich the uranium he bought from a Rastafarian in Green Market Square.

Then the bar was invaded by Angolans and Portuguese. I wanted to see the lads from Luanda give their former colonisers a damn good kicking, but once again history repeated itself. When I got up to go to the bar, an Angolan gentleman rushed over and offered to watch my stool for me. I called him a *kwerekwere* and chased him away.

I have since left the bar. Clive has had his stomach pumped and, as I write this, he is fashioning a crude sword from a dozen wire coat hangers. He is not dealing well with Japan's loss against Australia and is threatening to commit *hara-kiri*. I told him not to get blood on the carpet and sent him outside.

Today is retribution day. Today, Poland finally gets a chance to pay Germany back for a nasty little incident in 1939.

Appeasement, my ass.

13 June 2006

The Road to Hell is Paved with Estate Agents

That's it. I am getting out of Hermanus right now. My nerves are shot to hell. I have had enough of being terrorised by geriatric drug dealers trying to flog their black market Viagra every time I step out of the house.

My legs are scarred from getting caught in the crossfire of brutal Zimmer frame fights that break out every time Woolworths has a sale. I can no longer take the relentless calls from sex pests with Alzheimer's – the heavy breathers who cannot remember who they are calling or even why.

And now, to top it all, the whales are beginning to return and soon the town will be full of prurient voyeurs taking dirty photographs of these big fat exhibitionists fornicating openly in the bay. It is only a matter of time before whale porn becomes more popular than hormone replacement therapy. But before that sad day arrives, I will be long gone from this unholy den of vice.

I am going back to the city, to a place where TV critics describe films like *Desert Saints* as "an entertaining action thriller in which a hit man forces women to help him with his murders before killing them". Now that's entertainment!

I am going back to the city, to a place full of crack whores, toothless gangbangers and sleaze merchants of every stripe. And that's just the politicians. More worrying is that I once again find myself dealing with a dangerously unpredictable breed. The urban estate agent is not to be approached lightly. They do not sleep and they hunt alone. They are dangerous. Mark my words.

Some people – psychics and tow-truck drivers mainly – have a sixth sense. They have the ability to pick up on impending disaster and make a living from it. Estate agents are possessed of something far more freakish – a seventh sense. Through eye contact alone, they can tell whether someone has ever thought of buying or selling a property, no matter how fleeting that thought may have been.

But their powers extend beyond mere mind reading. They are also able to influence people to buy or sell through the physical act of touch alone. Two days after brushing against one of them, you will start having thoughts of moving. Within 24 hours, you will receive a real estate flyer in your post box. Three weeks later, there will be a For Sale sign outside your house and your wife will be shouting at you to stop drinking beer and help pack. It's beyond uncanny.

Forget about wooden stakes and silver bullets. The only way to avoid falling into their clutches is to rent. Estate agents do not waste their supernatural powers on those of us who rent. We are worthless to them. We are the untouchables.

But there are too many of us for them to ignore. We are an army. Sure, an army wearing borrowed boots, driving borrowed cars and living on borrowed time, but we are an army nevertheless.

And that's where I find myself. Fighting a rearguard action. Not too long ago, a copy of my ID and a reference from my previous landlord was enough. Now I need proof of employment, bank statements going back six months, a psychiatric report, three passport photographs, a certified copy of my family tree and two DNA samples.

A week ago I forged the lot and threw myself at their mercy. Fortunately, rental agents are not like normal agents. They are kept in isolation and permitted to mingle with the other staff at Christmas parties only. They are the wolverines of the real estate world. They are trained to kill and feed, kill and feed. And when they are not killing and feeding, they are cheating and lying in the hope that one day they will be released into the wild to bring down the really big game.

Last week I was permitted to inspect a property in Camps Bay so I put on a pair of underpants and brushed my so-called hair. Agent Orange said it was a snip at R15 000 a month. In my mind I said: "Are you an escaped lunatic?" In my voice, I said: "That's cool," thereby fooling her with my suave demeanour and cunning usage of colloquial slang.

Then she asked what I did for a living. I gave her the Gallic shrug and rolled my eyes. "I work from home." She tried to furrow her Botoxed brow but said nothing. Only the very rich and the very poor stay at home during the week and, as a confused young white South African, she was understandably reluctant to press me for details for fear of provoking a bloodbath.

Like a guide dog for the blind, she walked me through the house.

"Lots of built-in cupboards," she said, as I stared uncomprehendingly at the built-in cupboards. I instinctively took hold of her arm (nice coat, Labrador, probably) as she introduced me to the main bedroom and en suite bathroom. "This is the en suite bathroom," she said, in the event that I mistook it for the kitchen.

Then she led me into the lounge and pointed out the sweeping sea views, which I most certainly would have missed had I not escaped minutes before the Lord's Resistance Army could gouge my eyes out as punishment for trying to stop the child rebels from abducting my family in northern Uganda.

"So who owns this hovel," I said.

"A German gentleman," she said. I was about to point out the glaring oxymoron, but then recalled my mother telling me that if I had nothing good to say, I shouldn't say anything at all.

"What?" I shouted. "You expect me to stay here after what they did to Poland?"

I was talking World Cup, but I think she thought I was talking World War II because the tour ended pretty sharpish after that.

20 June 2006

The Great Cat Hunt

Ted called and asked if I wanted to go hunting.

"Of course," I snapped. "I haven't killed anything in weeks."

After filling the Thermos with hot coffee and whisky, I grabbed my AK-47 from under the bed and went outside. I soon got bored waiting and began pretending that I was about to shoot passing motorists. You would be surprised at the number of drivers who almost rolled their cars when they saw me. Silly people. When last did a white man shoot anyone with an AK-47?

When Ted arrived he told me to go back inside and switch the rifle for a handgun. I told him to stop being such a girl. "We are hunters, not sportsmen," I shouted, taking mock aim at his head.

"Whatever it is we are going to kill, we can kill more of them with this." I brandished the semi-automatic weapon with the ease of a Sudanese.

I have never seen the point of going hunting and coming home with just three or four animals. A good hunt is one that ends with your car full of dead things. They should be tied to the bumpers and strapped to the roof, lashed to the bonnet and packed in the boot. The smell of victory should linger in the air. Dogs and hungry people should run down the street after you in the hope that a carcass will slip from the car.

I knew that with a handgun, I would have to get within a metre or two of the animal if I hoped for a kill. And even then, it could take anything up to 15 shots to put it out of its misery. It is not so much that my aim is poor. The truth is that I don't really know what to aim for. I have no idea where animals keep their hearts, and I am not comfortable aiming for the head because when I am that close to my prey it feels more like an assisted suicide than anything else.

"You know the rule," said Ted, trying to pistol-whip my cerebellum with his Parabellum. "Small arms for small game."

137

Half an hour later we were on a ferry heading for the open sea. "We're going to shoot fish?" I asked dubiously. Ted laughed.

"Cats."

"Catfish?"

"No. Cats. Real live cats."

Then it dawned on me. Our destination was Robben Island. Our mission: to help eradicate the giant feral cats that were slaughtering penguins and terrorising the children.

Ted told me the SPCA and other anti-people organisations had fiercely resisted the idea of population control through the use of high-powered weapons, and instead had suggested that the cats be darted with a groovy drug like Pethidine, gently placed in silver boxes lined with red velvet and neutered in a soothing environment on the mainland.

The first SPCA patrol was decimated. Those who made it back refused to talk about what they had seen. One young man's hair turned snow white. Another lost his power of speech altogether. The leader of the group wept openly and spoke only of the "horror".

The order went out. Kill the bastards.

Ted stared grimly at the fast-approaching island. "They're out there watching us right now."

I eyed the other passengers from behind my reflecting *Soldier of Fortune* sunglasses. On board was a delegation of French-speaking people wearing matching red jackets that said they were in Cape Town for a pet food convention. Of course. The perfect cover for militant animal liberationists. They reminded me of Mad Mike Hoare and his band of mercenaries going into the Seychelles as fun-loving members of the Ancient Order of Frothblowers. I loaded a second magazine and took my gun off safe.

The ferry docked and everyone began making their way to the buses. Ted and I waited until the tour guards had their backs turned before ducking into the fynbos.

Staying off the roads, we made our way to Robert Sobukwe's old house. Ted, who knows his history, said the former PAC leader was kept apart from the others because of his annoying habit of singing in the shower and telling political jokes that only he understood.

We spent a few minutes admiring the sea view from his house and agreed that it was infinitely preferable to pretty much anything we had seen in

Gugulethu or Khayelitsha. The estate agents are right. Location is key, even if you are under house arrest on an island prison.

Just then I saw something quick and grey moving through the bushes. I fired off half a dozen shots, scaring Ted so severely that he had a little accident. I went off to inspect my kill while Ted inspected his pants.

There was no sign of a cat. Instead, a rabbit stared back at me. "Sorry," I said. He gave me the lazy eye and hopped away. We turned around and recoiled at the sight of hundreds more rabbits. Some were sleeping, others were twitching their stupid little noses, most were busy making more rabbits.

Ted suggested we shoot our way out but I told him we needed to save our bullets for the cats, so we kicked our way out instead. Not the brightest things, rabbits. They make good pets, but even better stew.

We made it all the way to the lime quarry without seeing a single cat. Plenty of buck, birds and tortoises, all of which would have been fair game had we been on a normal hunt, but no cats. We looked around the quarry where Nelson Mandela once worked.

"Not bad, really," said Ted. "Outside in the fresh air. Sound of the surf. Could be worse."

I had to agree. A real sentence would have been to work as a filing clerk for an insurance company in a fluorescent-lit office segregated into cubicles with a menopausal lesbian for a boss.

11 July 2006

Lebanon in Trouble
as Israel Menstruates

There is a little bit of Israeli in everyone. Not in the sense that the goyim are God's partially chosen people, because a lot of people don't believe in God. In their case, they will either burn in hell or have a jolly good laugh. Maybe both. Perhaps hell really is fun. It certainly couldn't be worse than here.

Some of us express our Israeliness by writing angry letters to the editor. In others, it manifests itself in the form of road rage. Then there are those who blow up the neighbourhood because someone's dog defecated on their lawn. It is all a question of precisely how much Israeli is in you.

Brenda turned very Israeli on Saturday night. I was watching the wrestling on TV and got so excited that I knocked my beer over and accidentally rubbed it into the carpet with my foot. She said something in tongues and tried to hit me with my Kavango war club, which in itself is nothing unusual. But when I went to get a fresh beer, she launched a pre-emptive strike that sent the animals fleeing and left me reeling with shock and awe. My beers were tossed like grenades into the street and the fridge is now lying at the bottom of the garden.

Women, far more than men, tend to overreact. Their responses are frequently way out of proportion to any given situation. To be fair, their loss of perspective and inability to control their inner Israeli is often the result of imbalances created by normal biological processes.

Right now it is clear to everyone of sound mind that Israel is about to have her period. When a country like Israel gets pre-menstrual, it is best to agree with everything she says and avoid making any sudden noises around her. When Brenda has PMS, it is the sound of another beer exploding in the lounge that drives her insane. When Israel has PMS, it is the sound of another Katyusha rocket exploding in Haifa that drives her insane.

I can almost understand why Israel has started bombing Lebanon back into the Dark Ages. A few years ago, I had a run-in with a Lebanese gang that was on holiday in Durban. Like Israel, I have always feared swarthy men who wear black leather jackets and lots of gold jewellery, but even Hizbollah would have rejected these heavies as too extreme. The Lebs are very scary people.

Look, I have nothing against revenge, especially if the alternative is to bottle up all the wrongs that have been done to you and then one day you wake up and decide to kill your entire family or join the ACDP.

Revenge is cathartic and goes a long way towards putting psychiatrists and other home-wreckers out of business. Even the Christians have long since given up turning the other cheek.

Look at what George W Bush did to Afghanistan when the leader of the Taliban *vloeked* his mother on CNN. God only knows what Saddam Hussein must have said.

At risk of sounding like a cat-hugging bunny-lover, I do have a problem with retribution when it is directed at the wrong people. Some may say there is no such thing as the wrong people – that we are all guilty of something or other, or certainly will be by the time we death-rattle our last – and that there is nothing like a damn good airstrike to make us see the error of our ways.

I am the first to agree that kids can be frighteningly naughty. Send them to their room without supper. Spank them if you must. Get them to learn the Koran or Torah off by heart. But dropping bombs on them is a bit much, even for an arch disciplinarian like myself.

But never mind that right now. What I find interesting is that Israel waited until the World Cup was over before sloshing gasoline on the fire. This is a shining example to publicists everywhere. What is the point of starting a holy war only for it to be bumped off the front pages by Zidane's headbutt? Come to think of it, the Italian who called the French skin-head's mother a skanky one-eyed terrorist whore probably caused the whole thing.

The point is, and I am sure there is one, we now have another unfolding drama to keep us in our armchairs and off the streets.

For your viewing pleasure! Replacing *Survivor Guatemala*! The United

Nations' Tightrope-Walking Toothless Wonders bring you, live and direct, Palestine, Syria and Iran versus America, Britain and Israel! Frontline tickets available from your nearest arms dealer! Hurry, hurry, hurry!

I was so excited by the blood and the flames that I dropped another beer and inadvertently changed channels while fending off Brenda's disproportionate response.

Beirut burning was replaced by our new fighter planes looking all shiny and Swedish. They were being towed down Marine Drive towards Ysterplaat Air Force Base. The moment the convoy reached Koeberg Road, heavily armed soldiers were deployed to run alongside the jets in case a hijacking syndicate had switched from Golf GTi's to Gripens.

The reporter said the jets would be used for peacekeeping purposes. Of course they would. What better way to distract the drug-crazed rebels of Central Africa than with a gut-churning display of synchronised barrel rolls?

But what are we going to use in times of war? I know. Send in the clowns! Bring on the contortionists! Men on stilts! We all need a good laugh and nobody wants acid rain on their parade, but the Lord's Resistance Army and other party-loving partisans learning to make balloon bunnies makes for terrible television and I, for one, would rather watch a dog fight on the Cape Flats.

Newflash: Latest reports from St Petersburg, Russia, indicate that the G8 everything in sight.

18 July 2006

A Gay Old Time on Freaky Friday

Brenda's 17-year-old niece, Roxanne, has finished her matric exams and is coming to stay with us over the holidays. When I told my unspeakable loinfruit the news, his face turned scarlet and he went all slack-jawed and glassy-eyed. I have seen that look before and it usually means trouble, so I smacked him sharply across the back of his head and said, "Get a grip, you dirty little pervert. She's related to you."

He started blubbing like a girl and looked at me accusingly. "So how come it's okay for homosexuals to get married and I can't even ..."

Hands trembling and heart pounding, I left the room before he could finish the sentence. His words hit me like a kick in the solar plexus and it all became horribly clear. This was going to be used as a defence in every trial involving monstrously aberrant behaviour of all shades.

"Your Honour, my client was under the impression that with men now being allowed to marry each other, it would be acceptable for him to hijack a bus taking disabled orphans to the beach, steal their money and clothes, abduct the supervisor and later roast him over an open fire outside parliament while wearing nothing but the hollowed-out head of a Shetland pony called Muff."

Friday is the day that same-sex marriages become legal. It is also World Aids Day. Let no one say the Constitutional Court lacks a keen sense of irony.

The love that once dared not speak its name is right now shaving its legs, drinking pink champagne and putting fresh batteries into the bullhorns. Cities and towns around this previously fine country have contingency plans in place to deal with spontaneous outbreaks of mincing, squealing and bitch-slapping.

Police in Cape Town say they will use water cannons to break up lesbian catfights and gay biker dogfights. A spokesman said that as a one-off concession, police would fill their tanks with jasmine scented rose water. Riot police have agreed to use sawn-off swimming pool noodles instead of rubber batons and officers have been issued with handcuffs lined with fake fur. Troublemakers will be hosed down with Eau de Cologne instead of pepper spray and the authorities will in all likelihood turn a blind eye to acts of aggression committed between consenting sado-masochists. Coprophiliacs will be expected to clean up after themselves.

Yea, verily, life will never be the same again. For a start, going out for a drink with the lads will be laced with an undercurrent that never existed before. Just when you think there's nothing left on earth that could possibly surprise you, Bruce from accounts follows you into the toilet and drops to one knee while you're having a wee. "Marry me," he says, giving you a good once-over. Being a red-blooded God-fearing hetero, your typical knee-jerk reaction leaves him on his back spitting out broken teeth. Who would have thought? Bruce, of all people.

It's bad enough women wanting to get married after the third date. Now we have to keep a close eye on our drinking buddies, too. Well, there goes the comradely arm around each other's shoulders while staggering drunkenly to our cars singing filthy songs about our wives and girlfriends. This once robust manifestation of male bonding is now open to serious misinterpretation and you simply cannot risk fumbling to get your key into the door if there is even the remotest possibility that your best mate will try to take you roughly from behind.

From Friday, it will no longer even be safe to play traditional macho blood sports like rugby. All that sweaty scrumming down and lunging for each other's legs is like foreplay to the tighthead prop who has made up his mind not to allow his ex-wives to put him off marriage for life.

I am also worried about Ted. Having known him for so many years puts me at even greater risk. For starters, he has spent countless nights slumped in a chair or sprawled in the flowerbeds listening to me expound on the psychology of women. Now, looking at it through a pair of rhinestone-studded spectacles, I can see how a healthy expression of misogyny could be misconstrued as an unhealthy attraction to people who aren't women.

Like most straight men, Ted got married so that he could have someone to cook his supper, do his laundry and have sex with whenever he wanted. He seems to eat okay and his clothes are generally clean, but the third pillar holding up that crumbling edifice of marital discord is calcified from years of neglect.

A partner's failure to fulfil his conjugal responsibilities is unlikely to ever be cited as the reason for a gay divorce. Gay men have sex all the time, even when they are feeling tired or emotional. And come Freaky Friday it's going to get even worse.

This weekend the country will be awash in proposals and engagements. The constant cry of consummation will wake up the babies and send stray dogs scattering and I think it is safe to say that anyone who fails to make it to the office next week is almost certainly gay and should be ridiculed mercilessly when they return.

However, I doubt that Ted would turn gay simply to get more sex. That would be a bit like converting to Judaism just to get more holidays. But I'm taking no chances. The next time he drops by for a drink, I'm going to make him wear my welding gloves.

And maybe a muzzle.

28 November 2006

The Lighter Side of Incest

The last time I saw Brenda's teenage niece, Roxanne, she had adorable blonde curls and was clutching a yellow teddy to her chest.

On Friday afternoon she alighted from the Mainliner bus at Cape Town station wearing a skin-tight purple halter-neck top, a pair of stiletto heels and a scrap of cloth that the southeaster had blown up against her hips. She had pink hair and was clutching a half-jack of vodka to her chest.

Brenda shrieked with joy. I shrieked with horror. Clive shrieked with unmitigated adolescent lust. By the time I got her back to the car, a bidding war had broken out between a gang of Nigerian crack dealers and the Congolese beaded wire cartel. Lagos Larry was offering 50 000 naira while Kinshasa Ken guaranteed her free French lessons and a position as Joseph Kabila's number two concubine. It was a difficult choice and I started haggling, but Brenda hooked her talons into my pants pocket and dragged me away while threatening to report them to home affairs. They were still laughing when we drove away.

Clive passed his final Rorschach exam at the institute a couple of weeks ago and, until Roxanne arrived, planned on leaving home to immediately embark on his career. At the time, he said he wanted to be a neurosurgeon and insisted on getting started right away. I gently removed the electric carving knife from his trembling hands and tried to talk him out of it by promising to get him an oxyacetylene torch for Christmas.

I sat him down and told him about the fascinating world of welding and explained that cutting and splicing large chunks of scrap metal was far more rewarding than cutting and splicing silly little neurons. Besides, neurosurgeons don't make showers of gold and silver sparks when they work.

Welders get to wear overalls and Darth Vader helmets. Neurosurgeons wear girly little masks and gowns. When welders screw up, their mistakes can be sold to the Kalk Bay hippies as avante garde objects d'art. When neurosurgeons screw up, their mistakes go off and join the Freedom Front.

I needn't have bothered, really. Clive said that while he couldn't wait to start welding, he wanted to get to know Roxanne a little better. I tried to encourage him to move out of the house at once, but Brenda intercepted us at the front door and sunk her teeth into the fleshy part of my hand, forcing me to let go of his throat and allowing him to escape upstairs where he quickly moved his mattress into Roxanne's room and locked the door.

I shouted to her to remain calm and set about kicking in the door with the one leg that Brenda wasn't clinging to. When I finally broke through, Clive was down to his scants and on his knees. Roxanne was applying glitter gel to his quivering lips. She looked at me with big blue eyes and told me that this kind of thing goes on all the time in Windhoek. "It's under control," she said.

Even Brenda seemed taken aback. I dragged my aberrant loinfruit from the room, kicking and screaming and protesting that Roxanne was his cousin. I bit him hard on the ear and told him that your first cousin is not the same as your first joint or your first assault charge or any of the other rites of passage that boys must undergo before they become men.

Like a dog reluctantly accepting that it is not yet strong enough to challenge the alpha male, Clive rubbed his ear and settled down after that. He apologised and asked if he could still get an oxyamphetamine torch for Christmas. I laughed and was on the point of correcting him when I realised what a great invention that would be.

I pushed him into his room, bolted the door and ran for my computer to see if anyone had come up with a device that could provide a rush of oxygen powerful enough to simultaneously counter the effect of amphetamines depleting the neuronal stores of dopamine in the mesolimbic pleasure centres of the brain. It was no good. Everything I punched in took me to sites that offered to show me pictures of Britney Spears with no *broeks* on.

I can barely look at Britney Spears fully clothed without wanting to tear my teeth out, and the prospect of seeing her fanny alfresco caused me to pour a whisky strong enough to make a grown man drunk.

The rest of the weekend was spent trying to get Roxanne to dress in something less likely to attract the attention of the white slave traders of Sea Point and to get Clive to dress in something more likely to repel the rear admirals who have been scouring the city for husbands ever since the Constitutional Court struck down Leviticus 20:13 (King James Version).

There are still three weeks to go before Roxanne returns to the land that God would have made in anger if he hadn't lost interest and moved to Somalia. Her blood runs with the wild horses of the Namib and the house vibrates with stampeding pheroponies.

For the first time in my life, I am afraid.

12 December 2006

A Long Walk to Fleadom

I woke up on Saturday morning, pulled on my black Levis, stuffed R500 and a flick-knife down my XXL James Small tangas, put the dogs in the car, picked up Ted and drove to Camps Bay beach. A few days earlier, I had called for a mass protest after local actress Terry Norton was arrested and dragged off the beach by a vicious Metro cop for walking her dog without a leash.

There were serious issues at stake here – issues concerning abuses of power, police brutality, rights to freedom of movement for dogs and so on. I was expecting an angry mob of at least a thousand people and all week I had been looking forward to a morning of anarchy and mayhem on a grand scale, with swarms of little dogs being chased by big dogs, big dogs being chased by riot police and riot police being chased by my own personal army of outraged dog-owners armed with tennis balls and Frisbees and other items designed with canine entertainment in mind.

Ted's job was to photograph the protest and bail me out of jail should things turn nasty. I had given him explicit instructions to record everything from the moment the police moved in with batons and teargas.

We couldn't find parking anywhere near the beach. "This is fantastic!" I said. "They've come out in their thousands." Ted looked doubtful and squeezed off a couple of frames of me hauling the dogs out of the car after we found a disabled bay outside a church in a side street.

One of the animals is a Zulu hunting dog, although if she is in the right mood she will go for pretty much any of the ethnic groups. The other is either a collie or a wolf, depending on which angle you look at it from.

So many people had turned up for the protest that we could hardly make our way down to the beach. I kept grabbing strangers by the hand and thanking them for coming.

On the lawn outside Café Caprice, Ted helped me up onto a concrete picnic table and I spread my arms, urging the crowd to settle down.

"Comrades!" I shouted. "Today we show the government that bylaws are effective not because they are enforced through fear, but because we choose to obey them. Today the government will see what happens when we choose not to. Once more unto the beach!"

I jumped off the table and onto the Zulu hunting dog who immediately sank his teeth into the person nearest to him. I tore the hound off and shook the old man's bloodied hand, congratulating him on becoming the first casualty of the revolution.

Struggling my way through the crowd and onto the white sand, the dogs bolting for the ocean, I was pleased to see Ted down on one knee firing off shot after shot of stunning action pictures that would almost certainly be syndicated to newspapers and magazines around the world. I punched the air with my fist and shouted, "Liberty or death!"

Making the international gesture for "follow me", I ran down the beach, trenchcoat flapping in the southeaster, and got about 20 metres before my left lung collapsed. Down on my hands and knees fighting to suck air into my good lung, a little white boy with red hair walked up and asked if I was okay. Suddenly he pointed to something behind my back. It could only have been a Special Task Force patrol closing in on me.

"War is hell, kid. Run. Save yourself," I gasped.

"Your dog's doing a poo," he said.

I looked around. There were no police. There was no army of brave men and women. There were no dogs. Just the colliewolf sniffing at a pile of kelp and the Zulu hunting dog in full squat. All around us were mounds of human flesh basted with coconut oil sizzling gently in the sun. Nobody was taking the slightest bit of notice. Even the strange boy with the faecal fixation had drifted off.

It was like that moment in *Saving Private Ryan* when Tom Hanks went deaf. I saw Ted run up to me in slow motion. His lips were moving but I couldn't hear what he was saying. He must have realised that I was in severe shock and started slapping me across the face. Then he grabbed me by the legs and dragged me into the surf while an in-bred redneck from Pretoria cheered him on.

The icy water brought me back to the harsh realisation that nobody had pitched up for the protest. Not one person cared enough to join me in sending a warning to the ruthless junta to keep its jackbooted thugs in check.

"What did you expect?" said Ted. "This is Camps Bay." He was right. It is the rich and powerful who engineer the status quo and you would have to be an idealistic fool to think they would ever challenge it.

Municipal bylaws exist to separate Us from Them. Bylaws affect vagrants and dogs and men who want to dance naked through the night to a heavy tribal beat around giant bonfires in their backyards while the women sacrifice goats to appease the moon god, Chandra.

Bylaws don't affect people who schnarf lines of Sao Paolo's finest off the dashboards of their Porsches before going in to the office to check on the latest Afghan heroin/Ukrainian hooker exchange rate.

But since you have failed me, from now on it's every dog for himself.

19 December 2006

The Last Outpost
at the End of the Empire

I would rather volunteer for the Ethiopian army and be permanently based in Mogadishu than spend another New Year with my in-laws. For a start, Islamic militants and drug-crazed Somali rebels are less likely to talk you to death. I will take a bullet to the head over torture by neurotic nit-picking any time.

It started shortly after we arrived at Durban's so-called international airport when Brenda's mother noticed we didn't have locks on any of our suitcases. After 20 minutes of telling me how fortunate we were to have had nothing stolen, I was ready to join the Benedictine monks so that I might devote the rest of my life to giving thanks for this life-altering miracle.

Instead, I reached into my hand luggage and pulled out a warm beer, sparking off a string of horror stories about roving gangs of feral street children preying on drunk people who, when they try to report the crime, are locked up by corrupt policemen and sodomised repeatedly in the cells before having microchips implanted in their brains and then smuggled out of prison to work as labourers on covert American-backed titanium strip mines on the KwaZulu-Natal north coast.

I was understandably reluctant to get into Brenda's heavily bearded father's pre-war Land Rover and go off to the Drakensberg for New Year, but she said she wanted to see mountains. Apparently Table Mountain was no longer good enough. She wanted a whole range of the stupid things.

Thanks to black labour and white guilt, the road to Underberg has remained in pretty good shape. Brenda remarked on how picturesque and peaceful the Zulu homesteads looked.

"Yes," said her mother, "that's what Piet Retief thought."

We rounded a bend and saw a car ahead with its hazard lights flashing.

A black woman was flagging us down. It's not unusual to see the natives selling things on the roadside in these parts and I said we should stop on the off-chance that she was selling her car. That way I could travel on my own and get lost and accidentally end up at the Wild Coast Casino where I would have no choice but to drink and gamble heavily.

Brenda's mother said it was a trap and that if we stopped we would be captured by local drug lords and forced to spend the rest of our lives leading marijuana-laden donkeys out of Lesotho at gunpoint. I was relieved to hear no mention of sodomy.

By the time we pulled over, a very small but intense civil war had broken out inside the car. The unspeakable ninny, Clive, was clutching at himself and shouting in his high-pitched girly voice that we were all going to die. Brenda was weeping and trying to wind up her window with a handle that kept falling off. Her mother had her father by the beard and was half in the driver's seat stabbing at the accelerator. I was laughing. Because that's the way I want to die. Laughing.

The woman at the side of the road took one look at this, ran back to her car, did a U-turn and raced off in the opposite direction. After that, nobody said much until we reached the lodge in the foothills of the southern Berg.

While everyone went off to check in to their rooms, I went off to check out the bar. The walls were covered with stuffed bass and trout. They all had impossibly big mouths filled with razor-sharp teeth. Well, all of them apart from the large-mouthed bass, whose mouth was inexplicably closed.

On the couch was a woman peeling a giant container of potatoes. She was singing, off-key, that old Percy Sledge abomination, *When a Man Loves a Woman*.

"They wired the wrong jaw shut," I whispered to the barman and asked for a glass of whatever the locals drink. He waved vaguely at the bottles behind him. "Fine," I said, "let's move from left to right."

After a whisky and a vodka, I put my feet up on an ancient gun dog that had shambled in and checked out the décor. Three flags were strung up above my head. One was Welsh, another was British. I was sitting directly beneath the South African flag – the one that our ex-patriots wave whenever the Springboks play at Twickenham. I quickly moved on to a cane and coke. On the far wall was a gilt-framed painting of a couple of stiff-necked

Redcoats rampant on horseback, gloating as the tattered remnants of a Zulu impi disappeared across the veld.

Foreign banknotes papered a wall behind the bar. A stuffed toy wearing a Sharks jersey slumped on the far end of the counter. To my left, a short-handled stabbing spear – Shaka's contribution to the global peace effort – was nailed to a wooden beam. Dangling from its tip was a black cap with the words, "Fuck Bob" printed on the peak. The side of the cap read, "Zim Farmer Supporter". Great. All the elements in place for a jolly good New Year's Eve bash.

Potato-woman looked up as the barman slid me a Klipdrift. "What you coming as?" she asked. This made no sense at all. Entire words seemed to be missing from the sentence. I thought it best to humour her.

I smiled and said, "What was was before was was was?"

She stopped peeling and said, "Excuse me?"

"Is," I said. She looked at me long and hard and I thought it best to leave the bar.

Later, arriving for dinner, we discovered that a fancy dress party had been planned. The hosts were thrilled. They said we looked just like one of those poor white Boer families that were incarcerated by the British in 1900. Then they gave us a bottle of cheap champagne and a table far from everyone else.

9 January 2007

Vatican Condemns Dakar Rally to Hell

Ted burst through my back door on Sunday evening brandishing a copy of the Pope's mouthpiece, *L'Osservatore Romano*.

"Listen to this," he shouted, opening the fridge and helping himself to a six-pack. "The Vatican is condemning it as a bloody, irresponsible, violent and cynical attempt to impose questionable Western tastes on the developing world!"

I tossed aside the latest edition of *Soldier of Fortune* and leapt to my feet. "Just what I was thinking," I shouted back, wrestling a beer from his hands. "How dare America come over here and bomb a herd of Somalian nomads and not even apologise?"

Ted gave me a flustered look and continued reading. "The trail of blood which grows longer from year to year … blahblahblah … underscores the undeniable component of violence that lies behind every attempt to export Western models to human environments and ecosystems that have little to do with the West."

By the time he had finished, there was beer on the walls, floor, ceiling and all down his shirtfront. It's not often that Ted gets this excited.

"Absolutely," I said, warily. "But it can't be easy telling goat-herders and Islamic fundamentalists apart when you're sitting in an AC-130 gunship at 10 000 feet in the middle of the night. Maybe it was just a simple …"

Ted guzzled on his can and waved the newspaper angrily at me. The headline read: "The Bloody Race of Irresponsibility."

"I agree," I said, quickly changing tack. "The Somalians are a bloody irresponsible race. Just look at their …"

Ted smacked me across the head. "That's not very Catholic of you," I said, forcibly relieving him of what was left of the six-pack.

"They are talking about the big race, you moron. The Dakar Rally. Not some inconsequential collateral flesh wounds inflicted in the holy war on terror."

Of course. I couldn't understand why I never saw it sooner. The scathing editorial was written a day after South African motorcycle rider Elmer Symons died during the fourth stage in the Morocco desert. I had never heard of Elmer Symons but I could see how the church might be upset. Symons had clearly gone over to Rome to be ordained as a bishop and was simply trying to get back home on his bike when he was unwittingly sucked into this perfidious riptide of motorised evil.

"This satanic race has claimed 49 lives in 29 years," said Ted, spraying beer on the cat.

"Five thousand died during the Inquisition," I said. "Another nine million in the Crusades. And they only had horses."

"It's not about the bikes," said Ted, adjusting his crotch. "It's about 500 depraved idol-worshipping foreign reprobates tearing up the desert and scaring the chickens. It's about exposing the natives to a perverted lifestyle that on the surface might seem a lot more fun than celibacy and mass."

I reminded Ted that the man formerly known as Joseph Ratzinger was once a member of the Hitler Youth, a high spirited little group whose members cheered with boyish zeal when Field Marshal Erwin Rommel went off with the 15th Panzer Division to have some fun of his own in North Africa.

"That was different," muttered Ted.

"Here's what I think," I said. "I think the Pope is a frustrated racing driver. All he ever owned was a VW Golf. Now he has a jet black Phaeton with a 450-horsepower six-litre W12 engine that he gets to drive to the supermercato and back once a week. I think he sits in front of his 108" plasma screen at the Castel Gandolfo nursing a limoncello and watching the Dakar Rally knowing that given half a chance he could take those arrogant French bastards."

Ted couldn't say anything because his whole face was bulging with beer. It looked like he was drowning.

"I bet you didn't know that Ferrari gave the Pope a $1.2-million donation in 2005. And that Michael Schumacher gave him a steering wheel mounted on a plaque that reads: 'The Formula 1 World Champion's steering wheel to His Holiness Benedict XVI, Christianity's driver.'"

Ted turned red and began hyperventilating violently so I went off to the kitchen to whip up a couple of Bloody Marys. "Best you make those Hail Marys, you heathen pig," he shouted after me.

When I returned, he grabbed his glass and began quoting from the newspaper once again. "The race and its sponsors betray a cynicism that ignores local realities. The wrecks of cars, trucks and motorcycles abandoned in the desert are rusty monuments to irresponsibility."

"Don't make me laugh," I said, opening up my throat valve and pouring the rest of the Bloody Mary directly into my stomach. "Africa is littered with monuments to irresponsibility. They are called gravestones. There are 144 million Catholics on this doomed continent and they are dying like flies because an old German man in a dress says condoms are the Devil's work. Don't talk to me about local realities."

We were both drenched in beer and our chins ran red with vodka-laced tomato juice. It wasn't a pretty sight.

"It's those infidel dogs over at Durex who are encouraging promiscuity." I stopped Ted in his tracks with a *mawashi geri* to the testicles and he went down like a sack of hammers.

"The Americans have started bombing the nomads, for God's sake. What difference does it make? What do you think is going to happen when they find out we have a Muslim for premier? None of us are safe anymore. "

Ted clutched himself and went pensive for a while. Then he threw up and said, "I planned on going go-kart racing at Killarney this weekend, but not if it means going to Hell."

"You'll be fine," I said. "Just don't forget your Saint Christopher."

16 January 2007

Bloody Mary and the Virgin Sacrifice

Brenda rolled over in bed on Sunday morning and squashed Boris the cat who woke up and sank his knife-like fangs into my naked buttocks. This is nowhere near as much fun as it sounds. In fact, it is an appalling way to wake up after a night spent in the dahlias trying to spot a comet that was allegedly tearing through the cosmos like some kind of incendiary bat out of hell. By the time I crawled into bed, there was plenty of vomit, but no comet.

My bum was so traumatised by this pre-dawn raid that I had to go to the kitchen and mix myself a Bloody Mary. Offering a silent toast to Karl Marx, the father of Stolichnaya vodka, I gulped down the opium of the masses and returned to bed. Brenda was awake so I pretended to be sleepwalking and collapsed in a heap on the carpet but she leapt out of bed and came rushing over to me, forcing me to pretend to wake up and protect my face and groin.

"You're bleeding!" she shouted, doing some sort of victory dance. Only it wasn't her victory dance. It was the dance that women do when they panic, a kind of running on the spot and a flapping of arms as if they were trying to fly away.

Apparently I had forgotten to wipe my mouth, as early-morning drinkers are inclined to do. I started laughing and inadvertently coughed up a piece of lemon. Soaked in tomato juice, it looked like a chunk of my lower intestine. Brenda aborted takeoff when I popped the lemon back into my mouth.

"You sick bastard," she said, dropping to one knee and rabbit-punching me in the kidneys. I tried to pacify her but she returned to bed, sobbing. With relief or disappointment, I couldn't tell. She spent the rest of the day subjecting me to a range of barbed comments designed to make me feel less of a man and more of, well, whatever it is that angry women reduce men to without quite driving them to the point where they are forced to cross that terrible divide and become lovers of their own sex.

Much later, when she thought I had been punished enough, or perhaps thought I needed a final crushing blow to send me over to the dark side, she put on a skimpy negligee and began doing what I assumed was yoga. I asked her to move so that I could watch the wrestling but she ignored me and continued with an unseemly display of stretching and splaying.

"I'm exercising my pelvic floor, in case you're interested," she said. The last thing I wanted to hear about was another of Brenda's flaws, but I reassured her that there were specialists who dealt with this kind of thing.

She stopped in mid-pose and said, "Do you even know where the perineum is?"

"Of course I do," I snorted, "it's two blocks from the Parthenon." Brenda made a harsh barking sound that some animals make before they attack, and said: *Absentem laedit cum ebrio qui litigat.*

"Exactly," I said. "Atthay isway atwhay Iway oldtay emthay!"

This was wonderful. Here we were communicating like a normal married couple. Then Brenda had to go and spoil everything by mocking my physique.

"Just look at you," she said, slipping out of the advanced locust position and into the very rude drinking camel position.

I glanced down at what was left of my body. My chest had slipped without me even noticing. Somehow it had joined up with my belly in the same unprincipled fashion that the Independent Democrats had joined up with the Democratic Alliance.

I left the room in high dudgeon and went to my den where I called Ted. "Code Red, Ted," I said.

He arrived bearing crates of Tafel lager and a mushroom the size of a Frisbee. I snatched the beers from him and threw the shroom out of the window. "Too many calories," I said. Ted was stunned. "But it was magic," he shouted. I patted him on the back. "If it's magic, it will come back to us."

Then I explained the crisis. "Maybe I should work out," I said, pouring a can of Namibia's finest down my throat.

"Nonsense," said Ted. "What you need is a cleansing ceremony. It's the latest in do-it-yourself absolution." He began mixing up a traditional cleansing beer made of traditional cleansing fluids. Ted said Jik was the new tik and passed me the Tupperware. I drank deeply and threw up.

"Now we need to kill something," I said.

"I was afraid of this," said Ted, reaching into his gay man-bag and pulling out a chicken that had seen better days. "Here it is. Here's your sacrifice. Kill this bitch and just watch your self-esteem soar."

I prodded the fowl. "It's not exactly a bull, is it?" Ted said a bull wouldn't fit into his bag and that if I didn't like it he would take it back to the N2 and set it free.

I didn't want to seem ungrateful so I thanked Ted and took the chicken. Most white people only know how to take chickens when they are lying docile and gutted in the frozen foods section, but not me. I grabbed the bird by the throat and addressed it in a stern voice.

"Listen, chookie. I'm an important man. I have no choice."

The chicken looked me in the eye and said, "I will die for your sins. But please make it quick."

I got such a *skrik* that I let it go. The bird made for the open window just as Ted walked out of the kitchen with my family's traditional Sunbeam electric carving knife.

We discussed killing something else, like the neighbour's yapping dog, but in the end we went down to the Spar and bought a braai pack. It was so much easier.

23 January 2007

Cry Havoc and Let Slip the Apes of Wrath

Ted called me on Saturday night, gibberingly drunk as usual, and told me a new study has revealed that male chimpanzees slap their girlfriends around as a way of keeping them on the straight and narrow. Then the line went dead.

The news got me thinking. Unlike witch-burning, wife-beating hasn't declined much in popularity among the less-evolved of our own species. Men who work with their hands (if they work at all) have for centuries used assault and battery as a way of ensuring that their women remained loving and faithful.

The landed gentry have traditionally controlled their women by hitting them where it really hurts – in their line of credit. Withdrawing Gold Card privileges is frequently more effective than bludgeoning. For a start, it saves on medical expenses and rarely leaves unsightly stains on the carpet.

However, educated men are increasingly incorporating a little violence into their disciplinary code of conduct. Some analysts believe this trend of mixing and matching is a direct response to Oprah's clandestine campaign to get Hillary Clinton into the White House and thus pave the way for women to take over the world.

Entry level wife-beaters need to remember that spousal abuse is no longer the brutal sport it was when our parents were young. The application of minimal force through the use of smart slaps has become the feng shui of home-based violence. The Japanese even have a name for it – they call it karate, the way of the empty hand – although they practise something else when it comes to killing whales.

Punches are passé and, to be honest, a bit rude. Traditional weapons like baseball bats and 9mm pistols are also on their way out as men discover that it is better to lie back and accept the gratitude of a repentant woman than it is to spend your evening filling out paperwork at the casualty ward or take off work to appear on homicide charges in front of a judge who could be drunk on power but more likely vodka.

The open-handed slap is the workhorse of domestic violence and remains a firm favourite among primates of all ages, from flyblown African villages to the castles of Constantia.

Sensitive, artistic men – architects, for instance – often take pride in utilising the full range of slaps as they apply to different situations. Unlike a semi-literate welder who comes home early and finds his wife watching Jerry Springer instead of doing the laundry. Rather than using a low-intensity bitch-slap with marginal wrist action, he opts for the big-swing straight-arm flattie-whack with full follow-through. This is the mother of all slaps and should be reserved for special occasions such as infidelity.

Should your wife be one of those skittish types who tend to bolt at the first sign of trouble, it is considered good etiquette to give her a head start. Two minutes is usually sufficient for the small to medium-sized woman. However, if she is one of those gargantuan behemoths whose idea of exercise is to open and close the fridge door 70 times a day, you might want to give her a bit longer. Like 20 years.

Husband-beating, on the other hand, is still in its infancy. This is largely because most men lack the capacity to appreciate the lighter side of physical abuse when they are on the receiving end. Unlike wife-beating, etiquette plays a secondary role in husband-beating. Because women are physically weaker than men, the use of blunt objects is not frowned upon.

However, if you are stronger than your husband, it would be only fair to rely on your innate weapons, i.e. your vicious tongue and supersonic voice, both of which can be equally damaging. You may also want to take a closer look at your sexuality. Marrying a man whom you can overpower with one arm behind your back sends disturbing signals on a number of levels. For a start, it suggests that you care not a fig for the traditional masculine/feminine divide. Fair enough. But be warned. Too much bullying raises a man's oestrogen levels. It's bad enough that he can't find your clitoris. Do you really want him to start misplacing the car keys as well?

If you are a normal woman, it is likely that you will have small hands and feet. These are useless when it comes to husband beating. As a relative of the cat family, you would do better to use your teeth and nails.

When you apply your teeth to your husband, his nerve endings will send out a message. Not, as you might expect, to his brain. The message first goes to his penis, which will then analyse the message.

Depending on how much he has had to drink, your husband will respond in one of two ways. Either his penis will interpret the biting as foreplay and he will become aroused, or it will forward a new message to his brain indicating that the biting is an act of war and that his penis wants no part of this terrible business.

Since you are meant to be disciplining him, it is unlikely that you would want his penis to misread the situation. Bite hard, but not so hard that you end up with a mouthful of flesh. That would be poor etiquette. Avoid quick, random bites. You are not a piranha fish. And steer clear of erogenous zones.

When it comes to men, this leaves you with two options – the top of his head (hard to grip unless you are a snaggle-toothed freak of nature) or the fleshy bit on his elbow. Anywhere else and you risk turning him on.

Disclaimer: I am not an advocate of domestic violence. Instead, I have always found that conflicts are best resolved through the use of cold, stony silences.

13 February 2007

Flying High
on Estates of Insecurity

I have always sworn that I would never live on a security estate.

They are loathsome places built on foundations of fear and inhabited by either victims of crime or people who expect to become victims of crime. They rarely make good neighbours. Those who don't carry unwieldy bags leaking trauma, carry panic buttons and cans of pepper spray. Normal conversation is impossible.

"Hi. How you doing?"

"How am I doing what? Who are you? Back off or I'll call the cops."

They should be called insecurity estates.

It is frequently freshly married couples who buy houses in these urban concentration camps without giving any thought to the fact that most violent crimes are committed by someone close to them.

Sooner or later, they discover the hazards of living in a controlled access environment. There are estates around the country ringed with barbed wire fences bearing the decaying remains of husbands who have attempted to flee from abusive wives.

Being married to the Antichrist, this was uppermost in my mind when the last landlord in a long line of many asked if we would rather go quietly or if we would prefer the sheriff of the court to help us move.

I wanted to round up the old gang, plant anti-personnel mines in the garden, board up the windows and wait for the posse to arrive, but Brenda said she would divorce me and I know from experience that it's cheaper to sacrifice your principles so I said okay, let's move.

Apart from having her bag snatched and me proposing to her, Brenda has never been the victim of a crime. That's why I couldn't understand why she wanted to move into a security estate.

"You'll like it," she said. Sure. That what Jim Morrison was told and two hours later he woke up dead.

The sign outside the estate said WELCOME. The spiked steel gate said quite the opposite. The guard looked at us. We looked at him. Instead of doing the sensible thing and opening fire, I opened my mouth.

"We are refugees fleeing the malevolent maelstrom of life," I said, spilling beer down my shirt. "In terms of the Geneva Convention, you are beholden to grant us safe passage."

Brenda evacuated the vehicle and approached the guard in a crab-like fashion. Whatever she said to him must have worked because he scuttled back to his cage and opened the gate.

Upon reaching the house, I immediately asserted my authority as the alpha male and informed Brenda that we would take it on appro for a six-month period.

This was like no estate I had ever seen before. Blade wire fences denied the bourgeoisie access from the north, east and south. But the western front was open to the sea. A midget with two broken legs could scale the fence that separated the house from the beach. Perfect.

The residential area allocated to previously disadvantaged individuals is a few kilometres away. Thanks to the all-pervasive lethargy and indolence that courses sluggishly through the veins of this great country, no house-breaker is going to walk all the way down the beach and then all the way back again through soft sand and piles of rotting kelp with my wide-screen television lashed to his back.

My new house is completely see-through. The lounge is surrounded by 21 glass doors that fold back on each other, giving the impression that the builders have yet to come along and put the walls up. I regularly walk into closed doors, proving the old adage that people who live in glass houses shouldn't get stoned.

There is a loo in the bedroom – not an en suite but right there a few metres from the bed – which is great if you're a coprophiliac with exhibitionist tendencies. And there is not a curtain in the house. It's like being on Big Brother without the morons.

Like all security estates, the streets are full of dogs and children. Fortunately, in these isolated parts, Vet's Choice is still being sold to dog owners with problem pets. All I need now is for medical practitioners to begin prescribing Doctor's Choice for problem children.

Apart from the crayfish poachers who infest the dunes every Saturday, there aren't many people around. Most of the houses on the estate seem to be holiday homes. Maybe not, though. Maybe everyone inside is dead.

It's hard to say in South Africa.

1 May 2007

Afraid of Dying Alone?
Take Someone With You!

My week started with a petrol attendant calling me *madala*. This would never have happened in the old South Africa. Back then, darkies knew their place. They didn't go around calling white men "old". They called them "baas" and everyone got along just fine.

It was only a vicious cold front that stopped me from exiting my vehicle and taking the uppity fellow to task. Instead, I opened my window a crack and demanded to know the reason for his insolence. He laughed, as only the freshly emancipated can laugh, and said he called me *madala* because I was *madala*.

I took a quick look at myself in the rearview mirror and got the fright of my life. I whipped around to ask Peter O'Toole what the hell he was doing in my back seat, but there was nobody there.

The attendant knocked on the window. He pointed at his hair. Then at mine. Of course. No wonder he thought I was old. He was clearly colour-blind. In my best Zulu, I explained to him that my hair was not gray, but dusky blonde. He laughed some more and said I owed him R200.

After handing over the cash, together with a hefty 20c tip, I took the revs into the red, slammed the stick into first and dropped the clutch. The car stalled with such vehemence that I flew from the seat and smacked my head into the windscreen.

"Madala," said the attendant, nodding his head in a sage-like fashion.

Rubbing my dented nut, I pulled out of the garage and into the path of an oncoming car. The enemy swerved and hooted and pointed violently at his eyes. "Yes!" I shouted. "You should get glasses!"

Driving home, I realised that the garage attendant hadn't been mocking me at all. In his culture, old people are revered. Their advice is sought after, their wisdom valued. Hell, if you live in the township, you can't buy a stolen plasma TV without getting the elders around to slaughter an ox to check that it's okay with the ancestors.

In whitey culture, old people are barely tolerated. They get elbowed aside on the pavement, cursed if they are driving – which they have no right to be doing – and lured into retirement homes on the bogus pretext that there is a very good chance they will fall head over heels in love with someone their own age when, in fact, all they are going to be doing is falling head over heels in the bathroom.

When our parents develop Alzheimer's disease, we look them squarely in the eye and say that we don't know who they are either and never visit them again.

White oldies have it good. If they were Eskimos, they would be expected to walk out into the snow and die of hypothermia rather than be a burden to the pack. We don't get much snow in these parts, but there's nothing stopping them from taking their Zimmer frames and going for a slow walk up Table Mountain where our economically disempowered muggers will happily dispatch them to the afterlife in return for a used colostomy bag and a well-thumbed pocket bible.

When I am more of a burden to my family than I already am, I will almost certainly remove myself for the greater good. The only difference is that when I leave the house, retirement home or asylum, I will have 15 kg of trinitrotoluene lashed to my chest to be detonated as and when I choose.

I don't see much point in going quietly. Dylan Thomas was right when he said it was better to rage against the dying of the light than to suffer the slings and arrows of outrageous fortune.

Nobody wants to die alone so why not take someone with you. Your old maths teacher, perhaps? Or a PT instructor from the army? Your boss? Perhaps a businessman who embezzled your pension?

What I'm trying to say is, don't waste your death on yourself. That's selfish. It wouldn't surprise me if something got lost in the translation of the ancient Jewish scriptures. Being selfish is wrong. Eating shellfish is fine.

Anyway. Twenty minutes after the garage attendant called me old, I went into a shop to buy half a loaf of bread and a bottle of methylated spirits. There was a man in front of me in the queue, also with dusky blonde hair. His cell rang and he looked at me and said, "You can go in front, sir."

Sir? I used to call my biology teacher Sir. When I was with my friends, I would call him a degenerate bum-fondling pig of a man. But in his class, I would call him Sir.

If President Mbeki had to walk through my front door right now, I would also call him Sir. But that's only because St John has made him God's ambulance driver.

Actually, that's not true. If our leader had to walk through my front door right now, I would scream like a girl, knock my drink into the keyboard and scramble for the nearest panic button. Once I had realised that he was after my vote and not my stereo, I would apologise and offer him a glass of absinthe which he would pretend to drink in the hope that I would see him as a man of the people.

Damn, it's cold. Perhaps that's why people are starting to mistake me for an old person. When temperatures drop below 15 degrees, my entire body shrivels up and I look like I'm suffering from progenia when, in fact, I possess all the instincts of a juvenile delinquent.

22 May 2007

Come to Australia and Get Blown – Skye High

Well-known mechanical engineer Chippy Shaik was quoted in a Sunday newspaper as saying, "I know fuck-all about any bribe or any money."

I, for one, believe him. Growing up in Durban, I had several Indian friends who would say the same thing whenever anyone called them after 10pm. It's an automatic defence mechanism – an instinctive reaction that goes back to a time when Britain ruled India with an iron fist wrapped around a bottle of pink gin – and does not imply guilt in any way whatsoever.

As far as I am concerned, the only crime Chippy ever committed was writing a doctoral dissertation on the "development of higher-order laminated composite structures under static and thermal loading". How dare he? This country needs genetically-modified food, thinner women and bottle stores that stay open on Sundays. We can't eat, drink or sleep with laminated composite structures, regardless of how they behave under pressure.

Chippy says he has had enough and is moving to Australia where people will understand his jokes. I know seven men and women who have been trying to get on to this fantasy island for years, but their applications always get rejected. I keep telling them that they need to engineer a situation in which they find themselves facing some kind of criminal investigation spanning at least three continents.

There is no point trying to get in to Australia on the grounds of being a clean-living, God-fearing person who is prepared to work eight days a week. This is a former penal colony. It is run by people descended from murderers and thieves, perverts and pickpockets.

If you understand static and thermal loading, the Australian authorities are frequently prepared to overlook your ties to the Cali cocaine cartel. Hell, you could even be married into Jackie Selebi's family, for all they would care. To get into Australia, you have to be wanted.

Right now, we have more important things to worry about. Colonel Muammar Gaddafi may or may not be bankrolling Jacob Zuma for president. Should we be concerned? Hardly. He's a colonel, for God's sake. He calls himself The Brother Leader and Guide of the Revolution, but he can't upgrade himself to general?

Zuma might have trouble balancing his cheque book but at least he doesn't live in a tent. I don't trust people who live in tents. That's why I don't trust Gaddafi. That's also why I refuse to climb Everest. Until they put up prefabricated cabins with underfloor heating in the death zone, there is no way I'm going near that treacherous lump of rock.

Another thing to worry about is that there is a rent boy by the name of Skye who has started naming his clients on the Internet. I need to make it clear that I am worrying on behalf of others.

After spending the last 10 years satisfying 2 500 politicians, preachers, sportsmen, entertainers, journalists and other lowlifes, the naughty bugger has decided to break the golden rule. And where is he living now? Australia. Funny, that.

Skye calls it his own personal truth and reconciliation commission, although I struggle to see where the reconciliation part of it would come in. So far, he has named 11 of his clients. He plans to reveal the names of another 39 over the next few weeks. The biblical injunction that it is better to give than to receive is cold comfort in times like these.

Skye provides a sphincter-clenching, blow-by-blow account of his skirmishes with a group of people who, if he had stretched it to one more, could have gone down in history as the Dirty Dozen.

I found it particularly disturbing that Skye spewed his catharsis in Afrikaans. It has been my experience that degeneracy on this scale is largely the preserve of those who speak in the tongue of the Queen. To discover that the great-great-grandchildren of those unbendingly heterosexual pioneers whose creaking wagons cut their trails into the earth have been up to such monkey business is almost too much to bear.

Don't get me wrong. I'm not judging anyone. But I am the product of a system based on the wisdom of Klein Calvin. My teachers told me stories of great bravery and sacrifice among the Afrikaner people. They told me of Wolraad Woltemade and Piet Retief, even though Wolraad's horse was the real hero and Piet wasn't all that bright. You want us to leave our weapons outside the kraal? Sure thing, comrade.

In those days, Boer porn did not exist. Men did it with their wives. In private. And always in the missionary position. Or so we were led to believe. Now, everything has changed. Skye's revelations have shattered an entire generation's worth of cherished myths. I want my money back.

The nail in the coffin of the camel whose back was broken by the final straw came when Beau Brummel announced his plan to turn Orania into a nudist colony. It's the Dutch coming out, I tell you. There is nothing a Hollander likes more than to take his clothes off, smoke a joint and fondle an underage girl from Cameroon. Make that Sweden. Africans are verboten in Orania.

Wrapping up, I would like to wish everyone a lucky strike on Friday. I am in a no-work, no-pay situation every day of my life, so I don't particularly care if civil servants get their 12% increase or if they get gunned down by the riot police.

Instead of suggesting that the ghost of Goebbels is manipulating our economy, Cosatu's chinless wonder should be pushing for a three-day working week. Nobody needs more money. More money just means more people trying to steal the stuff you bought with your more money.

Better to trade the money for time. With an extra eight weeks leave a month, everyone can go to Perth and toss a few prawns on the barbie with Chippy, Skye and JM Coetzee.

29 May 2007

James Bond 00 ...
... Oh, Who Cares?

Capetonians are forever complaining about streets being cordoned off, cars getting blown up, people plummeting off buildings and naked women running through the city.

This makes Cape Town sound a lot more fun than it really is. The sad reality is that all this excitement is carefully stage-managed for the benefit of 35mm Arriflex cameras.

People get shot in Johannesburg. Movies get shot in Cape Town. I'm not always sure who is worse off. Them, I suppose. At least we have the ocean.

Gracing the Mother City with his exalted presence at the moment is Daniel Craig, star of the latest James Bond movie. I never fully appreciated *Casino Royale* because halfway through it I went foraging for something to take the brutal edge off my Klip-nip and when I returned I discovered that I had lost the plot altogether. It seems I'm not the only one. From the moment Craig landed at Cape Town International Airport, he has been behaving like a highly-strung paranoiac in a poorly run witness protection programme. With all the ducking and diving between the terminal and the car park, I'm surprised his deviant behaviour never aroused the suspicions of our airport police. Okay, so I'm not all that surprised.

There is a disturbing similarity in the behavioural patterns of an American film star appearing in his latest movie and a member of the Americans gang appearing in his latest court case. Both go to extreme lengths to avoid being photographed. Both behave as they have something to hide. Both appear as guilty as hell.

While we know the gangster probably did kill the dealer who was muscling in on his turf, we also know that Chuck Norris has never actually killed anyone. Or so Hollywood would have us believe. However, plenty of B-grade actors have died in violent films, never to be seen in anything ever again. Countless extras have been gunned down in crossfire or mangled in car wrecks. Where are they today? Buried in unmarked graves across the Mojave Desert, that's where.

I suspect this is one of the reasons South Africa has become such a hot destination for foreign filmmakers. Deaths are so much more realistic when lead characters can use live ammunition without the producer having to worry about local cops following up on a missing persons report.

Soon after giving a non-existent pack of paparazzi the slip, Craig and his bevy of burly bodyguards arrived on set deep in the menacing slums of Bantry Bay. Frankly, it wasn't so much a set as a shiny new Range Rover parked outside an upmarket restaurant. Nevertheless, his fawning lickspittles moved like greased lightning to shield him from the prying eyes of the media.

The scene involved our hero sitting in the car talking on his cellphone. Then he stepped out of the car and said something to someone nobody could see. Controversial stuff and perfectly understandable that his people wouldn't want that kind of action splashed across the front pages of the local gutter press.

In a few months time, Craig will be trotted out to kiss the bums of film critics and talk show hosts in the hope of encouraging millions of people to fork over wads of cash to see him sitting in the Range Rover and possibly doing a bunch of other stuff.

I suppose the important thing is that none of us get to see him pretending to be someone else in a city that's not meant to be Cape Town. That could really ruin the magic for us.

For some actors, it seems certain roles become self-fulfilling prophecies. Judging from his recent behaviour, Daniel Craig honestly believes he is a secret agent.

In the space of a year, our very own Presley Chweneyagae went from playing the lead in *Tsotsi* to becoming one.

Today, Nick Nolte really is down and out in Beverly Hills.

Charlton Heston has become Will Penny, the aging, lonely cowboy he played in 1968.

And Paris Hilton is in jail, where she belongs.

In 1984 Arnold Schwarzenegger was a deadly cyborg known as the Terminator. In 2003 he became a deadly cyborg known as the Governor. The uniform is different but he remains the final arbiter of life and death.

Sylvester Stallone played a punch-drunk, steroid-guzzling meathead in *Rocky*, and today ... well, maybe he wasn't acting, after all.

And Tom Cruise went from being the junkie head of the Department of Pre-Crime in *Minority Report* to believing that the earth was once part of a Galactic Confederacy ruled by an alien tyrant called Xenu who stacked millions of people around volcanoes and blew them up with hydrogen bombs. And while John Anderton was a fictitious character, Tom genuinely believes he is an Operating Thetan on Level 7 of the Bridge to Total Freedom. Run, Katie, run.

The thing I love most about South Africans, apart from their inexplicable propensity for forgiveness and their extraordinary capacity for alcohol, is that they are not easily starstruck.

Sir Bob Geldof could walk down Adderley Street and anyone with a social conscience would offer him loose change for a cup of coffee. Charlize Theron wouldn't be able to get a room at the Mount Nelson because she looks like white trash from Benoni. Eddie Murphy would be mistaken for a car guard and, with her accent, Nicole Kidman wouldn't be able to get a date. Not after what happened in St Lucia. Last month, the famous piano-playing schizoid David Helfgott came all the way out from Australia and everyone ignored him because they thought he was Geoffrey Rush.

So you can relax, 007. Nobody is after you.

5 June 2007

Welcome to the All-Singing All-Dancing Strike

I am fascinated by the cultural differences that exist in this great country of ours. When I'm not busy being fascinated, it's all I can do not to pack a bag, grab my passport and run for the nearest airport.

Black people have a rich culture that involves ancestor worship, traditional healing, lobola, ritual slaughter (cows, sheep, taxi drivers etc.) and settling tribal disputes with machete fights at dawn.

White people have a culture that is rooted in sport, beer, fear, litigation and emigration.

Although I am always careful not to stereotype anyone, I think it is important to point out that industrial action is also an integral part of black culture.

There were times when Shaka's impis would come to him, usually after getting their asses whipped by the British, and threaten to down assegais unless they got danger pay. Being a reasonable man, Shaka would set up a bargaining council on a rocky outcrop just past Ballito.

If, for example, the warriors insisted on a two-goats-per-person-per-battle increase, and Shaka adopted an intransigent one-chicken-per-person-per-battle position, the dispute would be resolved by having the complainants thrown into the sea. Today, the CCMA has taken the place of Shaka's Rock.

Getting back to our cultural differences. When white people sing and dance, you can be fairly sure they're in high spirits and celebrating something or other – more often than not, their good fortune at having been born into the Caucasian race.

When black people sing and dance, there is no such certainty. What looks like a rollicking street party frequently turns out to be angry mobs of striking workers. When whiteys feel hard done by, they suffer in stoic silence. Well, those who aren't rich enough to move to Perth or stupid enough to join the Boeremag suffer in stoic silence.

Sometimes, one of them will come home from work, quietly murder his family and then blow his so-called brains out. Generally, though, they don't do much more than mope around the braai mumbling racial epithets through mouthfuls of boerewors and beer.

Darkies, on the other hand, are always ready with a song and dance at the first sign of exploitation. This is where the confusion sets in. To the untrained eye, it appears that the brothers and sisters are indulging in a bit of the old merriment, what with all the ululating and leaping about. I have seen Nordic-type tourists join in under the impression that they have stumbled across some sort of primitive ethnic festival. Whipping out their cameras and flailing their little white arms and legs, they rolled their eyes and shouted happy gibberish in the hope that it would pass for Swahili, blissfully unaware that the natives were not so much joyful as they were restless.

I always get a kick out of strike season, even though walkouts are on the whole a lot less entertaining than natural disasters, which, I might add, we don't get nearly enough of. Snow on the Berg comes a poor second to the stupendous adrenalin rush provided by a spine-rattling earthquake or pants-wetting tsunami. Those damn Asians have all the fun.

What has impressed me most over the past couple of weeks, apart from Geraldine Fraser-Moleketi's ability to keep a straight face every time she uses the word "comrade", is the dexterity that some workers have when it comes to the toyi-toyi.

To the uninitiated, this may look like a dance inspired by antediluvian firewalkers, but it's not. Far from it. Unlike the waltz or the marginally less gay tango, the complexity of the toyi-toyi lies in the synchronised vocal accompaniment that ranges from chanting provoked by the impact of economic injustices to screaming provoked by the impact of rubber bullets.

Watching the uprising from the safety of my lounge, it occurred to me that, while waiting for a government official to finish his pap 'n sushi platter and accept their list of demands, protestors should hold informal toyi-toyi contests.

It would be a way of keeping warm while simultaneously making a little extra cash, something everyone needs in these harsh no-work, no-pay times. Perhaps the department of arts and culture would like to sponsor the competition.

My money is on those who do some sort of physical labour for a living. These guys can toyi-toyi second to none, getting their knees right up past their ears. Teachers, on the other hand, tend to swing their arms a lot but aren't so hot when it comes to lifting their feet off the ground. That's the price you pay if your idea of a workout is lifting crates of beer and impregnating schoolgirls during lunch.

Funnily enough, hospital workers have emerged as the dark horses in the toyi-toyi stakes. Not so much the nurses because most of them weigh a ton, which is odd given the quality of hospital food, but the doctors have it down to a fine art.

I particularly enjoy watching the specialists. They toyi-toyi with a clinical precision that is unrivalled. And their balance borders on the sublime. A gynaecologist in full strike goes a long way towards restoring one's faith in the medical fraternity. Then there are those who are so uncoordinated that they can't wave goodbye without putting an eye out.

As a lapsed socialist born with two left-leaning feet, I strongly feel it is Cosatu's duty to help give these borderline dyspraxics a fair shot at making it onto the 7 'o clock news.

It is high time that Zwelinzima Vavi accepted his role as the working man's Arthur Murray. He needs to stop worrying about wage increases and focus on teaching white people to toyi-toyi.

Then – and only then – will the revolution be complete.

12 June 2007

Tongue-Thaied in Bangkok's Monsoon Madness

I couldn't write my column last week because a Burmese border guard threatened to shoot me if I attempted to enter his country. I tried explaining that I needed to get to an Internet café but he was having none of it.

With a shrug of his automatic weapon he indicated that the border was closed to Thailand. Then he began barking at me. "Yes, I know," I barked back. "You hate the Thais. But I'm not Thai."

Being almost two metres tall with blue eyes, you might think this would be self-evident. But when it comes to the Burmese, nothing should be taken for granted. I made the international gesture for "your government is a corrupt fascist dictatorship" and backed away into the huddle of souvenir shops that make up the small town of Three Pagodas Pass.

The other reason the column never appeared is because I missed my deadline by a day. In Thailand the year is 2550. You can see how one might get confused.

Brenda had taken the family on holiday. Her heart was set on the island of Koh Chang in the Gulf of Thailand. What a good idea, I thought. A vacation within spitting distance of the equator in the middle of monsoon season on a jungle-infested chunk of rock where nobody can speak English and the air is thick with Dengue Fever.

Not wanting to seem ungrateful, I kept my mouth shut and went off to pack. The unspeakable fruit of my loins was beside himself with excitement. He asked me about prophylactics and I smacked him sharply across the head.

"You rude little pig," I said. "This is meant to be a family holiday, not a sleazy outing to the fleshpots of Bangkok." Clive claimed he was talking about prophylactics to prevent malaria, but I could see in his dirty little eyes that he was lying.

Ten minutes after landing at Singapore International, I inadvertently shoplifted a newspaper from a bookstore that was busy opening. Brenda was appalled that I would do such a thing in a country where people get the death sentence for littering. Fortunately we were in transit and made our getaway before the airport police could put a trace on me.

Thailand's capital felt like Durban in February, only hotter and more humid with fewer Zulus and a different kind of Asian. The taxi was like a temple on wheels. Gold and silver statues of Buddha were glued to every surface. Garlands dangled from the mirrors. Flags flew from the aerial. Brenda asked the driver if he knew of any good hotels. I doubted that he made much sense in his own language so I told him to stop his nonsense and head for Khao San Road at once.

We had been awake for 30 hours and, judging by the way everyone was driving, we weren't the only ones. The entire city appeared to be functioning on a rich mixture of heroin and the divine guidance of the elephant god, Ganesh.

Khao San Road was once something of a hippy mecca for backpackers looking for spiritual enlightenment. From what I could make out, most of them were now looking for somewhere to get their hair braided or their willies massaged.

Brenda suggested we find somewhere to stay and have a little nap, but I told her a recent study had found that the best way to deal with jetlag was to stay up and drink beer until bedtime back home rolled around again. Oddly enough, she agreed to give it a shot.

Khao San Road is out of control. A kilometre long and packed with bars and stalls that spill out into the street. The motorcycle cops wear skin-tight stretch pants and surgical masks. Kamikaze drivers on three-wheel tuk-tuks compete with electric pink taxis, fruit vendors pushing carts and about a billion bikes ridden fast and hard by tattooed kickboxers and transgendered ladyboys. Pedestrians and dogs fill up the gaps. Tangles of thick black cabling hold the bars and guesthouses together.

After a few rounds of powerful Chang beer, Brenda and I were also in need of something to hold ourselves together. Half-mad with fatigue, it was only the inspired anarchy of Khao San Road that kept us going.

Switching to Singha beer, the waitress asked if I wanted grass. Right here? In the open? Brenda was watching me. "Fresh grass?" said the waitress impatiently.

"Yes, please," I said. Brenda gave me the Bangkok eye and said I would have to smoke it somewhere else. She needn't have bothered because the waitress went away and came back with a fresh glass. Brenda laughed so much she fell off her chair. Then the sky opened. Torrents of water sent the *farangs* (foreigners) scattering. The rain was warm. The air was hot. I sat and drank and laughed and melted in the monsoon mayhem.

Having successfully transcended jetlag we set off through the streets. Clive was terrified of going down the dark, reeking alleys but I told him to relax. This wasn't Cape Town. The worst thing that can happen is that you visit Patpong Road and buy a handful of fake emeralds. Or contract a deadly disease.

The Thais are too gentle or too afraid of being reincarnated as a rat to knife you in the ribs and take your camera. Almost every house has a small painted shrine in the front yard. I saw shrines that were worth more than the houses. The locals never even get angry because showing anger means losing face.

By the time we had found a hotel room with air-con and a flushing toilet, I had lost so much face that I could hardly see where I was going.

10 July 2007

Trains of Thought Collide at Hollywood's Death Railway

"You very handsome man," she murmured. "I love you long time." I looked deeply into her inscrutable Thai eyes but couldn't make out whether she was promising to love me until the day I died or until the meter ran out.

I never got a chance to find out because Brenda dragged me into a vibrating pink tuk-tuk. "Shanti guesthouse," she barked. Unaccustomed to taking orders from a woman, the driver looked at me for confirmation. I gave the patriarchal nod and he set off at a terrible speed through the backstreets of Bangkok.

Judging by my windowless cell, Shanti must be the way Thais spell shanty. A sign warned me to: "Be Aware of Fire, Rats, the Fan." Keen to avoid the shredding and burning that awaited me the moment I fell asleep, I suggested dinner.

The streets were full of fallen Thais reincarnated as curly-tailed dogs. Around a corner and in a makeshift boxing ring, a man in silky shorts tried to lure me into a Muy Thai contest. I was up for it and showed him my moves. Brenda apologised and helped me off the floor.

We found a restaurant on the banks of the catfish-infested sewer that runs through the city and I ordered a brace of Chang beers and a boiled serpent head in sour chilli soup starter. Brenda went for the roasted frog salad. Clive said he would try the fried Morning Glory. The dinner table conversation progressed from silent contemplation to a lot of shouting and hitting and being asked to leave.

I spent most of the next morning encouraging the serpent's head to leave my body in a calm and orderly fashion. Thais don't use toilet paper. They use handheld showers fitted to the wall.

I washed my bum, my face and my armpits and left the cubicle feeling like a new man.

But even though I was clean on my body, I knew that if I stayed in the city much longer I would sell Clive into child slavery, rent Brenda out to depraved German tourists and start my own opium trafficking business. Bangkok will do that to you.

Instead, I rented a car from Budget and had it delivered to the guesthouse. The driver handed over the keys and started walking off down the road. "Not so fast," I shouted. With the help of a 500 baht note and a little pressure on his phrenic nerve, the driver agreed to take us to the edge of the city.

We hadn't driven for more than a few minutes when I heard him say, "Stay right, go straight." He was out of the car before I could grab him.

The options of left or right were not immediately available. The car, a stupid little silver Al Goremobile, was wedged so tightly in a seething, brawling pack of taxis, trucks, bikes and tuk-tuks that all I could do was go with the flow.

Four hours later, we hit Kanchanaburi. Spraying warm beer over my comatose family, I told them to wake up and show a little respect for the dead.

Walking across the bridge on the river Kwai, I told Clive about the terrible tragedy that unfolded on this very spot way back in 1957.

"It was right here that British director David Lean shot one of the most overblown films of the 20th century. The set designer and thousands of his crew died during the building of a railway line between Thailand and Burma so that Japanese extras could be brought in from Rangoon."

Clive was so overcome with emotion that he broke free from my grip and ran to his mother who was some way down the track flirting with a Japanese imperialist thug masquerading as a tourist.

And that's when it happened. I walked over to put an end to this unseemly display of détente and the slitty-eyed Nip tried to finger jab me. It was only my lightning fast reflexes that kept me on the bridge and out of the river.

Later, Brenda claimed that he was merely trying to shake my hand. Yeah, right. That's what Hirohito said to whatshisname.

I marched the family straight off that Death Railway and checked us into a guesthouse where we ate steamed fragile pig's leg with coconut and lay awake listening to disco boats plying their sick trade up and down the river.

The next morning I packed up the family and headed for the Burmese border on a mission to free Aung San Suu Kyi, but the border was closed so we bought a bunch of chopsticks made from the last of Burma's teak forests and headed for Ayutthaya instead.

I wanted to stop at the Wat Pha Luang Ta Bua tiger sanctuary but Brenda pointed out that the guide book said it was risky for children. I pointed out that if I were Clive, I would rather be torn apart by Buddhist tigers and return a little closer to Nirvana than return to South Africa and be torn apart by agnostic murderers. I lost the argument by a margin of one.

Eight hours later I drove into Ayutthaya, the Thai capital for 417 years until it was destroyed by a Burmese biker gang in 1767. They trashed the temples, chopped the heads off the Buddhas and made it impossible for anyone to find a hotel in 2007.

It was dark. The streets were full of gilded elephants and godless transsexuals and Brenda was babbling about the melding of Sukhothai Buddhist influences and Hindu-inspired Khmer motifs. I was dishevelled, disoriented and drunk.

Just another summer in Siam.

17 July 2007

Riding Out a Gin Storm on a Pair of Killer Quad Bikes

We were somewhere near the Cambodian border when I found an English station on the car radio. The news was just ending. There had been a coup in Thailand. Brenda screamed and grabbed the wheel, almost sending us hurtling into a rice paddy.

It turned out that the coup was so, like, last year. But the army was still in charge and anything could happen. On the surface, life seemed normal. The bars were full of men pretending to be women, the rivers were full of fish pretending to be chicken and the streets were full of vendors selling fresh fruit and opium.

Coup schmoo. We were on our way to Thailand's second biggest island and it would take more than martial law to stop me.

I have always been partial to islands. There is something exhilarating about standing on one, knowing that at any moment it could sink to the bottom of the ocean or break free and drift into the shipping channel.

Steaming in on the car ferry, I got the sense that Koh Chang hadn't shaved or bathed in quite a while. It was covered in unsightly jungle and had obviously let itself go. I wouldn't be surprised if it had a drinking problem.

I pointed this out to Brenda and she said I was projecting. I checked my zip, but I wasn't. Odd sense of humour for a married woman.

The only road around Koh Chang is best tackled after three or four Mai Tais, the ingredients of which are freely available at roadside stalls. Easier to make than a Molotov cocktail, Thailand's national drink goes off like a car bomb in your stomach. It won't get onto CNN because the body parts stay inside your body, but there are other benefits that compensate for the lack of publicity.

Brenda fell instantly in love with a fishing village called Bang Bao. Consumed with jealousy, I demanded to know what Bang Bao could offer that I couldn't. Quite a lot, as it turned out.

Buried in a tangle of dive shops and marine abattoirs masquerading as restaurants, we found a guesthouse called the Buddha Bar. What luck. It's not often one gets the chance to drink with the sanction of a spiritual guide of Buddha's stature. That's the problem with Christianity. You just don't get places called the Jesus Bar. Funnily enough, a character called Bar Jesus popped up in the Bible but he turned out to be a bit of a con man and ended up getting cursed by Paul, which couldn't have been much fun at all.

The Buddha Bar felt like home should feel. I could lie on the floor looking out over the bay and have my victuals brought to me by an elegantly fading ladyboy with long black hair. My room was eight steps from the bar and we were the only foreigners there.

A soft rain began falling just as my plate of marinated frog's legs arrived. Happier than a Brahmin bull in Bombay, I was in the middle of composing an ode to the toad when the soft rain turned into a savage monsoon storm that never let up for six straight days.

Half crazy with crotch-rot and cabin fever, we were finally driven from the island.

Koh Samet, smaller than Chang, was only a couple of hours away but it was dry and the sun was shining.

Agnostic tradition dictates that any new arrival on an island lying within five degrees of the equator has to be consecrated by a blessing from St. Pina Colada. The saint was particularly effusive in his blessings on that day, and I insisted we hire quad bikes and race each other around the island.

Clive refused to take a bike on his own, preferring to sit behind his mother clutching on to her like some overgrown hairless marsupial with abandonment issues.

Being a woman, Brenda thought a race was a stupid idea. She pulled away sedately, then inexplicably opened up the throttle and rammed into the mountainside, almost snapping Clive's spine and causing me to laugh so much that I accidentally wet my *broeks*.

Later that evening we checked into a rambling affair called Jep's Place. It was on the edge of a road constructed from mud and potholes. Our cabin smelled as if something terrible, a German, perhaps, was curled up under the bed dying of Dengue Fever. I couldn't bring myself to look.

We slipped the brat a sleeping pill and took up defensive positions at the beach bar. All around us, sunburned *farangs* were staring out over the sea, wondering what in God's name had possessed them to bring their hookers on holiday.

"Yes, yes. I know. I'm paying you to love me long time. But what do you think Descartes really meant when he said *'cogito, ergo sum'*?"

"You buy more drink, I love you more long time."

Brenda ordered a gin and tonic. The waiter asked if we would prefer a bucket. A bucket of gin and tonic? Yes, please. It arrived in a green plastic bucket, much like the one with which I made sand castles when I was five.

Brenda said the quinine in the tonic would stop any malaria-packing mozzie in its tracks. She was right. The tonic worked like a charm. The gin, on the other hand, almost put me in traction.

Ten green buckets sitting on the table. And if one green bucket should accidentally fall, which it did, there would be nine green ... Hey! Let's check out the action on the other side of the island!

We spilled onto my quad bike, Brenda laughing and crying as South Africans are inclined to do when they travel abroad. Someone must have tampered with the steering, because no matter what I did, the bike veered repeatedly into the side of Jep's Place.

Eventually we gave up, went to bed and woke up just in time for our flight home.

24 July 2007

Fighting Off the Succubus & Sucking on Tequila

I quit smoking while on a camping trip to Solitaire in the middle of Namibia's nowhere lands ten years ago. It all began when I woke up in the early hours of the morning feeling as if I were in the middle of some sort of heart attack or brain attack. I fought my way out of the tent, half waking my girlfriend who seemed strangely unmoved by the fact that I was dying.

I put my head back into the tent to explain that I may be in need of urgent medical attention. However, the prospects of an untimely death were momentarily put on hold while my girlfriend's face morphed into something approximating a demon. Not one of those terrifying bowel-loosening demons, but more of a mischievous one, a succubus, perhaps. I took off into the night, naked and scared.

After stumbling through the desert darkness, she found me hours later wrapped around an anthill blue with trauma. Her face had returned to normal so I returned to the tent.

I was convinced that the episode had been caused by smoking. She disagreed, saying it was blindly obvious that the episode was caused by drinking one and a half bottles of tequila before bed.

"Perhaps," I said, "but I'm not taking any chances." I tossed the last of my cigarettes into the pristine desert and got us the hell out of there and back to Windhoek as fast as possible.

It was the best thing I ever did. I could taste food again, my skin cleared up, my teeth grew back, I learned to read Braille, appeared on Oprah and won two free tickets to the International Space Station. Indeed. The most incredible things happen when you give up smoking.

Some people, however, have reported negative side-effects after quitting.

Morbid obesity is one. Wanting to split your partner's head open with a blunt machete when they interrupt you is another.

In order to keep my weight down and stay out of jail, I decided to smoke only once my blood-alcohol level passed the 0.08 mark. Research has shown that while beer can also lead to the gratuitous eating of bar snacks and unprovoked outbreaks of violence, it's a lot harder when both hands are occupied.

I have just returned from Thailand where cigarette boxes are covered in the most appalling photographs of rotten lungs and putrefying hearts. I was so shaken that I needed a smoke to calm my nerves.

Last week a cold front sent my blood-alcohol level through the roof, so I rushed off to the shop on the corner and bought a box of Camel Mild. Right away, the hairs on the back of my neck stood up. Something was wrong.

The box was no longer yellow. Nor did it have my beloved one-humped camel staring vacantly into the distance. There was no tiny oasis. No little pyramid.

"What is this?" I asked the callow youth behind the counter. "A new box," he said. Damn your eyes, RJ Reynolds. How dare you bring out a new box without our permission?

I picked it up with long fingers and retired to my vehicle to study it at close quarters. The top of the good old box used to read: "Danger: Smoking Can Kill You." I always liked that. It meant I could lie on the beach and stare death in the face without having to go skydiving or scale some stupid rock face.

The top of the new box read: "Danger: Tobacco Is Addictive". Hmm. Perhaps all was not lost. In many ways, "addictive" is a far more erotically-charged word than "kill".

A lot of women are wary of a man who doesn't particularly care whether he lives or dies. For a start, it usually means he lacks the inherent ability to make any sort of real money. Certainly, they will sleep with him once or twice, but they won't have his babies or put him on their medical aid.

However, they can't resist a man who dabbles in something that could turn him into an addict. Then he becomes a challenge, someone to help, to nurse and, ultimately, to transform into a spineless robot who will slavishly do their bidding for all eternity.

I can live with the new warning. Then, on closer inspection, I noticed that the Camelus dromedarius had transmogrified into something Jackson Pollock might have spat out had his mouth been full of paint instead of alcohol when he rolled his car for the last time on August 11, 1956.

At the base of the box, the words Limited Edition were boldly printed. When I saw this I rushed back into the shop and bought several dozen packs. Bright blue background, funky pixellated camel, who could tell for how long these *objets d'art* would be available?

I turned the pack over and read the back. It said: "Nicotine in tobacco is a drug which acts on the brain and nerves. Most smokers are dependent on nicotine. That is why they feel uncomfortable and get cravings when they go without smoking for a while."

This is meant to be a deterrent?

We may as well stick up notices in gyms saying: "Women in oestrus act on the brain and nerves. Most men are dependent on women. That is why they feel uncomfortable and get cravings when they go without sex for a while."

Or post warnings in banks: "Money is a drug which acts on the brain and nerves. Most people are dependent on money. That is why they feel uncomfortable and get cravings when they go without having any for a while."

It's all a pack of filthy lies and if there were some other way for the human body to produce smoke rings, I would be there in a heartbeat.

31 July 2007

Trapped in a West Coast Panty Bar

The Mother City is a terrible place for a man to be during Women's Month. Whenever it rains, the gutters run pink with oestrogen and the bars fill up with lesbians. And there are still three weeks to go. Now, more than ever, problem wives and difficult girlfriends need to be isolated from the herd. Once they get wind of a movement, there is no stopping them. They will sweep through our cities like a great squealing tsunami, pausing only to get their hair done before laying waste to the country's confectionery stocks.

This doesn't bother me. Let them eat cake. But I know that once the gateau has been decimated, they will turn on us.

I had to get Brenda out of town fast, so I offered her an all expenses paid trip up the west coast. This is a region where women have long since won the struggle for equality. They do most of the work and bear the burden of responsibility admirably. Some of the most liberated men in South Africa can be found in these parts, sitting beneath trees gossiping and drinking like the women did before they freed themselves from the yolk of oppression.

We hadn't even reached Melkbosstrand before Brenda began demanding to know where we were going. I told her it was a surprise. Women love surprises, yet you wouldn't think so considering that most divorces are filed by women.

Passing Saldanha, Brenda held my last six-pack out of the window and insisted that I tell her. Faced with a hostage situation, I was left with no alternative. "Bosluisbaai," I said, watching the beers explode in my rearview mirror. "Bosluisbaai is in Namibia," Brenda barked, snatching the sole surviving Tafel from between my legs. I was outraged and called her a communist sympathiser.

"FW de Klerk," I shouted, "sold South West Africa to the terrorists for a dozen cows, five guns and a Nobel Peace Prize and to me it was and always will be a province of this great country!"

There are few things worse in this world than driving to Bosluisbaai in a rusting Hyundai with an angry woman and no beer as company, so I turned off at Paternoster. If you are into fishing villages full of deserted whitewashed cottages, fat unwashed policemen and motherless, quota-less fishermen with murder in their eyes, Paternoster is where you want to go.

I suggested we drive another few kilometres to Tietiesbaai. It seemed like a good place to spend Women's Day. Brenda was less sure and made me stop alongside the first white man we came across. He told us there was nothing at Tietiesbaai. Just another broken promise in the new South Africa.

Paternoster is a self-catering town without the catering. The shop sold ice, coffee and tins of hangover food. The bottle store was an alleyway that ended with a hole in the wall. It would have taken hours to pass my order through the burglar bars, but I pressed the buzzer regardless. Then, all of a sudden, nothing happened. So I went back to the car.

After much banging on doors and shouting in fractured Afrikaans, we occupied a cottage much like the Germans occupied Paris. Suffused with spontaneous romance, I tried to invade Brenda but she put up the French resistance so I offered to take her out in the hope that food would enhance her mood.

There is only one hotel in Paternoster. Any more and there would be trouble. I suggested a pre-dinner drink in the bar. Brenda was reluctant. "Come on," I said, "one drink can't hurt," knowing full well that hospitals, mortuaries, rehabs and maintenance courts are full of people who said the very same thing.

That bad old moon began rising the moment we walked into the bar. "Look at this amazing floor," I said. Brenda looked at the stained parquet. My diversionary tactic lasted all of four seconds. Then she looked up at a ceiling decorated with women's underwear. Bras and panties, as far as the eye could see.

Brenda was speechless just long enough for me to order her a double gin and tonic, which tempered her outrage much like petrol tempers a fire. Not that this country has any petrol. Plenty of outrage but not much petrol.

Trying not to blow our cover altogether, I ordered a triple klip 'n coke.

The barman, a misunderstood poet trapped in the body of an insensitive oaf, happily complied. Actually, that's not true. I could see that happily had never been a part of his emotional vocabulary. Primordial grunting, on the other hand, was right up there.

Brenda said the bar epitomised everything she found hateful in men. This wasn't at all what I had planned. I quickly pointed out that the low-flying lingerie bore the evidence of drunken signatures, indicating that the female clientele had voluntarily parted with their unmentionables. In that case, she said, the bar epitomised everything she found hateful in women.

This wasn't good. Now she hated men *and* women. I asked the barman for a shooter to calm things down. A Bob Marley was clearly out of the question. "How about a springbok," I said. He offered a gemsbok instead.

I told him I was game. He didn't get it, but we did. Over and over again. After the shooters, Brenda passed into the eye of the storm and all was right with the world.

Later the barman made us something called a Jelly Baby, which sent Brenda plunging back into the vortex. "What if," she said in a very loud voice, "this bar was decorated with men's underwear?"

It was a horrible image that stayed with me right until I went outside and aborted my Jelly Baby. Then we went back to our cottage and celebrated Women's Month by sleeping in separate beds.

7 August 2007

Malice in Wonderland

—'Protesting taxi drivers are claiming ownership of routes and have shut down a free transport service for University of Cape Town students. They say the Jammie Shuttle is "stealing" their business along Main Road and "taking food from their families mouths".' —news report

Rival taxi organisations in Cape Town have set aside their differences and succeeded in getting private vehicles banned from all roads leading into and out of the city.

This comes after taxi bosses managed to convince city officials that taxi wars were caused by people driving around in their own cars.

"I don't know why we didn't think of it sooner," said a taxi driver who would only identify himself as Tobias Shangaan of 17 Makakunya Street, Khayelitsha.

Many former motorists have already begun renting out their vehicles to the homeless.

"I don't mind the extra cash," said a Muizenberg resident. "The car radio keeps me awake at night but the battery has to go flat sooner or later."

Some people have given up their jobs rather than catch taxis. "I would sooner cut my own throat than get into one of those death traps," said a visibly angry Plumstead man who gave only his name, rank and serial number.

Mayor Helen Zille said that while she sympathised with former motorists, her hands were tied. "What can I do?" she said. "These people have guns."

In a related development, taxi drivers have mounted a campaign to shut down soccer moms running lift clubs in the southern suburbs.

Ashleigh Fillet-Mignon of Bishop's Court said she got the fright of her life after picking up her son, Bobby, and six of his school friends on Monday afternoon.

"I was running a bit late and the boys were worried that they would miss the kick-off. Bobby was in the front seat and Stevie, Paulie, Mickey, Donny, Ricky and Johnny were in the back. That's the nice thing about an SUV. You can really pack the kids in. Anyway. I was pulling out when this taxi came out of nowhere and cut me off." Fillet-Mignon said "at least 40 or 50" men emerged from the taxi and surrounded her car. She said the driver ordered the children out and made them line up on the pavement.

"He told them if they wanted to go somewhere, they should flag down a taxi. Of course they didn't know what to do. They're white, for heaven's sake. They have never caught a taxi in their lives."

One of the men then pulled Fillet-Mignon from her car.

"He said that my SUV was being subpoenaed. I told him he was talking absolute rubbish but he just laughed. Then he asked the ringleader for permission to shoot me so I thought I should keep quiet."

Fillet-Mignon said "about 30" of the men got into her car. What happened next took her by surprise.

"The man behind the wheel, a bald brute with some sort of tribal scars on his face, asked me where I wanted to go. I told him to take me to the Claremont police station but he said he couldn't do that so I told him to take me home. Somebody opened the back door and I got in. Then he picked up the kids and asked where they wanted to go."

Fillet-Mignon said it took over an hour to drop the children at their homes.

"It was an absolute nightmare. Johnny had to go to Rondebosch, Donny was all the way over in Newlands, Paulie had to be taken to Pinelands. And they were charged R5 each, which makes no sense when you think that Ricky lives just down the road and Stevie is in Wynberg."

Approached for comment on the incident, Bobo Nzelele of the Congress of Democratic Taxi Drivers said: "This is our route. These so-called soccer moms are taking food out of our children's mouths."

When it was pointed out that the passengers were only 10 years old, he said this was irrelevant. "A lot of children, especially non-black children, are very rich. They get plenty of pocket money to pay for public transport."

Nzelele said that lift clubs were "worse than apartheid".

Meanwhile, workers at the Green Point Stadium are once more threatening to down tools. Only last week, management gave in to their demand that a fleet of imported chauffeur-driven limousines be provided so that they could go shopping and clubbing after work.

"What could we do?" said Gussets & Girders MD, Column O'Beam. "These people have guns."

Now trouble is brewing again. Bulala Abelungu, president of the Union of Workers Working On 2010 Stadium, said there was another demand on the table.

"There are 800 of my members building this stadium and they have every right to play in the World Cup. Why should foreign people like Italy and France come here and benefit from our hard work?"

The union has given the South African Football Association until the end of next week to disband Bafana Bafana and send its talent scouts to the construction site.

"If Safa doesn't play ball, we will turn the site over to the Cape Minstrels. Don't push us too far."

Speaking from Zurich, Fifa supremo Sepp Blatter said: "What is wrong with you people? Don't make me come over there again."

In an unrelated development, Metro police are demanding the right to adapt their vehicles at state expense.

Top metro cop Bongoman Jonassole said it was unfair that firemen got to drive "big red trucks with ladders and hoses and things".

Speaking on condition of anonymity, shop steward Constable Wyfie Versmaak said: "These things they make us drive ... they just don't pull the bitches like they used to."

Versmaak said the Metro police also wanted more training. "We only ever go to court to give evidence or face charges. This is racial discrimination. We demand the right to wear gowns and be famous."

He said if the city refused to modify their patrol cars and let them practise as lawyers, the entire Metro police department would take to the bush and form a rebel army.

Premier Ebrahim Rasool said his hands were tied. "What can I do? They have guns."

4 September 2007

Osama Releases New Video to Celebrate Twin Towers Anniversary

Osama bin Laden's first video in almost three years has met with an enthusiastic response from al-Qaeda supporters, but there are others who seem less impressed.

Speaking from his home in Muizenberg, Hugh Spungen (19), said he preferred Osama's previous releases. "I thought this one was weak on rhetoric and lacked the open threats of violence which have made Osama the celebrity that he is today."

Spungen said the line, "... to escalate the killing and fighting against you", was a prime example of how the superstar was losing his edge.

"In his earlier stuff, Osama wasn't shy to open up with both guns. Now he's beating around the bush, so to speak. Who is this 'you'? It's all too vague and nebulous for my tastes," Spungen added .

Analysts say the likes of Spungen may have a point. Cordite Quaver of the Bellville Institute of Music and Security Studies agreed that Osama's latest release could signal a fresh approach.

"A few minutes into his video, Osama describes US President George W Bush as 'becoming like the one who plows and sows the sea – he harvests nothing but failure'. Osama's strength has always been in his rhyming couplets. By resorting to prose, as lyrical as it may be, it seems to me that he is taking his work in a new direction."

Quaver said the use of metaphor and allegory was dangerous in the sense that Osama risked losing support among his traditional fan base.

"Love him or hate him, the fact remains that Osama's pulling power lies primarily in his fundamental ability to think on his feet and shoot from the hip. I may be wrong, but I suspect his new style is going to bomb."

A Constantia arms dealer who gave his name as Mr X agreed that Osama was becoming complacent. He said he had watched this sort of thing happen before to other artists.

"Look at Eminem. Who among us will ever forget that line from *Mosh*: 'Stomp, push up, mush, fuck Bush, until they bring our troops home'. That was in 2004. Last I heard, Eminem was recording ringtones."

At one point in his 30-minute performance, Osama gently chides the American people: "You permitted Bush to complete his first term, and stranger still, chose him for a second term ..."

Cliffie Whigster, who wrote lyrics for the Blarney Brothers in the 1960s, said it was reassuring to see that Osama had not completely done away with form and rhythm.

"Term rhymes perfectly with term. It's a stroke of genius, in fact."

Commenting on the same verse, General Mikhail Sikorsky of the Fish Hoek Home for Retired Philatelists said he was intrigued by Osama's suggestion that the American people had "screwed up" by allowing Bush to finish his first term in office.

"This is revolutionary stuff," said a visibly excited Sikorsky. "When you think about it, why should the voters have to wait for elections before changing their leaders? Assassination should be one of the cornerstones of democracy."

Some say that Osama's new understated approach is the result of an increasingly reclusive lifestyle. Speculation was rife that he would put in a surprise appearance at the final round of auditions for Afghan Idol last month.

"I went all the way to Kabul but he never pitched," said one disappointed groupie from Mitchell's Plain. "Nobody has seen him since that nasty business in New York six years ago."

"He's losing touch with his fans," 14-year-old Minke van der Spuy said. Her sister, Bryde, agreed. "Osama needs to get out more."

Last week's global release of the multi-millionaire's 13th recording has also got the style gurus chattering. In his hugely popular 2004 video, he wore a gold robe over a white cloak. "Gaudy yet tasteful" was the general consensus.

Earlier, in a 2002 appearance, he sported a camouflage jacket which quickly became a hot fashion accessory for teenage boys and British troops involved in Operation Enduring Freedom.

His latest video, however, has come as something of a let-down to trend-spotters. After analysing the tape, Craigy Craig from Markham's in Cavendish Square said he felt "distressed" by Osama's new outfit.

"He certainly is looking good, what with the Botox and all, but a beige robe in a beige cave in a beige desert just doesn't do it for me. I don't know who is dressing this man but if it were me, I would have given him a big splash of yellow before turning the camera on. This is the home of the pashmina, for heaven's sake," said Craig.

While Osama might be dressing and speaking in muted tones, he has certainly made an effort in the facial hair department.

"I like the black beard," said a barber from Barberton. "I always thought the gray made him look too old. He's only 50 – why shouldn't he dye?"

But not everyone believes the new look is nothing more than a narcissistic indulgence. Former counterterrorism expert Joggie Spyker is adamant that the beard is false.

"This is no mid-life crisis. Osama has shaved and is probably living in a city where nobody has beards. If I were Bush, I would move the search from the Afghan-Pakistan border to the Sweden-Norway border."

On Sunday a White House spokesman described Osama as "virtually impotent". Dr Richard Dick, a specialist in the field, disagrees.

"Osama has five or six wives who have given him anywhere between 12 and 24 children. Bush has one wife and two daughters, both of whom are hell-raising gin junkies. No contest."

Meanwhile, a music producer from Islamabad has claimed that Osama and Eminem are collaborating on a new project titled, "Yo Ma's A Bush".

"This is something that will blow everyone away," said the source, who asked not to be identified.

Osama's manager, Ashraf Faruk al-Said Zubair al-Yaqoubi Husam al-Din, known in the industry as Dr Love, denied the claim as "malicious gossip" and urged the Bush administration to convert to Islam.

11 September 2007

Twisted Like a Koeksuster on National Braai Day

The loss of life on Monday was quite spectacular, even by our standards. Thousands of pigs, sheep, goats, cows and chickens fought among themselves for the honour of being the first to lay down their lives so that South Africans could celebrate National Braai Day in style.

The day was a resounding success. Gutters ran red with blood, dogs ran wild with bones and paramedics ran themselves ragged tending to the usual braai-related assaults, rapes and homicides. What a good idea it was to have Klipdrift as one of the sponsors.

Brenda wanted to do something to mark Heritage Day. Something different. Quite frankly, I couldn't see the point.

"We're white," I said. "We don't have any heritage." We did, on the other hand, have plenty of meat. It made far more sense to mark Braai Day. We arranged to meet Ted and Mary down at the beach where we could fall down without worrying about concussing ourselves. This is always one of the biggest hazards facing those who choose to celebrate Braai Day instead of Heritage Day. We passed a lot of families braaiing along the way. Many of them had taken over entire parking lots. Brenda wondered if arguments had broken out in homes across the Cape Flats on Monday morning.

"I want to braai in the parking lot in Muizenberg."

"Forget it. We're going to the one in Camps Bay."

"There's a new lot opened near the Waterfront. Can we go there? Please, daddy!"

I told Brenda there was a very simple explanation.

"A lot of coloured people regard their cars as members of the family. We wouldn't leave our child in a parking lot and go off and have fun without him, would we?"

Actually, I would, but I couldn't tell Brenda that.

Both Heritage Day and Braai Day are allegedly aimed at bringing South Africans closer together. In our case, it brought us a little too close.

Encamped on the beach, we had just finished our first case of Tafel lager and were wrestling a second kudu haunch onto the grid when we were forced to take up braai forks and fend off a pack of hungry darkies. Look, I'm all for unifying the nation and whatnot, but there are limits.

Engorged with dead animal and thoroughly beerlogged, we returned home to celebrate Heritage Day like the decent God-fearing patriots that we are. Heritage Day is a relatively new addition to the public holiday calendar. Prior to 1994, it was known as Right of Admission Reserved Day.

We agreed that the country has a fascinating array of indigenous fauna, all of which go well with one or other of the many indigenous sauces available in supermarkets everywhere.

Our flora, too, is not to be sneezed at. Unless, of course, you suffer from seasonal allergic rhinitis, in which case you have no business living here. Look at our national flower, the giant protea. Actually, I can't look at it for too long because I find it hostile and ugly. To be honest, I would rather look at roadkill.

Fynbos is unique to the Cape Floral Kingdom and you will be fined if you pick it. *Cannabis sativa* is unique to KwaZulu-Natal and you will be arrested if you smoke it. That's diversity for you.

The central image on our coat of arms is a secretary bird, a graceful creature known for launching random attacks on unsuspecting tourists. It specialises in pinning people to the ground and pecking their eyes out. Canada's national bird is the Common Loon. A bit like our national health minister, really.

The motto on our coat of arms is !ke e:/xarra//ke. Nobody outside of the /Xam tribe knows what it means. Most South Africans think it's computer code.

When it comes to the national animal, we have the springbok. France has some sort of chicken. Our rugby team is also called the Springboks. The French once accused them of playing like animals. This made us feel tremendously proud.

Our national fish is the galjoen. Like most hard-drinking South Africans, the galjoen is regarded as a creature that will fight to the death. Cooked over an open fire, however, galjoen tastes a lot better than the national drunk.

I am particularly proud of my heritage because South Africa is the cradle of humankind. So what if modern man emigrated to Australia as soon he could walk upright? We're still the cradle.

Our scientists have found blue-green algae dating back nearly four million years. Ted speculated that the slime was one of Badih Chabaan's earliest relatives. Let's see if he's still laughing with two broken legs.

I was fully expecting to receive one of the national orders that President Mbeki hands out at this time of year. Unbelievably, I was passed over once again. Morné du Plessis got one. So did Roland Schoeman. And Schalk Pienaar.

Apparently you have to be Afrikaans to get any kind of recognition in this country. As English-speakers, we are doomed. Even though our forefathers invented gin and tonic, lap dancing, airbags, the cat flap, shrapnel and the rubber band, nobody around here seems to care.

Oh, now I get it. Of course. It's far more important to reward a people who came up with jukskei, witblits, the Voortrekker Monument, the G6 artillery gun and a racial superiority complex so twisted that it makes their koeksisters look straight.

25 September 2007

Sergeant Van Der Pepper's Lonely Heart's Club

Oh, look. It's that month of the year again.

If it's October in Germany, it must be Oktoberfest – a time to pause and give thanks for not having been born a German.

In Namibia, October is known as "suicide month". Come to think of it, when I lived there every month felt like suicide month.

In South Africa, October is Transport Month. I only know this because I unwittingly helped pay for an enormous advertisement in a Sunday newspaper reminding me of this auspicious occasion. An entire page is devoted to an exciting calendar of events and I, for one, have no intention of missing the opening of the first bicycle shop in De Aar on 16 October.

I hope to have recovered from the excitement in time to attend the opening of the Thonyelani and Khombe Pedestrian Bridge in Bergville, KwaZulu-Natal, three days later.

If us taxpayers hadn't chipped in R500 000 for this ad, we might never have known about Transport Month. It would be churlish of us not to congratulate Minister Radebe on this fine example of money well spent.

October is also known as "break-up month". Wherever I look, I see relationships in tatters.

Cosatu is in tears because its duplicitous partner, the government, is unable to remain faithful for any meaningful length of time.

Justice Minister Brigitte Mabandla is citing irreconcilable differences as the reason for her divorce from a shattered Vusi Pikoli.

The ANC is threatening to split up with itself and even the local newspaper's Love Match column is heavy with heartache.

A lot of people are too shy to seek out their soulmates and playmates through the pages of a daily newspaper. Fortunately, I am prepared to help them out at absolutely no cost.

Here, then, are the advertisements for some of our country's favourite lonely hearts:

• Thabo Mbeki seeks trustworthy person for friendship and sharing of well-crafted metaphors. Must be familiar with the works of Pliny the Elder. Sense of humour not required but blind unquestioning loyalty a must. No chancers.

• Manto Tshabalala-Msimang seeks healthy fun-loving Christian who enjoys nights in on the town. Holding their own in a conversation equally important to holding their drink. Must be prepared to experiment with vegetarian meals in line with the national effort to find a cure for Aids. People taller than 1,5m need not respond.

• Brigitte Mabandla seeks needy, insecure companion for regular consultations and healthy working relationship. Must at all times show utmost respect for figures of authority and be unable to take any unilateral decisions whatsoever.

• Ngconde Balfour seeks extrovert with take-no-prisoners attitude for mutual sabre-rattling and lively exchanges of rhetoric. Must share an interest in red meat and movie classics like *The Great Escape*.

• Nelson Mandela seeks partner for scary, overbearing personal assistant. All races welcome.

• Irvin Khoza seeks 800 non-unionised labourers who enjoy spending time outdoors in the trendy Green Point area. Must enjoy working with their hands. Low self-esteem and a desire to please a plus.

• Ivy Matsepe-Casaburri seeks man or woman, race and age not important, with something good to say about Telkom. Luddites welcome.

• Jacob Zuma seeks machine gun in good working condition. Bullets a bonus.

• Schabir Shaik seeks sensitive medical professional to help secure 15-year stay in the presidential suite of St Augustine's Hospital. Friendship rewarded with non-repayable loans.

• Jackie Selebi seeks non-smoker with no hidden agendas or warrants of arrest. Must live by a moral code, especially the code of Omertà. Must also love police dogs.

• Helen Zille seeks support from genuine anti-drug Muslims, anti-alcohol teetotalers, anti-beef Hindus, anti-pork Jews, anti-sex celibates, anti-men lesbians, anti-doping athletes and anti-nuclear environmentalists. Race no problem but must be of voting age.

• King Goodwill Zwelithini seeks energetic non-virgin for robust fun. Race not important but Zulus preferred. Experience essential.

• Nosiviwe Mapisa-Nqakula seeks Malawian houseboy with legitimate papers. Strong arms, good teeth and a quiet disposition preferred. Must be prepared to work for love of work, not money.

• Mosiuoa Lekota seeks fellow militarist who loves walking on the beach, firing long-range artillery guns and flying in attack helicopters. Terry Crawford-Browne need not respond.

• Judge Nkola Motata seeks reliable company for after-work functions. Driver's licence essential.

• Robert McBride seeks reliable company for after-work functions. Driver's licence essential.

• Marthinus van Schalkwyk seeks middle class Pretoria couple for dinner parties. Black professionals only please.

• J Arthur Brown seeks wealthy widows for long walks up the garden path. Orphans welcome.

• Badih Chabaan seeks stunning Russian models to convert to Islam.

• Robert Mugabe seeks like-minded humanitarian for fireside chats. Must have an interest in politics, farming and blowing up the British House of Commons. Own car with own petrol essential. No whites please.

• Osama bin Laden seeks presentable, down-to-earth type unafraid to take chances. Ability to mingle unobtrusively in crowded marketplaces preferred. Must be a good listener and be able to follow orders.

• George Bush seeks Osama bin Laden.

9 October 2007

I Hear Dead People

Ted banged on my door on Sunday evening and said he had come to watch the rugby. "What rugby?" I asked. He called me an unregenerate abomination of a South African, which I thought a little harsh.

It took us an hour to transfer the beer from his car to my fridge and we almost missed the singing of the national anthems. For me, this is the highlight of any rugby match.

To watch these oafish mastodons clutching their hearts and singing like Umkhonto we Sizwe cadres is something that never fails to bring tears to my eyes. By the time I had picked myself up off the floor, the Argentineans were singing their own breathtakingly discordant anthem. Well, those who weren't blubbering like big hairy girls.

Earlier our team had run onto the field with whatshisname clutching one of those stuffed cuddly toys that you buy from Cardies when you're in trouble with your girlfriend. I was so embarrassed.

When Jake White was interviewed I couldn't hear a word he said because Ted was going on and on about the coach's startling resemblance to a cross between Michael Keaton and a meatball.

I was more concerned about the fact that women were allowed into the Stade de France. The French have really gone soft since World War Two. No wonder they got whipped by those English muffins.

Ted and I lost interest in the game before it even started. I mean, really. Argentina? They can't handle pressure.

Margaret Thatcher knows this better than most and she will have advised the boy, Mark, to bet heavily on the Springboks. Switching off the telly with a well-aimed beer can, Ted wanted to know if I was interested in having a little flutter on the race war going on in the judiciary.

"R500 on the darkies for a win," he said. "You're on!" I shouted. "The smart money says the whiteys will take this one."

Ted snorted. "Remember that while our lot were poncing about in wigs and gowns in the Old Bailey, recessing for roast beef and Yorkshire pudding, Shaka was wearing monkey skins and impaling dissidents on poisoned spikes."

He seemed to be suggesting that Shaka and Judge John Hlophe had studied at the same law school.

"There's no such thing as Zulu justice, you fool," I said.

"Right," said Ted. "Let's sort this out once and for all. We're having a séance."

This made about as much sense as anything else so I got a wine glass from the kitchen, dimmed the lights and pulled up a chair. Ted quickly filled the glass with whisky and ordered me to fetch another.

"We also need a Ouija board," he said, looking at me as if I were the only person in the neighbourhood who didn't have a Ouija board readily at hand.

"Trivial Pursuit will have to do," I said.

Facing each other across the dining room table, Ted said we had to hold hands and rest the middle finger of our other hand on the base of the upside-down wine glass which he placed in the centre of the board. Ted cleared his throat and closed his eyes. I gave his hand a reassuring squeeze and he reciprocated with a grip that splintered my metacarpals.

"Dullah Omar," intoned Ted in a voice that almost made me wet my *broeks*. "If you are here, give us a sign." I heard what sounded like a nervous cough. On closer reflection, I suspected it was Ted emitting a nervous trouser cough.

Then the glass began moving. I opened my eyes to see if he was playing silly buggers with me, but the expression on his face told a different story.

The glass stopped on Sports & Leisure, leading me to think that we had accidentally got Hansie Cronje on the line, but after a few seconds it continued on past People & Places and came to a halt on History.

Nothing happened, so I picked up a card. "Where did Napoleon fight his last battle?"

Ted screamed and snatched his hand away. "Relax," I said, "it's only me." He was outraged and insisted that if any questions were to be asked, he would do the asking. He had another shot of whisky to calm his nerves.

"Trivial Pursuit might not be ideal," said Ted. "Let's try channeling."

We closed our eyes once more. I was relieved that Ted was no longer trying to hold my hand. We sat like that for what felt like hours.

"Dullah Omar," said Ted, scaring me half to death all over again. "Did you give Judge Hlophe verbal permission to receive payments as a trustee of the Oasis Crescent Retirement Fund?"

Almost immediately, what sounded like Omar's voice came out of Ted's mouth. "Of course not," he said. "I was already working on my Bicycles for All campaign in the transport ministry by the time the fund was created."

Ted slumped over the table and didn't say another word. I shook him violently.

"Quick! Ask him if he knows anything about this Saturday's Lotto draw. Get the numbers! We need the numbers!"

But it was no good. Dullah was gone and Ted couldn't remember a thing. He said his head hurt and his mouth was dry. Apparently channeling and cheap whisky have similar side-effects.

With Ted unable to back me up, I knew the Black Lawyers' Association would never believe me when I told them I had horse's mouth evidence that their man was fibbing.

Actually, it's unlikely that the BLA would believe anything I told them. I could march into their offices right now and tell them the earth is round and they would denounce me as an imperialist Aristotelian lackey who wanted to deny others their democratic right to believe that the earth was flat.

I may as well give Ted his R500 right now.

16 October 2007

China Loves Us
– You Can Bank On It

When I heard that a Chinese bank had invested R36-billion in Standard Bank, my heart swelled with pride. They had chosen my bank. Not one of the others. They chose mine.

I shouted and laughed and turned up the music and danced with the cat. I began drinking hard and fast so that I could reach the place one must be in if one is to properly celebrate occasions of great importance.

I was less than three beers short of the place when the repellant fruit of my loins walked in. Right away he started blubbing like a girl. I asked him what was wrong and he said that when he saw me laughing and dancing, he thought something terrible had happened to his mother.

Reassuring him that Brenda was out foraging for victuals, I invited him to join me in a toast. I tossed him a beer and he caught it awkwardly against the side of his head. To cheer him up, I showed him how to open a beer with his teeth. It's a rite of passage for all boy-children

Spitting out bits of enamel, Clive asked what we were celebrating. I struck a noble pose and raised my bottle. "To China!" I shouted. The brat reacted as if I had rammed a cattle prod down his trousers.

Of course. I had forgotten. Something went terribly wrong during the early years of Clive's education. Instead of growing up to hate black people, he turned on the Chinese. None of his therapists have ever been able to explain how this happened.

I encouraged him to calm down through the judicious application of an inverted Indian deathlock, but, slippery with spilled beer, he wriggled from my grasp and took the moral high ground.

"China is taking over your bank and you're happy because why?"

I told him the benefits would be manifold. "For a start," I said, "with so much extra money, Standard Bank will stop robbing us. There will be no more bogus fees and trumped-up charges."

Clive snorted and called me an idealistic fool. I let it slide because modern parenting requires that verbal and physical abuse works both ways. Grabbing a piece of paper and a pen, he drew a picture of a dragon with a gaping mouth about to swallow what looked like a ping-pong ball.

"That's the earth," said Clive, giving me a withering look. "Interesting that you should say ping-pong. Want to know who the current world table tennis champion is? Wang Liqin, that's who."

Spittle flying from his angry teenage mouth, he shouted: "Don't you see? First ping-pong, then the world!"

I was speechless, mainly because I had never heard the runt string so much as a coherent sentence together.

"They invented the parachute, the cannon, the crossbow! They invented matches and gunpowder! Can't you see what's happening?"

I sucked on my beer and nodded wisely. "Yes," I said, "but they also invented stir-fried chicken with oyster sauce. That's damn good stuff."

Clive said I should read Sun Tzu's *The Art of War*. The closest I have come to reading anything by a Chinese writer is the menu at Tong Lok in Kloof Street and I intend keeping it that way.

"What about the gulags?" wailed Clive.

"Chicken, beef, gulags, I don't care. If it comes with oyster sauce and noodles, I'll eat it."

He broke another tooth trying to open a beer. "Here. Take mine," I said, giving him my empty bottle.

"Don't you see, father? There are 1,3 billion Chinese. All they want to do is get their hands on Africa's natural resources. Buying into the bank is their way of ..."

"Nonsense!" I shouted. "You watch. By Friday that surly cow at the Fish Hoek branch is going to cash my cheque with a smile and tell me there are no fees. She will say 'thank you and enjoy your day'."

"No she won't," said Clive. "But if she did, she'd say it in Mandarin."

The kid may have a point. It's common knowledge that Deputy President Phumzile Mlambo-Ngcuka was recently summoned to Beijing.

Not long after she got back, it was announced that Mandarin would be introduced at high schools around the country.

She also said that people of Chinese origin born in South Africa should regard themselves as Africans. Since we whiteys are having a devil of a job convincing the government that we are Africans, it might be easier for us to apply to the department of home affairs to be reclassified as Chinese.

The Hon. Dep. Pres. said that agreements were reached in several areas including agriculture. This is wonderful news even if it means having to fly to Shanghai to sink my choppers into a couple of meaty Durban mangoes and maybe a paw-paw.

She also said South African farmers were already in China teaching the peasants how to cultivate apples. Oh, please. When anthropologists uncovered the remains of Peking Man near Zhoukoudian, they found he had died half a million years ago while cooking some sort of duck casserole in an early version of the convection oven. Now we're teaching them to grow apples?

Are they teaching us how to harvest the organs of political dissidents? Let's trade. One fresh Falun Gong liver for two Granny Smiths. How much for Tokyo Sexwale's kidneys on the black market?

It's all starting to make sense. Ten years ago, the British gave Hong Kong back. The British don't return anything unless they are threatened with physical or financial retribution.

After meeting with the Dalai Lama the other day, American President George Bush said he was disappointed not to have been given "one of them free Tibet gizmos that everyone's talkin' about".

You think that's worrying? Check this out. China's boy-heavy birth rate means that by 2020 there will be 40 million frustrated bachelors on the streets. They can't all become monks. What you can expect, then, is the stealthy appearance of inscrutably inspired, motivated and involved gay bank tellers at a branch near you.

Welcome to the world's biggest Chinese takeaway.

Nkosi Sikelel' iAfrika.

30 October 2007

Scum King of the Estate Agents

I don't want to write about it. I really don't. The entire business makes me sick to my stomach.

I have just made my 14th move in 10 years. Looking at the devastation strewn across the lounge floor, I can see boxes that date back to the very first move. Some of them are marked 'important documents'. They are so important that they have remained sealed since 1997.

There is a box skulking in the corner with the words 'Ouma Sliced' on it. I never wrote that. It's printed on the cardboard. Even so, I'm afraid to open it. What if it's not rusks? What if it really is someone's genetically modified grandmother packed in neatly wrapped cutlets?

The beach house in Kommetjie is already a fading memory. Now, I have sweeping views of the squatter camp in Hout Bay. I can hear the Irish drinking songs and the gunshots quite clearly. Dogs bark relentlessly and sirens echo through the valley. It feels like home. What am I saying? That's the whisky talking. It doesn't feel like home at all. I wouldn't know what home felt like if it wrapped its arms around me and stuck its tongue down my throat.

Hadedahs standing waist high ram their deadly beaks into the lawn. They give me the lazy eye and scream in a hideous voice if I dare walk outside. I tried to set Boris the cat on them but the coward ran back inside and hid beneath the bed.

Brenda told me to leave them alone, that they are part of the natural environment. Let's see what she says when nature has her pinned down and is pecking at her eyeballs. That's assuming the squatters don't get her first.

Apparently only bereavement and divorce are more stressful than moving. What rubbish. Divorce is a happy occasion. You are lightening your load. Snakes shed their skins – we shed our husbands and wives.

It's a natural and beautiful process. As for bereavement, well, death is even more natural than divorce. It also helps to free up parking at the beach and stops the queues in Woolworths from spiralling out of control.

The stress, for me, does not lie in the actual moving. In fact I would say it's far more stressful for the movers. They are, after all, the ones hauling the excesses of the haves up and down flights of stairs in return for a tip that barely covers a chicken pie and a tik straw.

The real stress, as always, lies in having to deal with estate agents. It doesn't matter how specific you are in your needs, there are always those who will take you to facebrick atrocities with sinking floors and rising damp. Yes, it might be full of character, but it's also full of borer worms and the ghosts of murdered children.

One agent took us to a house and said: "The only problem with this place is that you will never want to leave."

Actually, sir, I will never be able to leave, whether I want to or not, because the garage is situated on a blind corner on a busy main road. The only way I would leave is in a body bag.

Brenda went to see a Tuscan villa. "You'll love it," said the agent. "It's perfect for the animals." And it was, if you enjoy sitting on the stoep watching your pets frying themselves on the electrified blade wire.

Who are these Tuscans, anyway? A race of midgets? I would have to put my legs out of the bedroom window to get a decent night's sleep and go to the toilet on my hands and knees and wee like a dog.

The rental? A snip at R13 000 a month. What in god's name is going on here? We rent because we cannot afford to buy anything remotely habitable. We are gypsies with high standards and strong socialist leanings. Don't mess with us.

But now that George Bush's war on terror, double-dealing on Wall Street and ongoing duplicitous machinations in the global oil industry have sent rentals through the roof, what are our alternatives? An upturned boat in Kalk Bay harbour? A hosepipe through the back window of my rusting Hyundai? Perhaps a stocking over my head and a visit to the nearest bank? What if a security guard wrestles me to the floor and finds a banana instead of a 9mm Parabellum down my trousers? Would my fellow convicts accord me the respect I deserve or would they mock me and taunt me and ravage me mercilessly in the showers?

One of our deeply caring banks says that the number of "non-performing home loans" has increased by 30% over the past year. I was trawling the Cape Flats last week looking for my dog when I came across a non-performing home loan. He was sitting outside his jerry-built hovel with his head in his hands. His four children and sullen wife were in the lounge staring at the empty space where the TV once stood. The non-performing loan told me that the bank was about to repossess his house. He asked if I could have a word with them. Get them to take the wife and children, instead.

There it is. Always has been. Small dogs get eaten by medium-sized dogs while the big dogs romp and gamble in the Elysian fields and, short of voting for the Communist Party, there is nothing I can do about it.

We have found somewhere to stay at a criminal rental and with a lease so long that it begs to be broken.

Right now, I need to apologise to all the estate agents I have maligned over the years. Their faults pale into insignificance compared to the agent we are dealing with at the moment.

He is an arrogant, vicious brute who single-handedly takes the reputation of estate agents to a level that I never thought possible. He is a lying, cheating thug who lured us into a defective house on a wave of false pretences and empty threats. I would name him right now, but let us rather wait for him to be named in court.

6 November 2007

The Naming of Teddies is a Difficult Matter ...

Ted came by on Saturday evening, despite me having asked him not to. Earlier in the day, Brenda had said she had a little surprise for me and I wanted to be alone when the moment presented itself.

I assumed she had come across my copy of the brilliant Dr Laura Schlessinger's book, *The Proper Care and Feeding of Husbands*, which I have been leaving in strategic locations around the house ever since it was published in 2004. The message in this visionary work of genius is simple. The key to a happy marriage lies in the hands of the woman.

All she has to do is follow a few simple rules: No nagging, stay in shape, let him go out with the boys, don't be neurotic, put him before everything else in your life, cook him a hot dinner every night and never say no to sex.

When I mentioned this to Ted, he laughed cruelly and said it was far more likely that Brenda was planning to lace my supper with the same stuff game rangers use to tranquilise elephants, after which she would grind mustard seeds into my eyeballs and chop off my willy.

It seemed improbable, but then again, until last week so did a Jacob Zuma presidency.

Brenda looked disappointed to see Ted stagger in under the weight of three cases of Tafel lager. "I'll get you next time," she whispered, shooting me a smile that would have made Aileen Wuornos flinch.

Surrounded by 73 of my best friends, I felt untouchable. "Not unless I get you first," I said, covering my crotch and moving in a crab-like fashion towards the safety of my study.

"Right," said Ted. "First item on the agenda – a toast to the ANC Women's League." I raised my bottle solemnly. No words were needed.

"Second item on the agenda – the naming of teddy bears." This sparked a discussion so heated that at one point it burst into flames. We joined forces and moved quickly to put it out with low-altitude beer-bombing runs that ruined the carpet but saved the house.

Ted said he was outraged when he heard that a British teacher, Gillian Gibbons, had been sentenced to 15 days in jail in Sudan after allowing her class to name a teddy bear Muhammad.

"Teddies are duplicitous creatures that bear allegiance to no-one," he said. "The infidel should have been put to death right there in the classroom."

I felt he was being unduly harsh. At the same time, anyone who voluntarily moves from Britain to Sudan deserves to be punished. On the other hand, she did come from Liverpool, a city that in many respects is far more brutal than Khartoum. Come to think of it, she's probably disappointed at not having got the 40 lashes instead.

Ted said he wanted to put matters right. He pulled out four soft toys from a bag at his feet and before I could stop him he poured beer over each of their heads. The fluffy cat was christened Jesus, the dolphin Buddha, the lion Krishna and some kind of marsupial missing one eye was named Jah.

"There," said Ted. "Now we're even."

Great. All I have to do now is come up with a way of pacifying the hordes of angry Hindus, Christians and Rastafarians who will march on my house this weekend.

"Third item on the agenda …"

"Forget the agenda," I barked. "Let's just watch television."

The 46664 concert was on. Perfect. We could relax and move on to the second case of beer.

A Muizenberg longboarder was on stage. He had a hearing aid in each ear and was strumming a guitar. "I've surfed with that dude," I said to Ted. "Nonsense," he snapped. "That's Peter Gabriel."

I was shocked. "That's the ANC's chief whip in the city council?" Ted gave me the lazy eye. "The other Peter Gabriel."

So it was. Between songs, the camera caught him drinking a cup of tea. The band sounded as if it were made up of people blowing on dog whistles. At one point, Pete stormed off stage. He was clearly unhappy with the sound. Ted said with all that tea he probably just needed to wee.

Then he came back and played something that drove the crowd wild.

Well, wildish. Okay, people clapped. Some simply stood and swayed. I would also sway if I had to smoke that awful Joburg *majat*.

Next up was Johnny Clegg. Or a reasonable facsimile thereof. He hasn't aged in 30 years. Ted said it was obvious that the cryogenics lab had thawed him out for the gig. His bald patch was bigger but liquid nitrogen does that to your hair.

Johnny was joined on stage by a gang of half-naked hijackers from Soweto armed with sticks and wearing yellow bandanas and running shoes. They sang a rousing rendition of *Impi*. The darkies in the crowd went crazy. The whiteys checked that they still had their passports on them.

After the ad break Nelson Mandela made his way onto the stage. People wept openly. They whistled and cheered and stamped their feet. They screamed and shouted and had unprotected sex with strangers right there on the field, so great was their joy.

Then he read his entire speech without glasses. I will always resent Mandela for making me feel old and feeble.

Later an American prima diva in a shimmering mini-skirt stopped short of pole dancing on her microphone stand and said: "Let me see your hands, people." Fair enough. I would also want to make sure that the audience wasn't armed.

A rapper called Ludacris did a set in which I didn't catch a single word. In an interview afterwards, he said: "Y'all know I have my own foundation back home – the Ludacris Foundation." We also have one. It's called the Friends of Jacob Zuma. You don't get more ludacris than that.

Oops. There goes my career.

4 December 2007

Dear Jacob Zuma ...

I was reading the Bible on Sunday afternoon while taking a break from drinking heavily and abusing my wife when I came across a story involving your namesake. The similarities were startling.

Jacob was the third biblical patriarch. You are likely to be the third democratically elected president.

Neither of you went to school.

Jacob had twelve sons with several wives and concubines. You're not telling how many children you have, but I'm willing to bet that your strike rate would make the other Jacob look impotent.

Jacob was a gentle man and so, I believe, are you. That business with the machine gun is simply something you have to do to appease the bloodlust of the voters.

One day, Jacob's brother Esau returned from the field faint from a lack of food. Seeing an opportunity, Jacob offered to sell Esau some lentil soup in exchange for the birthright which belonged to Esau as the older brother.

One day, you returned from the office faint from a lack of money. Seeing an opportunity, you (allegedly) met with Alain Thetard who (allegedly) offered you R500 000 a year in exchange for protection against a probe into arms deal irregularities.

Jacob's last 17 years were spent in Egypt. Your last 17 years will be spent in the Union Buildings. Or maybe Westville Prison.

Jacob died at the age of 147. It might be best for all concerned if this is where the similarities between you and your biblical counterpart come to an end.

I must congratulate you on getting the ANC Women's League to come around to our way of thinking. You have done a magnificent job of getting so-called women's issues off the national agenda and back into the bedroom where they belong.

You, Jacob, are a man of the people. Do you mind if I call you Jacob? Of course you don't. You are such a grassroots type of fellow that you would probably object to the formality. Jake it is, then.

Jake for President. It has a nice ring to it. And why not? You have demonstrated that you possess what it takes to lead this fine country. For a start, most men are too afraid to have unprotected sex with an HIV-positive woman. But not you, Jake. You showed the world that real men don't discriminate. You showed us that real men treat all women equally. Your disease is my disease. Or, as the Spanish say, *su enfermedad es mi enfermedad*.

You, more than most, have a firm grasp of the axiom that powerful men have powerful libidos. And you know all too well that the one is meaningless unless used in conjunction with the other. Bill Clinton understood this. So did the Kennedys. Tony Blair, on the other hand, was clueless. This is why his foreign policy was generally a limp, flaccid affair.

You have paid your dues, Jake. You have paid your R12 a year to be a member of the ANC. And you are nothing if not an upstanding member. Sure, there were tough years in which R12 was not always easy to come by. But there were also the good times – times when you knew you could make a call without worrying about whether your telephone records were going to be subpoenaed by the Scorpions. A time when you could ring up an old buddy in Durban and say: "Hey old buddy, you wouldn't have a million or two to spare, would you?" And your old buddy would say: "Sure thing, Jake. But whatever you do, please don't use your position as deputy president to secure me an arms procurement contract."

Everyone has to borrow money at some point in their lives. I've borrowed money in the past. Perhaps not on the same scale as you, Jake. After all, R40 for a bottle of Klipdrift doesn't really compare.

But once again the gods of good fortune smiled on you. The man you borrowed from is spending 15 years in jail. I have to repay my debts or risk getting my legs broken.

Thabo is clearly jealous of your ability to sing and dance, often at the same time. You stand up in front of thousands of people and sing revolutionary songs about your machine gun. Thabo stands in the shower and makes up songs about his trip to the World Economic Forum.

You have a pretty Indian girl as an advisor. Thabo has Essop Pahad.

Your middle name is Gedleyihlekisa. Thabo's is Mvuyelwa, a full six letters shorter than yours.

You are 100% Zulu. Thabo is 100% Xhosa. I am 60% Dutch, 20% British, 5% Scottish and 15% street.

A last word of advice. Don't trust Winnie. She says she is trying to get you and Thabo to play nicely, but I am convinced that her eyes are on the prize. You can't trust a woman you're not sleeping with. If I were you, I would move quickly on this.

Run, Jake, run. 2009 is your year.

I'll be in a bar watching your inauguration with pride, even it does happen to be a bar near my new home in Wagga Wagga.

Yours truly,

Ben Trovato

(Shadow Minister of Information)

11 December 2007

Vultures Circle the Lame Duck of Limpopo

I don't trust Jacob Zuma for the simple reason that he is bald. Shaving your head is a deeply unnatural act for anyone but a cancer patient. And even then it had damn well better be a serious cancer, like brain or lung. None of this pancreatic nonsense. And you can forget about skin.

A head without hair is like a tortoise without a shell. It's not something we want to look at. Bald people polish their heads. How sick is that? Floors and cars are polished. Not heads. What kind of world would this be if we all started shining our heads? I can already see the signs outside hair salons. "This week only – wax and polish R35!"

Anyway. Forget the heads. I'm sick to death of the entire shameful business. Four thousand people get to decide who will become president? I have never heard such nonsense.

I was sorely tempted to drive up to Polokwane and give that mob of two-stepping, power-saluting megalomaniacs a piece of my mind. The first thing that stopped me was not having the faintest idea where Polokwane, or even Limpopo, was situated. The second was that I am white and would have stood out like a nudist at a Baptist convention.

Come to think of it, being white would probably not have been an issue at all. There's a very good chance that this is the first time in our country's history that so many darkies have gathered in one place without once blaming us blue-eyed devils for some or other human rights atrocity or malfunction of government.

On April 4, 2006, I announced my intention to run for president after which I wrote: "However, I may have to reconsider if the ANC does not desist from behaving like a rabid dog that has sunk its teeth into its own buttocks and is now preparing to begin the messy business of devouring itself."

Talk about premature premonitions. I never knew it then, but 20 months ago the ANC was merely licking its buttocks, softening them up for the real devouring which begins this week. Put on your headphones and turn up the volume, for the terrible sounds of slavering and crunching will surely drive you mad. The philosopher king should have let lying dogs sleep. Now the Kraken is well and truly awake. By firing Zuma, Mbeki gave the masses – that bottomless pit of doomed humanity – a figure to rally around. Everyone loves a singing, dancing martyr. And it doesn't matter that Zuma's not educated. By all appearances, he is concealing two brains beneath that giant burnished cranium.

When Thabo Mbeki returns to Pretoria it will be on a pair of webbed feet and crutches. Jacob Zuma will leave considerably taller than when he arrived. He will be followed by a feral pack of acolytes who will win our sympathy by once again demonstrating their pitiful inability to walk normally. These people belong in calipers, for God's sake, not government. And those brave souls who allowed their names to be attached to Thabo's List? What of them? Alas, not even Oscar Schindler could save their careers now. Uneasy lie the heads of Trevor, Joel, Terror, Manto and a host of others. The Night of the Long Knives is not far off.

Circling like a winged hyena, his glittering eyes hooded and fangs a-drool, the lappet-faced Mo Shaik keeps his scavengers in tight formation. Wait for my signal, boys. The duck is lame. Soon, he will stumble and fall. The water is pink. Wait until it turns red. Red like the colour of Comrade Blade's flag.

Where once the spirit of noble revolution prevailed, the spirit of Judas Iscariot now hangs heavy. Trusted delegates who once gave voice to the voiceless have mutated into Janus-faced quislings, their actions dictated by duplicitous promises of positions and power. Fifth columnists from the third force are buying their way into the hearts of the fourth estate with offers of free beer and finely-tuned snacks. Democracy is being gang-banged right before our eyes and there is nothing we can do to stop it.

All we can do is put our faith in the words of Bob Marley. "Jah will never give the power to a baldhead," he sang in *Redemption Song*.

But then his dreadlocks fell out and he died of cancer.

18 December 2007

STILL ON THE RUN

All Skinned Up
and Ready to Wed

Afew months ago, when Jacob Zuma was wriggling about all slippery-like in his rape trial, he was interviewed by a television reporter while participating in one of the many traditional blood-letting festivals which take place in that rotting mosquito-infested swamp they call KwaZulu-Natal.

He was half-naked and draped in leopard skins accessorised with springbok offcuts and a splash of lion. Speaking of his trial, he told the reporter: "People must not think I'm an animal." I laughed so much that I fell off the couch and had a small accident in my *broeks* and had to tell Brenda that I spilled beer in my lap.

Zuma was on television news on Saturday evening. He was getting married. Again. And again he was dressed as a leopard. Animal tails dangling from his waist like a terrible carnal kilt covered his legendary manhood. He looked magnificent. Like some sort of rare animorph hybrid. Which, of course, he is. But instead of falling under the Convention on International Trade in Endangered Species, *Jakobus Zumaensis* is protected by the ANC National Executive Committee.

This time, Zuma didn't speak to any reporters. He didn't have to, because something far funnier happened. He was crouched on the ground sniffing the air and intently studying the movements of his prey. His long tail swished flaccidly in the grass. He appeared disinterested in the weaker ones in the herd, the ones who were swaying their skinny little hips to the sound of an unseen drum. The one he had his eye on looked fit and healthy. Plenty of meat on those bones. She smiled coyly and waved her traditional umbrella in the air, setting up a tsunami of flesh that undulated up and down her well-fed body.

Zuma's eyes narrowed. His tail stiffened. In a flash he was up on his padded Reeboks, flailing his fighting stick and moving with an agility befitting the spirit of the animal that rested lightly on his shoulders.

Clearly a graduate of the Johnny Clegg School of Dancing, Zuma raised one leg and slammed it to the ground. Then he raised the other leg and slammed it to the ground. Then he lost his balance and fell over. Yes! That's the kind of president I want. The kind who can topple over, legs in the air, belly unfurling like a miniature mudslide, and still laugh like a madman.

I was disappointed to see that nobody had bothered to give him a machine gun as a wedding gift. Instead, our future leader had to make do with a stick. I've got a stick, for heaven's sake, and that's the reason people don't take me seriously. A man of Zuma's stature deserves more than a stick.

After eating a cow, his delicate bride made a start at shedding the extra 250kg by dancing with her new husband. Photographs in the anti-revolutionary Sunday press made it appear as if Zuma were about to use his stick on the future first lady.

Like most men who dabble in domestic abuse, my first thought was: "She must have done something wrong." I studied the pictures closely. In MaNtuli's mouth was one of those whistles that women carry in their handbags should they come across a rapist who would rather turn himself over to the police than listen to the sound of a cheap plastic whistle. At least, I think it was a whistle. For all I know, it was a marrow bone she was sucking on.

Then I saw it. Number One Wife had forgotten her top! She remembered to bring her shield and panga along, then pitched up wearing nothing but a skirt, a family of meerkats and her 44E bra. Zuma's relatively modest 44B chest wobbled in outrage. MaNtuli blew her whistle. Wobble. Whistle. Wobble. Whistle.

Outside the kraal, security men in sheepskin suits wrestled with a naked woman who kept shouting: "It takes 40 dumb animals to make a fur coat but only one to wear it! Get your hands off me! I'm Stella McCartney!"

The guards thought she was an escaped mental patient, which she is, and offered to give her a goat if she left quietly. Stella took the goat back to England and gave it a new home in a verdant pasture where, three hours later, it was crushed by Prince Charles's horse in the Royal Beaufort Hunt.

The little red fox laughed to see such sport. Then the German short-haired pointers found the fox and things weren't quite so funny any more.

Meanwhile, back at the wedding, MaNtuli was draping white beads around her beloved's neck as a symbol of her acceptance of him as her husband. *Beads?* Who does she think she's marrying – John Lennon? Beads are for hippies and queers.

Comrade Jacob, if you're reading this, make sure your next wife drapes a string of great white shark's teeth around your neck. On second thoughts, you probably want to avoid anything associated with the colour white. Get the locals to string you a necklace of black mamba teeth. It's the least they can do. After all, you've been stringing them along for years. Husbands throughout the Nkandla district must be sick and tired of hearing how wonderful you are.

"Zweli, why can't you be more like Jacob? He pays his children's school fees, he gives them pocket money, he flies his family to Cuba for holidays, he buys groceries and nice clothes. And he's always got petrol in his car."

Zweli shrugs his shoulders. He knows the old Zulu truism: Never fear when Schabir is near. He also knows what happens when a tick bird gets greedy and eats the cow.

Zweli takes another hit from the paint tin and smiles.

8 January 2008

Schnaai the Beloved Country

With the growing number of civil servants on what President Thabo Mbeki euphemistically calls "extended leave", we should stage some sort of event to recognise those who have excelled in the fields of fraud, corruption, racketeering and so on. It could be loosely based on the Oscars. Or the Golden Globes.

The idea came to me after it was reported that Jackie Selebi became the fourth senior government official to be given the chop by Mbeki.

Nominations for the 1st annual Golden Chop Awards are pouring in. Right now, Jackie Selebi is a hot favourite. Selebi will be remembered for his shockingly realistic portrayal of South African police chief Jackie Selebi in the highly acclaimed drama, *Schnaai the Beloved Country*.

Few among us will ever forget the sight of Selebi playing Commissioner Selebi, resplendent in his blue uniform, hand squarely on his heart, proudly reciting the SAPS Code of Conduct.

I would like to share with you, if I may, my favourite line from that memorable performance: "I undertake to work actively towards preventing any form of corruption and to bring the perpetrators thereof to justice."

Later, Selebi's character breaks away from the script and delivers one of the most poignant ad-libs ever heard: "Let us stand together. Let us take hands. This is our country – we will not allow any criminal to take control of it."

That was seven years ago, almost to the day, and Selebi's tour de force still leaves me gasping with disbelief. Mark my words. The smart money is on Selebi to win this year's Golden Chop for Best Actor.

Industry insiders report that Selebi is slated to appear later this year in the legal drama, *Gun with the Wind*. Co-starring Glenn Agliotti as The Dealer, Clint Nassif as The Canary and Brett Kebble as The Dead Guy, this complex production is likely to take months to wrap up.

Meanwhile, opening at the Pietermartizburg High Court in August is a production bound to capture the imagination of all South Africans. Billed as a musical thriller, *The French Connection* stars Jacob Zuma as The Defendant and Pierre Moynot as The Representative. The cast includes 218 minor characters, some of them experienced thespians in their own right.

Zuma plays a simple Zulu man, Jacob Zuma, who rises to high political office only to be led astray by The Indian, an unscrupulous businessman played by seasoned method actor Schabir Shaik. After Zuma is fired by The President, played by Thabo Mbeki in his first major role outside the depressing sitcom, *Plato's Republic*, he taps into an angry vein of popular discontent and stages a breathtaking comeback. But there's a terrible twist in this tale. A powerful group of vigilantes known as the Scorpions set out to destroy Zuma. Drawing on the tactical skills he acquired as a young herd boy, Zuma fights back with every weapon at his disposal.

More complicated than *The Matrix*, scarier than *Night of the Living Dead*, funnier than *Friends*, *The French Connection* will make you laugh, it will make you cry, it will make you wish you lived somewhere else.

Jackie Selebi and Jacob Zuma are two of the country's most popular entertainers. Let's take a look at some of the highlights of their colourful careers.

Before being hired to play the commissioner of police, Jackie Selebi was employed by the department of foreign affairs. It was as South Africa's ambassador to the United Nations in Geneva that he learnt the subtle art of diplomacy. That he moved in such refined circles and engaged with some of the world's sharpest minds was evident during a conversation he had with Sergeant Jeanette Mothiba hours before taking up his new post, when he walked into her charge office and demanded a vehicle and a driver.

The official Independent Complaints Directorate records reflect:

"It is alleged that the suspect (Selebi), during the course of a conversation at the Brooklyn Police Station charge office on 30 December 1999, called the complainant a 'bladie voken chimpanzee' and told her to 'shut-up her mouth'."

After investigating Mothiba's complaint, the ICD decided that the insult was not sufficiently serious to warrant prosecution. ICD executive director Neville Melville put his finger on it: "Unlike 'baboon', 'chimpanzee' is not commonly used as an insult. The definition in the *Collins Concise Dictionary and Thesaurus*, 'an intelligent small black ape of central W-Africa', does not really assist."

Then, a month later, Selebi was charged with intimidation after threatening to fire a sergeant who was involved in some kind of agricultural dispute with his uncle. In an interview at the time, Selebi said: "These allegations are too difficult to counter with the truth ..."

With such a watertight defence, it was little wonder that the case fell apart. Selebi's best lines:

"These hands are clean."

"I will never be arrested."

"As President of Interpol, I am ready to serve all members of the international police community in every area of crime-fighting."

"I am stepping down in the best interests of Interpol and out of respect for the global law enforcement community."

Unlike Selebi, Jacob Zuma is ... on second thoughts, I really can't be bothered. Let's cut straight to his best lines:

"I don't feel comfortable if I'm not honest."

"I start from basic Christian principles."

"Same sex marriage is a disgrace to the nation and to God."

"I am not in a race to become president of the country."

"It (a shower) ... would minimise the risk of contracting the disease."

"Bring me my machine gun."

15 January 2008

If it Breeds, it Leads

Finally. At last. The heathens from the hinterland have returned to their loathsome lairs. They have driven up prices, frightened the children and left our beaches awash in broken brandy bottles and rusty fish hooks. Slowly, our bars, beaches and mortuaries are once again filling up with locals. That's the good news.

The bad news is that September will see a whole new generation of mewling, puking brats being extricated from the loins of women whose idea of celebrating the birth of Jesus Christ was to drink heavily and fornicate relentlessly with complete strangers, none of whom were me.

Some women couldn't wait, apparently, and were dropping their drawers as early as March. On December 25th, the lead item on the evening news was a story about the first baby born on Christmas morning. A reporter spoke to the teenage mother in hushed, reverential tones as if she were interviewing the Virgin Mary and not Mary from Manenberg.

Instead of being interviewed, this wretched strumpet should have been dragged from the maternity ward by the Procreation Police and charged with wilfully copulating without due regard for the consequences. She should have been publicly flogged, not put on national television and lauded as some sort of evolutionary miracle worker.

There is nothing on the statute books that says I can't go to Bellville for the weekend and impregnate three hundred unhappily married women. Given the statistical probabilities governing twins and triplets and the fact that I have sperm with the tenacity of tiger fish, I could easily fertilise five hundred embryos by Monday.

But let me have three beers to calm down afterwards and the first road-block I hit, I'm treated like a common criminal and thrown into jail to have my bottom ravaged by a fighting general in the 28s.

I once tried to get a free dog from an animal shelter and a woman with the face of a diseased kidney said she would first have to inspect my property to see that it was suitable for the skanky *brak*. Obviously I couldn't have her poking around my house. It's barely fit for human habitation, thanks to Brenda's aversion to housework.

I showed her my ID to prove that I was 100% Caucasian and therefore genetically disinclined to harvest the hound's organs for muti or cross-breed it with a leopard so that I could win the Friday night fights in Mitchell's Plain, but she was having none of it. No inspection, no dog. I threatened to burn the place down but she bared her teeth and I left quickly.

So I can bring newborn babies into my house by the armful without any kind of inspection, but not a dog?

This country is full of people too stupid to even pass their driving test and yet they are entitled to create humans without passing a single test. What manner of dystopian hell are we living in?

Speaking of which, I've just had my parents staying with me for the last two weeks. They live in Durban and got married at 20 – my fault, apparently – and they have been together for 50 years. That's their fault. They arrived in a white-trash motor home with two senile Maltese poodles and a long line of cars that had been trying to overtake them since Umtata.

I never know where to take my parents when they come to Cape Town. They don't gamble or smoke dope, nor do they catch fish or ride bicycles. So I took them to Cape Point where the two oceans don't meet and the wind threatens to pick you up and dash you against knots of Waffen-SS veterans who approach the walk to the lighthouse with the same single-minded determination that Hitler approached Poland.

The reason I avoid Cape Point is the same reason I avoid Mount Everest. You get to the top, fall to your knees, cough up a little blood, shout at the sherpas, or in this case, the Germans, and look at the view.

Unless you're prepared to adopt the lotus position and chant *om mani padme hum* in the hope of achieving enlightenment, I have always found that scenery can generally be dealt with in 30 seconds or less, particularly if there's a chance that a rogue baboon could come along and rip out your throat just as God is about to reveal himself to you.

We also went camping in the Cedarberg. Since my parents insisted on bringing their geriatric poodles along, it had to be a dog-friendly campsite. As everyone knows, the only campsites that take dogs are those run by in-bred Afrikaners battling to save their farms from being repossessed by the bank, the government or the foetal alcohol victim with no front teeth who lives in the shack down by the dam.

We paid R50 per person and R50 per dog. For that, we got a patch of ground that looked like it had been cleared with napalm. The only way I could survive the 40 degree heat was to drink gallons of warm beer and strip down to the camouflage print shorts that Brenda gave me for Christmas.

I have steered clear of military gear ever since I sent out the wrong signal and lost us the war in Angola. What can I expect for my birthday – a pair of night vision goggles? A steel helmet?

The early onset of tick-bite fever, or what my mother called alcohol poisoning, forced us to flee after only one night. Back home the filthy southeaster raged for six days, causing the family to turn on one another like a pack of caged lab rats.

At one point, my mother shouted: "Where's that old bastard?"

"He's reading the paper in the garden," I answered.

She gave me the lazy eye and said: "I'm talking about the dog, not your father."

I need a holiday.

22 January 2008

No Power to the People – Amandla ... A-Where You?

There is nothing worse than a half-arsed disaster.

Nobody wants to hear about how you narrowly escaped being crushed in a deadly avalanche. They want to hear about how you were swept away by tons of ice and snow and survived for three weeks by eating your own fingers.

Nobody cares that you live in the only house still standing after a tornado has levelled your suburb. Nor do you want to suffer the indignity of almost drowning. There are few things more embarrassing than a lifeguard dragging you onto a beach full of curious holidaymakers who gather around taking side bets on whether or not you're going to make it, and then regaining consciousness to discover that the near-death experience has provoked a spontaneous event of a priapic nature in your Speedo. Not that this has ever happened to me, of course.

But if a killer backwash had to sweep me out into False Bay and I saw a lifeguard swimming towards me, I would quickly fill my lungs with water and sink my teeth into my arm in the hope that the blood would attract a great white shark rather than suffer the indignity of being laughed at by a pack of grizzled longboarders.

My point is this. Eskom and the government are doing a pathetic job of creating a full-blown disaster. I feel deeply ashamed when I think that the international community is watching. Sudan has civil war. Eritrea has famine. Mozambique has floods. Zimbabwe has Robert Mugabe. We have power failures. The lights are on. Then they're off. On. Off. On. Off. It's as if some gin-quaffing, horse-riding, SUV-driving mommy's little spoilt brat is somewhere out there, face covered in ice-cream, flicking a switch up and down just to annoy the hell out of us.

Ban Ki-moon: "Have you found that naughty kid, yet?"

Thabo Mbeki: "Still looking, Mr Secretary-General."

Maybe it's Jackie Selebi's kid. That would make sense because the newspapers have forgotten all about him and the treacherous band of brigands who are steering this country with the same single-minded determination that kamikaze pilots steered their planes in the Pacific.

Let us not be known as a country that does things in half measures. We are part of a continent renowned for spectacular crises and disasters. We have had the most magnificent genocides, the most fabulous conflicts. We don't walk around saying things like, "Shoo, that was quite a drought. Anyone got a spare glass of water?" Of course we don't. We suffer quietly in large numbers and then we die splendidly right there on CNN.

So please stop calling this power glitch a "crisis" and stop demanding solutions. It only encourages the craven dogs to issue yet another press release.

What I want is for Eskom, the government or Selebi's kid to cut the cable. Pull the plug. Sever the connection. Spank the monkey. Do whatever it takes to turn this bitter-sweet comedy into a genuine catastrophe. The entire country must be plunged into darkness without further delay.

Only then will the world sit up and take notice. Once the CIA satellites report that South Africa has disappeared off the face of the earth, other countries will start taking us seriously. They may even want to help. Or quite possibly celebrate.

Electricity is heavily overrated and has caused nothing but trouble ever since it was invented in Philadelphia by a village idiot called Benjamin Franklin who thought it a fine idea to fly a kite with a key tied to it in the middle of a violent thunderstorm. He was burnt to a crisp, naturally, and the government was quick to confiscate all the keys in the country but nobody could get into their houses so they rescinded the ban on keys and outlawed kites instead. It was decisive action like this that helped turn America into the superpower it is today.

Without electricity, the industrial revolution would never have happened and there would be no such thing as the five-day working week or Jeremy Cronin's poetry.

Also, my friend Ted Kaczynski wouldn't be serving four life terms in a Colorado jail.

We don't need electricity because it has been around for only 150 years and we are still programmed to survive without it.

I think a lot of you are afraid right now because you don't really understand electricity. I mean, you struggle with your tax return, right? In a nutshell, electricity is made up of atoms. Each atom has a centre consisting of protons, neutrons, a bottle store and a Spar. That's all you need to know.

Some people will try to tell you that electricity is a part of nature. Do not believe them. If this were true, wouldn't you just go into the bush and harvest sacks of the stuff? I know I would.

Static electricity was discovered as far back as 600BC when Thales of Miletus wrote about amber becoming charged by rubbing. If truth be told, I reckon it was Amber who filed charges against Thales. Stand in one place for too long in Athens and even today you will have an ancient Greek rubbing himself up against you in no time at all.

Meanwhile, people are complaining that the blackouts are preventing them from working. Imagine that. There are some in this country who stamp and curse when they are forced to leave the office and sit outside in the sun smoking and drinking like normal people. You should be ashamed of yourselves.

And while I'm at it, without electricity you ladies wouldn't have the vacuum cleaner, the dishwasher or the microwave oven. And yet you still treat us like vermin.

How dare you.

29 January 2008

Too Much Junkie Business

Heath Ledger's memorial service was held in Los Angeles on Sunday.

For those mental midgets who would rather read a book than *heat* magazine, Ledger is the man who single-handedly brought peace to the Middle East and then discovered a cure for cancer while ending the civil war in Sudan.

Reading the gushing obits, I got the impression that he must have died after heroically plunging into a piranha-infested river in an attempt to save a group of disabled children whose school bus had been swept off a low-lying bridge in a remote area inhabited by man-eating wolves.

On closer inspection, it turned out that Heath died after heroically plunging into a sack full of drugs. His greatest accomplishment was spending 90 minutes pretending to be a gay cowboy.

His memorial service was, by all accounts, not to be snorted at. Dozens of film stars turned up in the hope of meeting 'Fernando', Heath's closest and most trusted dealer. Heath's father, acting inexplicably out of character for an Australian, delivered a eulogy that was strangely lacking in the words: "That useless junkie bastard got what was coming to him." Instead, he spoke of the terrible accident that befell his son.

Yeah, I had a similar accident once and it got me six months suspended for three years.

Meanwhile, two US entertainment channels have folded under pressure from Heath's friends and agreed not to broadcast a video of the poor misunderstood thespian at a drug orgy saying: "I used to smoke five joints a day for 20 years." Cumulatively speaking, that's the equivalent of sitting down and smoking an elephant made entirely of marijuana. No wonder he needed sleeping pills.

How is it that unreconstructed dope fiends like the beaver-faced Amy

Crackhouse, the man-guzzling boozehound Lindsay Lohan and *Time* magazine's Mother of the Year, Britney Spears, can earn the respect of a nation by publicly confessing their predilection for high-octane alcohol and powerful narcotics?

And should they voluntarily agree to go into rehab, how is it that they are lauded as national heroes and portrayed by the media as role models for the youth of today?

Take this line from *The Daily Telegraph*: "Ledger's former school, Guildford Grammar School, has offered to hold a memorial for Perth's homegrown movie star."

That's right, kids. Bring your homegrown down to the school hall and we'll all gather round to suck on a giant hubbly-bubbly and give Perth's favourite stoner the kinda sendoff he woulda wanted.

If I had to tell you that on Sunday night I had trouble finding my keyboard beneath a mountain of cocaine and heroin, none of you would write to the paper blaming the editor for putting me under the inhuman strain of having to deliver a column week after week. All that would happen is that the police would raid my home, steal my stash and force me to pay protection money for the rest of my life.

Ted has just walked through my door empty-handed. I pretended not to know him and was about to press the panic button when he whistled and stood back. An Irish Wolfhound came bounding into the room wearing saddlebags with a six-pack of Tafels lashed to each of its heaving flanks.

We sat down and the dog brought us a beer each. "Good dog," I said. "The best," said Ted.

I told Ted that *People* magazine was reporting that Britney hadn't slept since Thursday and that the national guard had blocked off the road and cordoned off the airspace so that the paramedics from the funny farm could come for her with minimal interference from the running dogs of the yellow press.

"That's more than JFK got," said Ted, signalling the dog to bring him another.

I told Ted that America had set a new standard for understanding and forgiveness and that there was never a better time to take drugs anywhere in the world, with the possible exception of Ventersdorp.

The dog seemed to understand. He trotted over to Ted and presented his rear, much like a pedigree would present at Crufts. Unlike a judge at Crufts, Ted reached in and withdrew a small plastic bank bag.

"Is that what I think it is?" I said.

"Yes," said Ted. "It's the cell number of the Eskom guy. The one who decides who gets shut down and who doesn't."

I tried to grab it from him because this kind of information is worth millions, but the dog intervened on the basis of some sort of dumb allegiance to its master. In the ensuing melee, the number was lost. I accused the dog of having swallowed it and was preparing for a rudimentary disembowelment when the hound outsmarted me with an intelligence belying his Celtic heritage and bounded off towards the freeway, thereby restoring my faith in his Celtic heritage.

Ted told me to forget the dog and instead focus my psychic energy on swinging Super Tuesday Barack Obama's way. I thought he was speaking in tongues and slapped him hard against the side of his so-called head. He apologised and then, when my back was turned, he headbitted me, which is the same as being headbutted except the aggressor sinks his teeth into your head.

Ted relinquished his grip when I shouted out Hillary Clinton's name. He fell back like a wounded animal. "Are you telling me that you would rather have a white woman than a black man rule the free world?"

"Yes!" I shouted, wiping the blood from my eyes. "I have always felt safer in the hands of a white woman than a black man."

Ted was incensed. He said there would be nuclear war with the first irrational mood swing and Africa would go to hell in a handbasket while she spent all her time colour-coding the Oval Office.

Then he spat on the ground three times and left.

5 February 2008

The Terrible Confessions
of a Teenage Loller

I pulled up at the traffic lights on Sunday and spotted a beggar stringing his way through the cars ahead of me. I quickly wound up my window and recited the Driver's Prayer: "The Lord is my shepherd, I shall not want this raggedy misfit to come unto me; he maketh me lie down in my seat so he cannot see me; even though I drive through the valley of the shadow of death (Fish Hoek), I will fear no evil as long as the robots turn green before he reacheth me."

Unfortunately the robots weren't working. Nor was St Christopher, the patron saint of travellers. Does God and his peeps still take Sundays off? And why do the orthodox churches depict St Christopher with the head of a dog? Everyone knows that dogs make notoriously bad drivers. Their snouts give them a blind spot bigger than a bus, and their steering sucks.

The beggar reached my window and, like a boil that sets up home on one's bottom, refused to go away. Then he transgressed one of those invisible boundaries that separate the rich from the poor, or, in my case, the poor from the indigent. He knocked on the window. I struggled to release myself from my seat belt so that I might leap from my vehicle and beat him around the head until he begged for mercy. It was then that I noticed he was no ordinary beggar. This one was white.

We don't see many poor white people on the streets of Cape Town, which is a damn good thing because this would not look good in the eyes of Fifa. Having unruly packs of darkies clogging up the intersections is bad enough, but toss in a few white faces and Sepp Blatter would take the World Cup away from us faster than you can say "elitist Swiss bastard".

I don't have much sympathy for a white beggar because if he really wanted a job, all he would have to do is claim to be a nuclear engineer and Eskom would hire him in a flash. A blinding, white flash. Followed by high-speed thermal winds that would suck your eyeballs out and strip the flesh from your body.

I was about to give this fallen specimen of a once proud master race Eskom's postal address when he gave me the lazy eye and said, "I don't like begging but it's better than stealing, right?" I was appalled by his crude interpretation of passive-aggressive behaviour and tossed a R5 coin over his shoulder. He threw himself athletically beneath the wheels of a passing cattle truck and I drove away.

Later my mother called and said, "I've got your report here." I quickly cut the connection to buy time to think up an excuse but she called right back and said she had been going through piles of junk that constitute a record of my childhood and had come across my old school reports.

Here's what my teacher said at mid-term in my first year: "An intelligent pupil but unfortunately doesn't always give of his best."

Give of my best? I was six years old, for God's sake. Not weeing in my shorts in the middle of finger-painting was a remarkable achievement.

Things barely improved by primary school. "A great pity that such an intelligent child is so disinterested in his work. He should adopt a more serious attitude to his lessons." The principal, clearly in on the conspiracy to ruin my life, added: "A capable pupil but seldom exerts himself. Enjoys reading."

So why didn't they just give me a pile of books and a mattress at the back of the class? Everyone would have been happy, especially my mother, who, despite the warning signs, insisted on taking me to the library three times a week. That's where the rot set in.

Standard 3: "Arithmetic is his weakest subject and he must be watched." Nobody ever rescinded the order and I can feel their eyes on me right now.

Mid-term Std 5: "Has not yet learned self-discipline. Fidgety, talkative and inattentive. Art – not interested. Handwriting – weak. Neatness – slapdash."

End of year Std 5: "A boy with lots of ability who is too lazy and too lacking in interest to make use of it. Good at English with a wide general knowledge. Careless in arithmetic. Always lolling in class, rarely sits up properly and generally shows a lack of interest."

Yeah, that's my dark secret. I was a pubescent loller.

Standard 7 brought a litany of abuse: "General science: Could do better. Maths: Adopts a negative attitude. History: A very poor result. Geography: Extremely weak. Geometrical drawing: More effort required. Afrikaans: *Moet harder werk*."

The hanging judges of standards 8 and 9 sent me home with reports guaranteed to get me a whipping.

"His disastrous maths and history marks indicate all too clearly a grave lack of effort, a situation which must at all costs be remedied. History is a learning subject and 17% speaks for itself."

As for my matric results, well, they earned me a ticket to the army where I cost us the war in Angola.

Sorry about that.

12 February 2008

One Squirrel Monkey on a Stick and Two Sauteéd Swans, Please

Brenda was reading the newspaper when she spontaneously erupted with laughter. I didn't know it was laughter at the time. It's a rare sound in these parts. I thought she was erupting with something dark and potentially dangerous so I hit the floor and rolled beneath the lounge table where I curled up in the foetal position and lay there like the craven coward that I am.

When I realised I was in no immediate danger, I crawled out pretending that I had dropped something valuable. Brenda pointed out that I didn't own anything of value, forcing me to go on the offensive. I demanded to know what all this frivolity was about.

She said she had come across a story about a suicide bombing in Afghanistan that killed 80 people. I fell to my knees, tears streaming down my cheeks. Brenda gave me the lazy eye.

"You haven't heard the really funny part yet," she said. "The bomber blew himself up at a dog-fighting competition."

"What?" I shouted, on my feet in an instant. "Dog fighting is an ancient and honourable sport enjoyed by kings and commoners alike. It is a cultural tradition no different to gay-bashing or Jew-baiting."

Brenda would have none of it. She is a big fan of dogs and believes that anyone who goes to dog fights deserves to get blown up. This is why Hillary Clinton must not become the next American president. Women act according to their emotions. For all we know, Hillary still nurses a poisonous well of bitterness towards men who cheat on their wives and that, once she is in the White House, she will issue a decree stating that male adulterers shall be stoned to death. By the time her hunger for revenge has been sated there will be seven men left in America, none of whom will be her husband.

It could be worse. Barack Obama might get elected and order the immediate incarceration of all white people. The boy has the look of the Mau Mau about him, I tell you. Come to think of it, the US could do with a little Kenya-style democracy.

As we speak, America is in the throes of a sub-prime mortgage crisis. I don't understand what this means, either. Where I come from we use blunt machetes to achieve a greater understanding of things. There is nothing like a little hacking and bludgeoning to shed light on a complex situation, and the best way to end this incomprehensible crisis is for Washington to wake up to the sight of several hundred half-naked black men wearing reflecting sunglasses and red bandannas screaming in Swahili and manning swivel-mounted machine guns welded to the back of stolen stripped-down bakkies.

I switched on CNN to calm down and saw a headline that read: "Bush in Africa." Well, duh. There would be, wouldn't there? These *yanquis* really need to get out more. What next? Ice in Antarctica? Rivers in Brazil? Desert in Australia?

It turned out that with the finish line in sight, the Supreme Commander has decided to be extra nice to the savages. Something to do with needing a legacy, apparently.

The doe-eyed anchor informed me that Bush is on a six-day, five-nation tour of Africa. That's a tour? Sometimes it takes me six days just to find shoes.

Tanzanian President Jakaya Kikwete called Bush a good friend of Africa. Bush scratched his chin and the CIA sniper shrugged and lowered his rifle.

The leader of the free world told the leader of the flea world that he was putting up $700-million towards the fight against Aids. That's rich, considering that the disease was started by two men in tight shorts and moustaches having hot green monkey sex in a San Francisco bathhouse.

I went to fetch a beer from the fridge and when I came back Bush had been replaced by something even more disturbing.

"Right now, Russia is angry," said the anchor. I dropped my beer and shouted at Brenda to run for the underground bunker. She shouted that I hadn't built it yet. We stood there shouting at each other as couples do when they have only a few minutes left before the nuclear warheads land.

I was relieved to discover that Russia is not angry with everyone, but only Kosovo, a country the shape of a bloodstain and the size of Benoni. It was part of Serbia until about 8.15pm on Sunday evening when the Albanian moonshine kicked in and a rowdy mob of gypsies dressed as parliamentarians fired their guns into the air and declared Kosovo a country.

The Serbs are outraged. Ten years ago they gave the Albanians a damn good kicking and told them to behave. And now this. You don't want to upset the Serbs. They are like white Hutus.

Russian President Vladimir Whatshisface said that independence without UN approval would encourage secessionist breakaways around the world.

This is the moment I have been waiting for. I hereby declare myself Life President of the Republic of Hout Bay. I also hereby appropriate Lichtenstein Castle as the seat of my government and take great pleasure in announcing that the residents of Imizamo Yethu will make up my Cabinet of 15 000 ministers.

The riding of horses is outlawed and the World of Birds will be converted into an exotic restaurant for the starving masses, offering affordable weekly specials such as Baked Buzzard, Tawny Tandoori Owl, Sautéed Swan, Flambéed Flamingo, Squirrel Monkey on a Stick and, on Sundays, Boiled Pot-Bellied Property Developer.

Our flag will feature a perlemoen and crossed screwdrivers and our anthem will be whatever you feel like singing when drunk. Our national animal will be the brown rat and our national flower, the *cannabis sativa*. Our coat of arms will be just that – coats fitted with holsters; one gun per coat.

Applications for citizenship are now open.

19 February 2008

Eat Like a T-Rex, Drink Like a Bastard

It looks like a scene from *Attack of the 50 Foot Woman*. Thousands of cars abandoned halfway up pavements, on yellow lines, in the middle of the road. No sign of the terrified drivers. And that's just the parking lot. Inside the airport, things are far worse.

My airline has one person behind the desk and 100 people in front of it. Most of them seem to be children suffering from some sort of mental illness that make them behave like hyperactive howler monkeys.

I ask for the bulkhead seat and she looks at me as if to say: "You dumb brute, that seat was booked five years ago."

There are two hours to kill before boarding. If this were Miami, those two hours would be spent getting a full body cavity search from a couple of Cuban reactionaries. But nobody wants to blow up my airline. Well, nobody apart from the ordinary folk who use it on a regular basis.

So I find the bar and order a beer. After every beer I move to a different seat so that whoever is monitoring the security cameras will think I am a new arrival having his first drink.

I do this because once upon a time there were three not very wise men who prevented me from catching my flight. They said I was a potential danger to the crew, the passengers and quite possibly myself. I had spent almost 12 hours waiting at Johannesburg International Airport for a flight to Atlanta and only fell off my stool at the very end. The more I pointed out that aircraft seats were equipped with belts to prevent this very thing from happening, the more they seemed to not want me to fly.

But this is now. Comes time for checking in and I brace myself for the alarms. I am one of those people who trigger metal detectors irrespective of what I'm wearing or what's in my pockets. It's like a default setting.

Sure, I have a steel pin in my ankle but let's face it, how many South Africans don't have a piece of metal imbedded in them these days?

By the time I make it to seat 749b, there is just enough room in the overhead locker to squeeze in a pack of playing cards. I am wedged between two people who look like they were personally responsible for causing the famine in Sudan.

It's not long before a cabin attendant with big white teeth and small black moustache sashays up to me. He stands in the aisle, eyebrow raised, lips pursed, one hand on his hip. Wagging a slender finger at me he quickly bends down. I scream and cover my crotch. In one fluid movement he whisks my hand luggage away to another part of the plane where the rest of the cabin crew can rifle through it at their leisure.

I turn to the lardaceous blimp next to me and ask her to promise that if I lose consciousness she will make sure that Freddie Mercury over there doesn't give me the kiss of life. Big mistake. The human zeppelin interprets this as a sign that I want to chat and babbles incessantly from takeoff to landing.

If you had to turn to the person behind you in a bank queue and ask where they were from and what they planned on doing once they left the bank, they would think you were an escaped lunatic. Why is it any different on an aircraft?

Later the pilot saunters down the aisle in his shiny black shoes, dripping gold braid and oozing charm all over the young girls travelling alone. For airborne taxi drivers who work in the public transport sector, pilots are delusional to a disturbing degree.

Fortunately not all aeroplane drivers suffer from the Shuttleworth-God complex. There are those who guzzle double brandies until sunrise and then repeatedly stall the plane on the runway, getting themselves banished to the domestic redeye routes where everyone is drunk and nobody really cares if they live or die.

The meal arrives and I have to eat it with little arms, like a Tyrannosaurus Rex. There is not enough food to make even a bulimic throw up so I order more beer and focus on directing waves of hate at the young mother two rows in front of me.

Women with babies should be banned from flying, if not placed under house arrest. I don't pay filthy amounts of money to have a colicky blob destroy my central nervous system by screaming from one airport to the next. And I don't care if its poor little ears hurt. I also get pressure in the head but you don't hear me carrying on like that.

I am not usually prone to air rage because I know which drugs to take to prevent it, so I lie back, put my headphones on upside down and try to cover myself with a blanket made for a circus midget. That's when the feral pack rat in front of me hits his recline button crushing my kneecaps and causing my beer to fall into my lap. Quick, more drugs. Ah, that's better.

The last stop on Dante's infernal itinerary is reached when the plane lands. I am the last person to board the bus to the terminal. They call it a terminal because that is where it all ends. In tears, usually.

I am the last person left standing there. Then one of my suitcases makes a fashionably late appearance and the carousel shudders to a halt. There is no sign of the second bag.

The Airports Company of South Africa needs to contract out its ground services to the Saudi Arabians because Roman Dutch law is clearly not working.

It's time to start chopping off hands.

26 February 2008

And the Oscar for Best Worker in a Domestic Drama Goes to …

Brenda went out early on Saturday morning and came home with a young black woman. This was a fantastic turn of events. "Where did you get her? What's her name? How much did she cost?" I babbled feverishly.

Apparently there was a special on at the taxi rank. Some sort of mid-summer sale. Two for the price of one. I told Brenda to go right back and fetch the free one but she said one was more than enough.

I went over to get a closer look. Teeth good. Muscles strong. Five fingers per hand. She lowered her head and I rapped sharply on her skull three or four times. No echo at all. Always a good sign.

"*Cuál es su nombre?*" I asked her. I know more Spanish than Zulu or Xhosa even though I have never even met a Spanish-speaking person. I reckoned that since they are all foreign languages, she would know what I was saying. Apparently not. She simply stood there and stared at an old bloodstain on the wall.

I turned to Brenda. "There seems to be something wrong with this one. I think you should take her back. Did you get a receipt?" Speaking slowly and deliberately, I said: "Who are you?" She stared at the floor and said in a small voice: "EC790548."

"Not your serial number!" I shouted. "Your name. *Il vostro nome. Jou naam.*" This time she seemed to understand. She put her hand out and said something unpronounceable in an Eastern Cape kind of way.

"Kwaai Lappies," I said, pretending to shake her hand. "That's a lovely name."

Brenda rolled her lazy eye, informed the tall, dark stranger that the bedrooms were upstairs and left for work without so much as offering to make me breakfast.

Once I was certain that Brenda had driven off, I washed my teeth, brushed my face and went into the master's bedroom. Kwaai Lappies was on her hands and knees. Another good sign.

I had my kit off in a flash. Flexing my one functioning bicep, thrusting my chest out and sucking my stomach in, I struck a pose that is irresistible to women. I can only hold this position for around seven seconds and by the time Kwaai Lappies realised I was in the room, I had deflated considerably.

She scooped up my trousers and shirt, stuffed them inside a grubby pillow slip and walked out pretending that she wasn't at all impressed with my physique. After recovering from the rejection, I put on a fresh outfit and began tracking Kwaai Lappies. I picked up her scent in the kitchen and eventually found her doing the laundry in a room that I never even knew existed.

For a married man there is nothing more exciting than seeing someone else do the housework. Brenda stopped doing it a long time ago. Apparently something to do with me inadvertently making a remark about it being women's work.

This was a historic occasion and needed documenting, if only to prove to Ted that I hadn't cracked and cleaned up the place myself.

I fetched my video camera and began following Kwaai Lappies wherever she went. It wasn't easy because she was a fast mover, but I was overjoyed to find that she was a natural and needed very little direction whatsoever.

She moved effortlessly from washing the crusty dishes to scrubbing the squalid floors to scooping up the festering cat vomit. I got it all in one seamless tracking shot. Capturing a low angle of Kwaai Lappies scouring the toilet bowl while bathed in natural light was a shot that most cinematographers can only dream of.

Although her sense of timing and grasp of character was generally excellent, the bathroom scene took several takes because there was so much dirt and grime ringing the tub that it looked like the high water mark in Durban harbour.

At lunchtime I took a well-deserved break from filming. Salmon roses and a bottle of Pongracz for the crew; bread and tea for the cast. Well, it would have been if Brenda had remembered to buy bread and tea. I was on a tight budget and Kwaai Lappies didn't seem to be the complaining type.

After lunch I lay on the couch and shot a lot more footage of Kwaai Lappies transforming my filthy home into something you might expect to see on *Top Billing*.

Around sunset I called it a wrap and told the budding starlet that she had been magnificent. She asked for a lift to the taxi rank, forcing me to tell a little white lie about there being no petrol in my car.

"The exercise will be good for you, Kwaai Lappies," I said, sinking back into my imitation leather couch.

I was pleased with the day's work. Kwaai Lappies had been successfully integrated into my home and I had discovered a new career. The French have a name for my style of filming. They call it "*cinéma vérité*". Cinema of truth.

When Brenda came home I slipped a Rohypnol into her gin and tonic, pretended to take an interest in her day, then helped her into a chair and played her the video.

Instead of complimenting me on my stylised *mise-en-scène*, she called me a stinking racist pig and threatened to turn me over to the Human Rights Commission.

"Why don't you move to the Free State and join the Rambo nation?" she barked, scaring the cat and setting off every dog in the neighbourhood.

"The *Free* State?" I laughed so hard that I had a little accident in my *broeks*. Brenda was appalled.

"Don't worry," I said. "Kwaai Lappies will take care of it."

4 March 2008

This is Simon's Town – Not Bloody Poland

The recent police attack on bars in Stellenbosch has left me horrified. I am still struggling to understand how the cops can swoop on three student drinking holes and only find two joints and a pill. What kind of students are we dealing with here? If these had been bars frequented by UCT undergraduates, the police would have needed a fleet of garbage trucks to remove the drugs.

Were these Stellenbosch kids even drinking? I doubt it. If they had been, surely they would have fought back instead of cowering and whimpering like a litter of freshly whipped puppies. Even the bouncers were curled up beneath the pool tables.

I have seen the video footage and, to be frank, I feel ashamed to call myself a South African. Have we become a nation of craven curs? Where was that indomitable Afrikaner spirit that kept 40 million darkies in their place for all those years?

It's a damn good thing that Stellenbosch is no longer a breeding ground for the country's leaders. Imagine that lot in power. The entire Cabinet would hit the deck at the first sign of trouble. Malawi would be able to invade us.

A policeman is not, in principle, permitted to shoot you in the face simply because you refuse to listen to him. But if you are a student in a bar at 2am and you're not drunk and have no drugs on you, I would say that an officer would be within his rights to shoot you in the leg at the very least.

Given that police are coming into our bars and causing mayhem, we need to go out there and meet them on their own turf. We must not sit back and wait for them to come to us. If you are angry about something or feeling sexually frustrated, go to your nearest police station and ask to speak to the most senior officer there. Once he is within striking distance, slap him hard. If you have pepper spray, use it. You do not have to provide a reason for your actions.

If he insists that you explain yourself, tell him you have reason to believe that there are weapons and drugs on the premises. He will blush furiously and encourage you to leave quietly because he knows you are right and there is nothing he can do about it.

Right now I have more pressing matters to attend to. There is a crisis of terrible proportions unfolding on the Cape peninsula and nobody is doing a damn thing about it. Let me be blunt. Germany has invaded Simon's Town.

Ted and I discovered this on Thursday night when we tried to get a drink at the Seaforth Hotel. The usually empty verandah was jammed with burly, cropped-haired brutes braying and barking in a harsh guttural tongue. A fast-moving pack of Aryans beat us to the last free table.

"This isn't Poland, you *herrenvolk* bastards," shouted Ted. I dragged him back to the parking lot and explained that the German navy had been invited to come over and play with our navy for a bit.

Hungry for revenge, we returned to Simon's Town on Saturday with the aim of sinking one of their frigates. Ted carried a concealed hammer and I lashed a small screwdriver to my thigh. What we hadn't bargained on was getting caught in the middle of the South African Navy Festival.

We approached the gates to the base expecting to be strip-searched. Instead, a surly knave thrust a programme into my hands. It warned us not to bring any weapons into the area. From where I stood, I could see two 35mm twin-barreled guns, four 20mm Oerlikon cannons and eight Exocet surface-to-surface missiles. Damned if I was going to surrender my screwdriver.

Some festival it was. Boerewors rolls and battleships. A bagpipe band and a couple of tatty submarines up on bricks. Lots of screaming children. Millions of blowflies swarming around the ThyssenKrupp signs.

But we weren't there to have fun. We were there to deal a crippling blow to the German navy. Ted asked a black man in a waiter's uniform to bring us two cold beers but he claimed to be some sort of high-ranking officer on the SAS Isandlwana and threatened to report us to the military police.

We came across dozens of people queuing to get on board the SAS

Amatola and tried in vain to get them to protest. "Don't you understand," I shouted. "You helped to pay for this monstrosity. Wouldn't you rather the government had bought you a house?"

Apparently not. All they wanted to do was see the guns up close. They deserve to be poor.

Eventually we found it. A humourless gray hulk. The *Einsatzgruppenversorger*. "Catchy name," said Ted. At the foot of the gangplank was a mat. The progeny of one of Josef Mengele's less successful experiments told us to wipe our feet before boarding. I expect the ship would have to be quarantined if a speck of African dirt found its way on board.

There were too many slack-jawed gawkers around for us to scuttle the ship and in the end I had to settle for scraping my car key along one of the metal doors.

We hurried off to catch an event billed as Dry Dock Flooding but it turned out to be nothing more than water pouring into a big hole with none of the screaming and drowning that usually accompanies a good flooding.

After that I wanted to see something called Tug Ballet but Ted said that if the Germans were involved it was probably a euphemism for synchronised masturbation.

Thoroughly miserable, we went back to the main street and holed up in a bar called The Nelson where we were joined by two ladies with no front teeth, three young girls with five toy handguns between them and a two-year-old who said, "fucking cops" when she heard a police siren outside.

18 March 2008

Gladly, the Cross-Eyed Bear

Ted dropped in unexpectedly on Easter Sunday. He was in a shocking condition.

He said it all started on Good Friday when Mary forced him to watch SABC 1. "Grounds for divorce," I said, pouring him a shot of cheap whiskey. "You should move quickly on this."

Ted shook his head glumly. "It gets worse," he said, dribbling ethanol down his shirt. It turns out that Mary made him sit through a gospel music extravaganza called *Joyous Celebration*. "Cruel and inhuman punishment," I said. "Take her for everything she's got."

But that wasn't the end of it. After an hour of what Ted described as "a living hell on earth", Mary went to bed leaving him sitting there paralysed from the neck up. Before he could regain the full use of his brain, the next programme came on. It was *Kill Bill Vol. 1*, the most gratuitously violent film ever made.

Between gulping whiskey and crying uncontrollably, he said he soon began noticing disturbing similarities between Quentin Tarantino's gorefest and the story of Jesus.

He said that Uma Thurman was obviously the Virgin Mary. After Mary fell in with a bad crowd of right-wing Christian soldiers called the Deadly Viper Assassination Squad, she mysteriously fell pregnant after spending the night with David Carradine who was made up to look like Joseph. Coming to her senses, she fled to Bethlehem where she hooked up with a wandering minstrel and agreed to marry him but on her wedding day a jealous Joseph pitched up with a posse of three wise guys and shot her in the head.

Mary woke up from a coma five years later and went off to the Gaza Strip where she killed a bunch of Palestinians out of revenge and then discovered that her baby, Jesus, was still alive and then the movie ended.

Ted was clearly in a bad way. He was shaking so much that I had to hold him down and pour the whiskey into his mouth and rub his throat so that he could swallow without choking.

Then he bit me and screamed, "Jesus is out there somewhere. We have to find her!"

There was only one way to snap him out of his confusion. We had to stage our own Passion Play. This was, after all, the one day of the year on which people could get away with anything as long as it was done in the name of God.

"Listen to me," I said, biting Ted on the back of his head. "You need to get your perspective back. The first thing we need is a cross."

We trawled the house and came up with enough bits of wood to cobble together a decent-sized cross. Ted seemed disappointed. "Mel Gibson's cross was much bigger."

"So was his budget," I said. "Now lie down so that I can nail you to it."

Much like in biblical times, this simple instruction sparked a terrible argument. I explained to Ted that the human hand had tiny soft bones in it that provided no hindrance to a steel nail.

"Besides, people are doing this right now in the Philippines and they don't feel a thing."

Ted looked skeptical. "That's because they have drugs." Fine, I said. Let's have some drugs. So we did. Everything seemed much clearer after that.

Ted kept moving his feet and I kept missing the nail so he agreed to be tied to the cross with two pairs of fur-lined handcuffs that have been in storage since my honeymoon.

He insisted that I flagellate myself so I went off and dug out the whip that has also been in storage since my honeymoon. I had to use it on Ted several times to encourage him to stand up and carry the cross like a real man.

"Now I have to betray you," said Ted. "Call me Judas." Without warning he lashed his mad, foam-flecked lips to mine. "Open your eyes," he whispered. "You're not meant to be enjoying this."

I gave us both a quick flagellation to cleanse us of the unholy spectre of the love that dare not speak its name. "Yea, now we shall visit the 14 Stations of the Cross," I said, "starting at Fish Hoek station."

It took us a while to get there because people kept asking if we were in the Two Oceans Marathon because if we were we should know that it ended last Saturday. I cursed them in rudimentary Aramaic and whipped them soundly.

Exhausted, we stopped at a church and pounded on the door until a priest opened it. He wouldn't let us in. "We're not open till six," he said.

"We have come a long way," said Ted.

"Give us the body of Christ," I said.

"I don't have it," said the priest.

Instead, he gave us a bottle of wine and half a loaf of bread and told us to bugger off.

By the time we reached the station I had flagellated the shirt clean off my back and Ted was on his hands and knees. So far so good.

"Two tickets to Golgotha, please," I said.

"You can't go to Gugulethu from here," said the heathen behind the counter.

A man in a yellow bib gave us the lazy eye. "You can't bring that thing on the train."

"Back off, Barabus," I said, threatening him with my whip.

We went outside and sat on a bench. "Now what?" said Ted, shifting his cross irritably.

"Dunno," I said. "Can't remember how it ends."

I uncuffed Ted and we sold the cross to a Congolese car guard and went across the road for a beer.

25 March 2008

An Open Letter to Supreme Commander Robert McBride

Dear Robert,
Do you mind if I call you Robert? Obergruppenführer McBride sounds so formal. Besides, I feel like I already know you since we both have ties to Durban. I used to drink in the bars along the beachfront and you used to blow them up. Had I not been in a state of penury on the evening of June 14, 1986, I may well have been without my legs today.

On the other hand, a physical disability these days goes a long way towards getting one into some or other company's quota of cripples, even if one happens to be the colour that dare not speak its name. Brenda has offered to lop off a limb or two but, to be honest, I don't really want a job that badly.

Glancing over your criminal record, I was surprised to learn that Umkhonto we Sizwe managed to recruit anyone at all in Durban. What with the stifling humidity and powerful marijuana, it was only after I grew up and moved to the west coast that I realised apartheid even existed.

What was worse for you? Being on death row or being married to a lawyer? I always had my doubts about that Paula. Since you're divorced, you probably discovered that women who fall in love with convicted killers aren't altogether right in the head.

After your unfortunate car accident in December 2006, your second wife, Nina, told the media you were "very lucky to be alive". Wives often behave irrationally when their husbands return from year-end functions, but at least she stopped short of actually killing you. If it had been my Brenda, you would have got more than just snapped ribs and a head wound.

About that accident. Don't let it get to you. Anything can happen when you suffer from a medical condition such as ours. Just the other evening I went out with a friend and we ended up in a parking lot sharing a bottle of his diabetes medication. By the time the sun came up my blood sugar levels were so high that I had to drive home with one eye shut and my head out of the window.

Everyone rolls their car at least once in their lives and, quite frankly, I'm surprised you haven't told the court about how you had to swerve violently to miss the child who ran out into the road after his soccer ball. That damn child is everywhere. One time he even caused me to veer into a crash barrier and rip open the side of my mother's car. And that was at 3am. I blame the parents.

Thank God some of your more trusted Metro police officers arrived at the scene of your mishap and threatened to shoot those interfering whiteys if they called the South African Police. I've been at braais where I have come close to gunning down family members who have tried the same thing. When the party gets going, the last thing you need is the real cops barging in and spoiling all the fun.

A word of advice. Don't lose control of your court case. Witnesses are saying you are a man to be feared. Keep it that way. If you hear testimony that is not to your liking, walk swiftly to the stand and dose the witness with a prolonged burst of pepper spray. If the magistrate was trained in exile, this will count in your favour.

You have also been accused of running your department like the Mafia. This is not a negative thing. The Mafia is one of the most successful organisations in history and after the trial I expect you will be declared life president of the Black Management Forum. On the down side, this would probably mean having to trade your 9mm pistol for a laptop.

By all accounts you run a tight ship up there in the hinterland. Only three officers out of several hundred at your year-end function were drunk enough to have imagined that you polished off several bottles of whisky in the space of an hour or so. They are a disgrace to the force and should be summarily fired at.

Compared to your guys, ours are a bunch of big girls. Just the other day, a dog had a spontaneous bowel movement right there on the main road in Sea Point and a vigilant member of the Metro police encouraged its owner to clean it up by ramming her head into a wall. What good is that? Everyone knows the use of minimum force does nothing to engender respect for the law.

If this crime had been committed in Johannesburg, your lads would have broken both her arms, planted heroin in her pockets and extorted money from her for years to come. That's how the law should be enforced. There's too much pussy-footing around in Cape Town.

By the way, are you aware of the striking coincidence that you, the chief of the Ekurhuleni Metropolitan Police, share a first name with the man who founded the British Metropolitan Police? Robert Peel's men were known as 'Peelers'. Have you ever thought about changing your name to Robert Piel? Your men could be called 'Pieletjies'.

Anyway, enjoy your administrative leave, whatever that is, and I hope to see you back in the driving seat soon. With Jacob Zuma as president, Tony Yengeni as minister of finance and you in charge of safety and security, this country will never be the same again.

Yours truly,
Ben Trovato.

1 April 2008

An Identity Crisis Leads to Violence and Almost-Sex

I was looking for my ID book – not, as some of you may think, so that I could prove to the bartender that I was old enough to drink – but so that I could go to the bank and prove that it really was me who was stupid enough to keep doing business with them.

I searched the house and found nothing. Well, I found a room containing two large metal machines with round windows and a bunch of buttons – probably useless Korean-manufactured time machines that Brenda bought on eBay. But no ID book.

I went so far as to accuse Kwaai Lappies of pilfering it. "Kwaai Lappies," I said sternly. "Have you stolen my ID book?" It is important to be forthright with these people. It's the only language they understand. Had I to ask her if she had *seen* my ID book, I would be bogged down in a confusing maze of primitive metaphysical reasoning. Of course she has *seen* my ID book. I leave it lying around all the time. But if she admitted to having seen it, she would be hard pressed not to tell me where it is. If she said she hadn't seen it, I would know she was lying and be left with no choice but to hand her over to the police for a little low-key torture.

As it turned out she simply said, "No" and continued ironing. A brilliant answer that left me flat-footed and speechless. I expect she was trained in the Soviet Union.

I would have strapped her into my homemade polygraph machine if Eskom's relentless power surges hadn't blown the gizmo that administers electric shocks.

When Brenda got home from work, or wherever it is that she goes during the day, I asked her to give Kwaai Lappies a full body search.

"Rendition is also an option," I said.

A strange look passed across Brenda's face. One that I hadn't seen before. I moved in with the speed of a striking cobra and began gnawing on the back of her neck. Sadly, it was not the look of an aroused woman but rather that of a guilty one.

She broke my hold with an elbow to the epiglottis and said, "I put your ID through the wash."

The full horror of the situation struck me. Home Affairs. Riots. Mayhem. People dying of starvation right there in the queue. I broke down and wept. Well, I tried to but real men don't weep so I just scrunched up my face and made my shoulders shake.

"How could you?" I shouted. Instead of falling to her knees and performing hasty amends, she said: "Any more of that and you can do your own laundry." I couldn't think of anything to say to this despicably unfair riposte so I put on my wounded face and looked out of the window.

The heartless cow relented and said that since she had to renew her driver's licence, we could go to the traffic department in Grabouw and home affairs in nearby Caledon where there would be no queues.

As some sort of concession, Brenda let me drive. I proceeded to do so, fast and recklessly. By the time we reached Grabouw my testosterone levels were so deep into the red that I could have killed a small buck with my bare hands and then drunk its blood and worn its skin.

But Grabouw is not ready for this even though the town is known only for its boerewors.

The traffic department looks like a police charge office only with better security. Thick glass partitions prevent you from grabbing the clerk by the throat. On one wall is an Arrive Alive poster. Below the words, "Dangerous Sleeping Habits" is a photograph of a man soundly asleep on a railway line. He has a pillow under his head and a train is one second away from cutting him in half.

I always thought a dangerous sleeping habit was when you caroused until dawn and at around 11.30am your boss walked in to find you sprawled under your desk drooling into the corporate carpet. Apparently I was wrong. Apparently a dangerous sleeping habit is when you swallow four caps of zopiclone with a litre of vodka and take half your bed down to the tracks.

I discovered that my driver's licence had also expired. Quite a while ago, actually. Unless one is apprehended for some sort of violation, which never happens nowadays, how is one meant to know these things?

I try to avoid eye tests. You wouldn't know it by looking at me, but my vision is afflicted with pterygiums, an astigmatism and a red/green colour blindness which makes every robot a potential death trap. The examiner passed me and I tripped over her seeing-eye dog on the way out.

With our hands stinking of fingerprint ink and industrial solvent we pulled in at the home affairs office in Caledon. It shares a wall with a butchery, which is handy if you are taken with the urge to gnaw on the hindquarters of a lamb while waiting to be attended to by one of the four women who studiously avoid the public, the ringing telephones and the inexorable passage of time.

I began to get an understanding of what it must be like to be Captain Invisible or, as the Catholics would have it, to be assigned to the hell of the damned. I performed an impromptu limbo dance right there in the hallowed halls of home affairs, but still the purgatorial gatekeepers ignored us.

I left when Brenda started shouting and swearing. On my way out I passed a box of government-issue condoms at the door. How frightfully clever of them. All thoughts of homicide turned instantly to thoughts of sex. I no longer cared about my ID book. All I wanted to do was ravage Brenda right there in the parking lot. I even blew up a bunch of them to make the moment more romantic.

Of course it never worked. Mixing sport and politics never does.

8 April 2008

When it Comes to the Siesta, Spain can Learn From Us

B y the time you read this, I will be gone. Not, as some of you may hope, to the afterlife, but to somewhere far more erotic. Spain. And not a moment too soon, either.

There is blood in the water and darks shapes are circling. Treachery is afoot and it's time to get out of town.

Spain seemed like a good bet because it is a lawless country with no police and a handful of corrupt politicians in charge. Hang on. That's us. Spain is a well-run democracy full of beautiful women with fiery temperaments and a rebel movement that can't really be bothered to blow up too much stuff.

Brenda seems to be under the impression that the trip is going to be some sort of second honeymoon. Well, I suppose it couldn't be any worse than the first. What am I saying? Of course it could. At least we survived the first, even though I will carry the scars with me for the rest of my life.

I have been trying to interest Brenda in bullfighting but she says it is a cruel and barbaric sport practiced by cruel and barbaric people. I told her that if she insisted on talking like that in Spain, I would have her arrested by the Guardia Civil. Then I showed her a picture of the famous bullfighter Manuel Rodríguez Sánchez in his tight, sequined trousers and scarlet cape. Her eyes glazed over and she began breathing heavily. I quickly pointed out that a bull by the name of Islero gored him to death in 1947. She seemed disappointed.

"Don't worry about that," I said. "Wait until you see me in action." If there's one thing that will rekindle the guttering flame of passion, it will be the sight of me leaping over the barricades and single-handedly challenging a giant Córdoban bull to do his worst.

Obviously I won't hesitate to reach for my ankle holster and whip out the old 9mm Parabellum if *el toro* gets too cheeky. That's how we South Africans fight wild animals. None of this girly sword stuff for us.

Apart from an inexplicable reluctance to gun down their wildlife, Spain is very similar to South Africa in many respects. They had General Franco. We have General Mbeki. The Basques and the Boers both want their own homeland. We have Vladimir Tretchikoff who was influenced by his mother, they have Salvador Dali who was influenced by lysergic acid diethylamide. Their street life is as vibrant as ours in Khayelitsha or KwaMashu except that in Barcelona people generally don't wind up in hospital, jail or the mortuary after a good night out.

I read on a website that "Spanish men tend to maintain eye contact with females for longer, although this does not mean anything". Yeah, sure. "Hey amigo, I'm just taking your wife for a walk down the beach. Relax. It doesn't mean a thing."

The rules of the road seem similar to ours: drive as fast as you can on whichever side of the road has the least amount of traffic and stop only for petrol.

When it comes to the winter solstice, "the tradition in Spain witnesses the jumping of men over men which is a symbolic representation of victory over illness". In Cape Town we have men jumping on top of other men which is a symbolic representation of a society going to hell in a handbasket.

Spain is known as a wine-drinking country. We are known as a country that drinks wine, beer, brandy, vodka, cane, ethanol, formaldehyde and, if it's very late on a Friday night, blood.

Another fine tradition we share with Spain is the siesta. The only difference is that while the Spanish close their shops and offices for a few hours in the afternoon and go home to sleep, our people keep theirs open and sleep right there on the counter in front of us.

The money might take some getting used to. Thanks to the likes of Tito Mboweni, a couple of sheiks with more wives than they can handle and a bunch of narcissistic coked-up teenagers in the New York Stock Exchange, the rand is like Monopoly money compared to the euro.

I bought a wad of the stuff on the black market last week. And please understand that I don't mean black in any pejorative sense. Even though some of my best friends are white they have close ties to the black market, which must count for something.

Thousands of our money got me a few brightly coloured notes with boring pictures of old buildings on them. This trip is going to cost me a fortune. With beer coming in at around R35 a pint, I doubt that I shall have much left over for luxuries like food and accommodation.

Never mind second honeymoon, I have a strong feeling this is going to end in Brenda being deported and me clinging to the legs of a Flamenco dancer, begging for refugee status.

15 April 2008

Mickey-Finned by Ben Dover

My holiday in Spain got off to a fabulous start. It began when our pilot had a stand-up fight with his boyfriend and consequently delayed our flight from Cape Town to Johannesburg by half an hour.

Not a particularly great amount of time in terms of evolution and the universe and stuff like that, but just long enough for us to reach Iberia's check-in counter eight minutes after it had shut.

"No," said a yellow-vested man with the face of a stupid person. "You can't get on the plane." Even though it's only leaving in an hour? Even though. But we have already checked our luggage through from Cape Town to Madrid, we said. The stupid face assured us that because we had not checked in, our luggage would not have been put on the plane.

"Take it up with SAA," he said.

So we joined a long line of other unhappy people at the SAA counter and were told that they could put us on the next flight to Madrid – in two days' time. Brenda was outraged and began threatening people who didn't even work for the airline.

All they could do, said the man with the "do I look like I care about your problem?" expression, was to put us up in a hotel. But, oh dear, all the hotels in Joburg are full so you're going to have to stay in Pretoria. The hotels in Joburg are not full. This is simply SAA corporate code for "our R50-a-night rat-infested hovel in Hillbrow is full".

We were handed a voucher for a taxi to the "hotel" in Pretoria and went off to recover our luggage from the bowels of the airport. A man who looked like a second-hand duffel bag checked his computer and said that our luggage was on the Iberia flight.

The next day we woke up in Pretoria and our backpacks woke up in Madrid. I shall spare you the litany of horrors that were inflicted upon us during the 12 hours we spent at Oliver Tambo International, but after much begging, pleading, threatening and weeping, SAA grudgingly agreed to put us on a flight to London. Anything was better than another night in Pretoria, even if it meant arriving in a completely different country to the one we had originally planned on visiting. I began to understand why Qantas had the longest queues of all.

After decompressing in the smoker's lounge, a cheerful place where you could fall down dead and nobody would care, we were herded into our pens at the back of the aircraft. We landed at Heathrow at dawn, dressed for sunny Spain. The temperature outside was 3°C. So much for global warming. Brenda shivered and cursed and every time she turned on me I gently deflected her wrath back towards SAA, where it belonged.

We spent our first night in Paddington and wondered how our bags were enjoying Spain. Reeking like homeless people, we went to a Lebanese restaurant and had a terrible fight after Brenda accused me of being transfixed by the belly dancer.

"What belly dancer?" I said, taking another mouthful of empty fork and knocking my beer into my lap.

The next day, reunited with our backpacks which were looking relaxed and tanned, I told Brenda that I was taking her to the East End. To a place called Rotherhithe where I used to live in a squat because back then I couldn't afford to pay even the smallest amount of rent.

Our cab driver, born in England, oddly enough, warned me that the area had changed since I was last there. "Most of us cockneys moved out when the Pakis moved in," he said. "We're out in the shires, now."

The shires? Isn't that where the hobbits live? I dared not ask for fear that he had something against hobbits, too.

Rotherhithe had certainly changed. The slums where I lived had been knocked down to make way for rows of yuppie flats made of ticky-tacky. Where were the punks? The skinheads? The drug dealers? The people who once made this such a fantastic place to live?

And so it was that in the space of a few years I went from staying in a filthy squat to staying in the Rotherhithe Hilton. Funny thing, life.

The next day Brenda suggested we get the hell out of London but I had received certain information that the Camden Crawl was on the go. Billed as three days of anarchy, it seemed silly not to be there for it.

Brenda was a bit tense at first but it wasn't long before she was so relaxed that she ran off down the middle of the road and got her nose pierced by a girl with purple hair. I remember being awash in beer, loud music and police sirens. That's it. London was killing us. We had to get out. So we caught the train to Dover, a town like Muizenberg but with even less hope.

For the first time, we had to shoulder our backpacks. After about 30 metres I started feeling like a tortoise walking on its hind legs with a giant shell made from lead. I complained and moaned and bitched non-stop until Brenda hailed a taxi just to shut me up.

Later we walked up some stupid mountain to get to a castle where posters pretended that Dover was on the frontline in the first world war. I could see the troops hunkered down in the Horse & Hare as the first wave of bombers came over on their way to London.

"Woz that a plane, mate?"

"Nah, that's the number 19 bus, that is."

"Orl right, then. Your round."

No wonder Britain lost the war.

We holed up in the White Horse pub, a crumbling edifice built in 1345. The walls of the bar were covered in graffiti from people foolish enough to have swum the English Channel. This made me uncomfortable so we went out the back where a very drunk man told us that Mandela was a terrorist and should never have been released. This made Brenda uncomfortable so we drank up and left quickly.

Later that night we trawled desperate Dover for a little action. The Funky Monkey looked promising, what with its sign banning "chunky rings and heavy jewellery" but it was closed.

The Louis Armstrong was open and for possibly the first time ever, we were the youngest people in the bar. The patrons were there to listen to Bill Barnacle's Jazz Band, drink sherry and reminisce about the war.

My notes stop making sense at this point because around midnight, Ricardo with a bandaged hand joined us and, when I wasn't looking, slipped something nasty into my beer. By the time the bar closed it was as if my spine had turned to jelly. Brenda poured me into a taxi and we went back to the hotel whereupon I deposited my supper in the bath.

And the holiday was only just beginning.

29 April 2008

Welcome to Europe – Parking Full

I t was a relief to leave Dover, a nasty little town full of white supremacists and sociopaths who slip date rape drugs into your beer and then send you home with your wife.

Ferried into Calais, we hefted our backpacks and set off in search of a bravish new world. We hadn't gone more than 20 metres when Brenda said, "Whose idea was this?" I was staggering under the weight of my pack. Any attempt to speak would have left me utterly drained.

We reached the bus station and while Brenda was studying the time-tables I slipped off and hired us a car. From then on our backpacking holiday consisted of us parking outside hotels and backpacking to reception.

Brenda was delighted when I told her that our days of roughing it were over and we made for the parking lot. "What the hell is that?" she barked. "I thought you said we had hired a car." Apparently in Brenda's world, a Renault Clio doesn't qualify as a car.

The only way to drive a gay car is hard and fast and soon we were barreling down the road to Paris while our fellow motorists waved their arms about and shouted words of encouragement.

"I love the French spirit," I said.

"You're on the wrong side of the road," Brenda said.

My plan was to park in Versailles and catch a train in to Paris. "You would be a damn fool to take a car into the centre of Paris," I said.

"Isn't that the Arc d'Triomf?" said Brenda.

Damn! Versailles, like so many towns to come, was simply not where the map said it would be. With Brenda playing the role of Henry the Navigator, I'm not surprised.

I drove straight into 15 lanes of traffic rotating at high speed around the Charles de Gaulle circle. There were no visible markings on the road and no form of traffic control whatsoever. There are motorists who have been trapped in the inside lane at the Arc d'Triomf ever since the Americans liberated Paris.

Brenda said we should get out of the mayhem and head for the hills but I said I wanted to spend one night in Paris. "I bet you do," said Brenda, giving me the lazy eye.

All the on-street parking in Paris is taken by residents who use public transport and only move their cars if someone in the family has to be rushed to hospital for open-heart surgery. Everyone else parks underground.

After numerous verbal incidents with excitable French drivers, we found an underground parking outside some kind of old church.

"That's the Notre Dame Cathedral," said Brenda. She knows these things.

After we had parked in the bowels of France and returned to the surface of the planet, I saw an old man pretending to be a hunchback. I laughed and laughed. "Good one," I said, pointing at his hump. He tried to spit on me and Brenda said, "I don't think he is pretending."

Brenda insisted that we check into the Notre Dame Hotel because it was on the Boulevard San Michel and she wanted to feel like she was the one Peter Sarsted was singing about. I gave a hollow laugh. "I suppose next you will want to study at the Sorbonne and get the Aga Khan to give you a racehorse and show off your topless suntan ..."

Brenda said I was being ridiculous, which I take as a compliment these days. We went for dinner at a restaurant staffed by waiters so inconspicuous and guarded that I wondered if they thought we were Germans and they were still in the Resistance.

Our meal plus a few drinks came to a very reasonable 150 euros. It only becomes unreasonable when you convert it into rands.

For reasons which make no sense, our drive through Europe turned into something akin to the Paris to Dakar Rally. Right through France, ours was the fastest car on the road. Not a single person overtook us. Well, one or two tried but I managed to shut them out.

By the time we reached the Spanish border I had a renewed respect for the Clio. Brenda showed no signs of renewed respect for me.

I was relieved to see that all borders had been scrapped between

European Union countries. The last time I was here, I was travelling with a couple of South Africans who duped me into stuffing a bag of contraband down the front of my trousers. I was frisked by a border guard and came within a finger's breadth of a Spanish jail, deportation and, ultimately, a crushing look of disappointment on my mother's face.

San Sebastian is the first Spanish town you hit after leaving Biarritz. It seemed to have grown enormously since I last set foot in the place. "So have you," said Brenda.

Spain has a rich history of colonisation, invasion, conquest and reconquest by everyone from Phoenicians to the Visigoths to the Moors and, finally, the Christians who seem to have dug in for the long haul.

In Spain there are no new parts of cities. There are only old parts and really, really old parts. These are the ones we stayed in.

After checking in to a pension that looked as if had last been inhabited by a collective of anarchists on the run from General Franco's thugs, we hit the tapas bars with a vengeance.

Brenda tried to teach me some Spanish but it started off badly. "For example," she said, sighing heavily, "whisky has a different gender to beer." I laughed like a sick goat. "After drinking the stuff, so do I." She seemed unimpressed by my sparkling wit.

Keen to sink my choppers into a Spanish fish, the waiter said there was only hake on the menu. Of course. You have depleted your own stocks and now you want to give me a South African fish that was caught by Spanish pirates plundering our waters. I drew myself up to my full height, which wasn't much since I was on my knees.

"How dare you?" I shouted.

"*Que?*" said the waiter.

"Exactly," I said, knocking my beer into Brenda's lap.

The next morning we did a high-speed dash across northern Spain, stopping only to slap and kick a petrol pump that refused to give us fuel. They have a peculiar system in Spain. You fill up your car and they trust you to go into the garage and pay. That would work really well in South Africa.

We reached Santiago de Compostela at dusk. This ruined city is ruined ever further by dozens of shops selling Jesus on a T-shirt, Jesus on a mug, Jesus on many different kinds of crosses. Plastic Jesuses. Silver Jesuses.

Wooden Jesuses. Every kind of Jesus you can imagine. Except smiling. Nobody ever makes a smiling Jesus.

Someone else who is big in Santiago is St James. So big, in fact, that Christians will often walk 800km just to get their hands on a plastic version of their hero. They call it "walking the Camino". Personally, I would rather walk the plank.

On closer inspection, it turned out that the Christians hijacked the walk from the pagans who would make the trek to the coast to copulate on the Rocks of Fertility. Christians will say this is a pack of lies but there must be a reason why the gift shops are also full of plastic witches on broomsticks.

We found a hotel next to the cathedral. Brenda said she liked it because it used to be a convent and she used to be a convent girl. That night, Brenda asked if I would help purge her of all the Catholic guilt she had accumulated over the years. I had my trousers around my ankles before you could say "Hail Mary".

Standing at reception the next morning, I overheard an elderly American tourist ask the desk clerk if an exorcism had taken place in room 307 the previous night.

"In a way," I said softly. "In a way."

It seemed only right to leave at that point, so we shimmied into the Clio and pointed our noses in the direction of Portugal. We wanted to spend a few days on the Algarve but when we got there we couldn't find any parking so we carried on driving and before we knew it we were at the end of the country. The British have annexed the Algarve. I cannot understand why the UN is doing nothing about it.

Henry the Navigator bent over her map and said, "Look. An island. I bet it's deserted. We should go there."

"What's it called?" I said.

"Ibiza," she said.

6 May 2008

The Noshing of the Bulls

"**B**efore we head for the forgotten island of Ibiza, we need to go to bull country," I said to Brenda. I have always wanted to stab a bull through the heart and slice off its ears so that I may nail them to my study wall as a conversation piece.

As in every other city bigger than Fish Hoek, we got repeatedly and hopelessly lost seconds after taking the turnoff. If Columbus had hired a female navigator, Jamaica would be called America today.

Eventually we came upon what the Spanish laughingly call the "historic centre" of Córdoba. Brenda prefers to stay in these areas because they have "character". Give me a break. Old buildings are like old people. If you've seen one, you've seen them all.

I simply cannot stand before one more crumbling edifice heavy with statues of sad-faced people and say, "Hmm. That really goes back." History has very little significance when one travels without guide books of any kind.

What did intrigue me in Cordoba was the Mesquite. When I first saw the name, I thought it was a strip joint and was wondering how I could give Brenda the slip for a couple of hours, but it turned out to be a giant, cavernous structure built, oh, I don't know, about a million years ago.

It was constructed by the Moors and for a long time was used as a place of worship by both the Jews and the Muslims. At some point the Knights of Santiago got wind of this unseemly arrangement and rode hell for leather to Cordoba where they killed everyone in the name of Christianity and converted the mosque into a cathedral.

Today they charge tourists an entrance fee and warn them against being unduly impressed by the godless Moorish architecture.

Like the rest of Spain, Córdoba was stuffed to the gills with Catholics. There was no room at any of the inns and the sidewalks were jammed.

Apparently only a damn fool arrives in Córdoba in early May without reserving some sort of accommodation.

The city was gearing up for a marathon of festivals ranging from celebrating the cross, the onset of spring and, I think, the ham. These people love their ham. They string it up by its back legs right above your head, but it's difficult to relax when you're worried about the hindquarters of a pig landing in your lap just as you order your next beer.

The Spanish also love their children despite them being infinitely more nasty than falling ham. Give me Spanish ham over Spanish children any day.

Ham is at least disciplined and rarely speaks out of turn. In fact I would go so far as to say that Spanish pigs behave better than Spanish children, even as they prepare to sacrifice themselves so that we may gnaw on their scrumptious buttocks. The pigs, not the children.

In Africa, if you come across a lion cub in the bush you run like hell because mom or dad can't be far behind. In Spain, if you come across a couple between the ages of 16 and 50, you run like hell because their children can't be far behind. They will be shrieking or crying or doing something that will set your teeth on edge and make you want to commit unspeakable atrocities upon their swarthy little heads.

We have the Pope to thank for this appalling state of affairs. Spain would be a far more pleasant country to visit if the men didn't think they would burn in hell for putting a latex sock over their willies every time they felt horny.

Making matters infinitely worse, Córdoba was also full of latter-day Visigoths. These travelling barbarians might have swapped their swords for ice creams and prefer to think of themselves as Germans, but you only have to look into their faces to know that they come from a terrible place in history.

Seeking refuge in the restaurant at the end of the Mesquite, Brenda amused herself with a jug of powerful sangria while I fired off several frames from the old Nikon whenever something caught my eye.

A comfy chair, cold beers, warm tapas and an endless supply of sultry, underdressed Andalucían women in the cobbled roads. This was travel journalism at its best.

The sangria went to Brenda's head and she asked me when exactly I planned on fighting a bull. "Fight?" I laughed. "Forget fight. Fighting is for sissies. I'm going to *eat* one of them wild beasts."

I stared unflinchingly into the eyes of the waiter and said, "Bring me the *rabo del toro*. Pronto." The crowd in the restaurant fell silent. Somewhere in the back streets a fiery-tempered flamenco dancer rattled her castanets and an old war hero riffed on his 12-string Ibanez. Buzzards circled overhead and a boy with a goat stopped to watch.

Ten minutes later the waiter returned. He set the mound of steaming bull before me and moved quickly for the safety of the bar. As the guitar solo reached its dizzying crescendo, I fell upon my plate and devoured the animal with consummate skill and courage. Not to mention relish and gusto. Rising up to my full height, not easy in a sitting position, I stabbed my fork into a fist-sized chunk and fell back, exhausted.

"*Olé!*" I cried.

"*Torero!*" responded the crowd.

"*La cuenta!*" shouted Brenda.

After the bloodied remains of my conquest had been removed, I offered to buy Brenda a pair of boots. "We have to eat them *and* wear them," I said. "It's the only way to get any respect around here."

I found the perfect pair in a seedy shop down a blind alley for just 15 euros. Brenda said she doubted they were made from real leather. "Nonsense," I said. "I'm talking genuine bull, here."

I explained to her that her bull had probably taken one look around the ring and said, "You want me to do *what*?" then promptly died of fright. Boots made from gay bulls will obviously be cheaper than boots made from bulls that kill three matadors and two horses and then jump into the stands and start goring the crowd. I could see Brenda was uncomfortable with the idea of wearing boots made from an effeminate bull so I changed my story rather than risk paying more.

"Or," I said, "it's more likely that your bull walked up to the matador and said: 'It's because I'm black, isn't it?' Then he refused to fight and was dragged around the back and shot in the head because nobody likes an uppity bull.

"Think of him as a Martin Luther King bull."

13 May 2008

The Willies, My Friend, Are Blowing in the Wind

I had reservations when Brenda suggested we catch a ferry to Ibiza. Not the kind of reservations that sensible people make when they go on holiday, but more the kind that make you think twice about going to an island renowned for its wild sex and drug-soaked parties.

I was anxious. What if we couldn't find the parties? Or worse, found the parties but weren't allowed in because we talked funny and dressed like homeless people?

Brenda resolved my quandary by stepping through the doors of Iscomar's office in the harbour town of Denia and buying two one-way tickets to this wicked isle of sin. One way? I raised an eyebrow and gave Brenda a quizzical look. She asked if my stomach was playing up again.

The ferry was oddly empty. So was Ibiza. When we landed, a chromium-plated platoon of dangerous bikers was waiting at the docks. As we disembarked a police siren cut through the air. Instead of making a run for it, some of the bikers hopped off their Harleys and started grooving to the mad, swooping sound. Then a cop joined in, waving his bullhorn in the air and howling like a dog.

"Yeehaaa!" I shouted, waggling my hips like Britney Spears. Everyone stopped and looked at me. Brenda made the international gesture for mental instability and quickly led me away.

The streets were virtually deserted and everything was shut. "Maybe these fiesta fiends only get out of bed when the sun goes down," I said hopefully. Sadly, that was not the case. We had once again run aground in the middle of a public holiday.

This kept happening to us. What were the odds, for heaven's sake? After all, Spain only has 342 public holidays a year.

Wherever we went people were either asleep or drunk in the name of Jesus, an assortment of virgins or sundry patron saints of flowers, horses, chickens, fish, wine and ham.

We sat down at a pavement café and, surprisingly, got served within four hours. This is the average length of time one spends trying to rouse a waiter in what the Spanish euphemistically call the low season. I think they left the 's' off low.

"I don't want a tortilla," I said sulkily. "I want to gobble a fistful of methylenedioxymethamphetamine and dance like John Travolta from dusk to dawn." Being the sensitive man that I am, I left out the bit about wanting sweaty, semi-naked Balearic wenches to throw themselves at my feet.

Later, trawling side streets that hadn't been upgraded since the Phoenicians were here in 654BC, we came across a shop renting out scooters that were last ridden during the Second Punic War. I chose one that was relatively free of Carthaginian blood stains and we spluttered off in search of hotbeds of abject hedonism.

Ibiza was bigger than I thought and we both ended up with sore bottoms for all the wrong reasons. Still and all, it's a scenic enough island and most of the beaches have bars on them, which is more than I can say for our country where metro cops wrestle you to the floor and smash your head in if you open a bottle of wine anywhere outside a designated venue licensed by the state to sell alcoholic beverages.

We had only been there a couple of days when I discovered that the island's autonomous government had introduced legislation forcing nightclubs to close by 6am. This was outrageous and I insisted that we leave before the fascists put us under house arrest. We fled to Formentera, a far smaller island half an hour's boat ride away.

A cold front had moved in so we hired a car designed for midgets and set out on a voyage of discovery that took all of 20 minutes. Formentera makes Craggy Island look like Borneo. I even saw the spitting image of Father Ted pass us on his bicycle.

"This place is deader than a stillborn sheep," I said over a jug of sangria at a lonely beach bar. Brenda's eyes widened and her jaw dropped. I thought she was having some sort of chemical reaction to the sangria so I quickly polished it off. "Look behind you," she gasped.

And there, willy a-flap in the breeze, was the reason people come to

Formentera. He was hung like a convicted killer and strolling brazen as you please past the bar. Quite put me off my tapas, it did, so I dragged Brenda back to the car and we found another beach. This one had naked women on it which made me feel considerably less appalled.

I took my trunks off and stood there for a bit but the sensation that a police sniper was drawing a bead on the back of my head was too much to bear so I put them on again and went for a swim feeling like an overdressed pervert.

Two days later we arrived in Barcelona. Well, not so much arrived as got sucked along in a raging torrent of cars, trucks and bikes and then spat out at Columbus's statue at the bottom of the Ramblas. We parked underground and I took Brenda to see where I had once holed up in the narrow back streets of the Barrio Gottica. I was horrified to see the changes.

"Where are the doe-eyed hookers? The hash dealers? Where are the Moroccan muggers in Nike running shoes?" All gone. Swept away when the city hosted the Olympics, an old man told me.

"It was better under Franco," I said.

20 May 2008

What a Long Strange Trip it's Been

I get back from Spain and the first thing I see is a picture of a man in flames on the front page of the newspapers.

My first thought was that Eskom had finally given up and people were setting foreigners alight just to keep warm at night. I imagined families chatting about their day while huddled around burning Somalis, the kids doing their homework by the flickering light as dad chucks a fresh Zimbabwean on the pile.

My second thought was, "That can't be it. What's wrong with you?" I got a firm grip on myself and set about getting to the bottom of this peculiar business.

I thought I had the hang of it after about nine seconds of skimming the local papers, but then Essop Pahad, the Dalit responsible for keeping flies, journalists and international opprobrium off our non-resident president, complicated matters by saying: "We need to understand that xenophobia has historically been used by right-wing populist movements to mobilise particularly the lumpen proletariat against minority groups in society."

Of course. It's blindingly obviously that the Boeremag is behind this. For a start, the violence has all the hallmarks of an organisation known for its raw cunning and razor-sharp intellect. Ever since police inadvertently uncovered their brilliant plan to lure all the darkies out of the country by leaving free food along the highways, the right wing has been looking for interesting new ways to mobilise the lumpen proletariat.

Cut to:

Union Buildings – Night.

Mbeki: What happens to a dream deferred? Does it dry up like a raisin in the sun? Or fester like a sore, and then run?

Pahad: I would say that society's dynamics become manifest in the dynamics of the reciprocal connections created between reality's myriad facets.

Mbeki: Johnnie Walker?

Pahad: Certainly.

Mbeki: From each according to his ability. Cheers.

Pahad: To each according to his needs. *Nazdarovya*.

I hesitate to write in any great depth about the recent events instigated by that Afro-Saxon quisling, Morgan Tsvangirai, to force Zimbabweans to go home and vote for him, because I am not altogether convinced that there is a lighter side to xenophobia. Let me just say, though, that I think we should spare a thought for all the families out there who have been left without their Malawian houseboys and other imported factotums of that ilk. Good help is damnably hard to come by these days.

And so, to matters more serious. It is with a heavy heart I inform you of circumstances necessitating that I relinquish this valuable piece of literary real estate with immediate effect.

More than a quarter of a million words. That's what I have given you over the years. And what have I got in return? Vicious abuse. Death threats. Liver damage. Offers of marriage. Many of you never failed to let me down in your steadfast refusal to send steaming wads of cash when I was at my weakest.

Then there were the others – the ones who showered me with kind words and indecent proposals. Thank you. Some of you will be hearing from Brenda soon.

To those who mailed me mind-altering substances to encourage me to continue writing, if I could remember who you were you would not be forgotten.

Ultimately, the responsibility for all of this nonsense must fall squarely on the head of Chris Whitfield, who, as editor of the *Cape Times* in 2002, over-medicated one winter's evening and rashly agreed to let me loose on the op-ed page.

When I sent off a carefully crafted and highly emotional e-mail informing him that I was laying down my pen after 65 straight months, he was so devastated that all he could manage was a single word.

"*Nooit*," responded Whitfield. A man of few words, indeed. One word less and he would be a man of no words at all. I can only imagine that the wracking sobs and floods of tears precluded him from saying more.

The incumbent editor, Tyrone August, has courageously fielded much of the fall-out generated by this column and I have no doubt that the Freedom of Expression Institute will want to award him some sort of medal in the near future. That's it, then. My work here is done.

Time to saddle up the old dromedary and limp off into the sunset.

Adios, bandidos.

27 May 2008